What Works (and Doesn't) in Reducing Recidivism

What Works (and Doesn't) in Reducing Recidivism

Edward J. Latessa
University of Cincinnati

Shelley J. Listwan
University of North Carolina, Charlotte

Deborah Koetzle
John Jay College of Criminal Justice

ELSEVIER

Amsterdam • Boston • Heidelberg • London
New York • Oxford • Paris • San Diego
San Francisco • Singapore • Sydney • Tokyo

Anderson Publishing is an imprint of Elsevier

Acquiring Editor: Pam Chester
Development Editor: Ellen S. Boyne
Project Manager: Julia Haynes
Designer: Tin Box Studio, Inc.

Anderson Publishing is an imprint of Elsevier
225 Wyman Street, Waltham, MA 02451, USA

Library of Congress Cataloging-in-Publication Data
A catalogue record for this book is available from the Library of Congress.

British Library Cataloguing-in-Publication Data
A catalogue record for this book is available from the British Library.

ISBN: 978-1-4557-3121-3

For information on all Anderson publications
visit our website at http://store.elsevier.com

Typeset by TNQ Books and Journals

Printed in the United States of America

14 15 16 17 18 10 9 8 7 6 5 4 3 2 1

Working together
to grow libraries in
developing countries

www.elsevier.com • www.bookaid.org

Dedication

To my family: Sally, Amy, Jennifer, Michael, and Allison
Edward Latessa

To my children: Jackson, Sam, and Owen
Shelley Listwan

To my Mom: Roz Faber
Deborah Koetzle

Contents

Preface

During the past several decades, research has demonstrated that rehabilitation efforts can be effective at reducing recidivism among criminal offenders. However, researchers also recognize that treatment is not a "one size fits all" approach. Related studies indicate that effective services should be designed to target criminogenic needs of offenders while also recognizing other personal needs (e.g., sexual abuse issues) and potential obstacles (e.g., no transportation) faced by offenders. Interventions are most effective when they have clear targets and are guided by theories of criminal behavior. Offenders vary by gender, age, crime type, and/or addictions, to name but a few, and these individual needs must be addressed by providers. Finally, issues such as leadership, quality of staff, and evaluation efforts affect the quality and delivery of treatment services. This book attempts to synthesize the vast research for the student interested in correctional rehabilitation as well as for the practitioner working with offenders. Although other texts have addressed issues regarding treatment in corrections, this text is unique in that it not only discusses the research on "what works" but also addresses implementation issues as practitioners move from theory to practice, reentry into the community, as well as the importance of staff, leadership, and evaluation efforts.

Finally, as should be evident to anyone who has worked or studied in corrections during the past 20 years, the work of Don Andrews, Paul Gendreau, and James Bonta has helped turn the corner for correctional rehabilitation. We are proud to be standing on their shoulders. We are also grateful to our colleagues, Dr. Paula Smith, Myrinda Schweitzer, and Ronen Ziv, for contributing the chapter on what works with sex offenders. In addition, we thank everyone at Elsevier, especially Ellen Boyne and Pam Chester, for their support, prodding, and putting up with us.

About the Authors

Edward J. Latessa is Director and Professor of the School of Criminal Justice at the University of Cincinnati. He received his Ph.D. from The Ohio State University in 1979. During the past three decades, he has published more than 140 works in the areas of criminal justice, corrections, offender assessment, juvenile justice, and program evaluation. He is coauthor of seven books and has directed more than 150 funded research projects. He served as President of the Academy of Criminal Justice Sciences in 1989–1990 and has received numerous awards.

Shelley Johnson Listwan is Associate Professor in the Department of Criminal Justice and Criminology at the University of North Carolina at Charlotte. She received her Ph.D. in Criminal Justice from the University of Cincinnati in 2001. She has also served on the faculty at the University of Nevada, Las Vegas and Kent State University. Her areas of interest include corrections, criminological theory, psychology of crime, and victimization. She has authored several articles and books in the areas of prison victimization, problem-solving courts, and correctional rehabilitation.

Deborah Koetzle is Associate Professor in the Department of Public Management and the executive officer of the Criminal Justice Doctoral Program at John Jay College of Criminal Justice, the City University of New York. She received her Ph.D. in Criminal Justice from the University of Cincinnati in 2006. She was previously on the faculty at University of Nevada, Las Vegas. Her research interests center on effective interventions for offenders, problem-solving courts, and the use of social media by police departments. She has authored several articles in the areas of problem-solving courts, risk assessment, and program evaluation.

Online Resources

Thank you for selecting Anderson Publishing's *Criminological What Works (and Doesn't) in Reducing Recidivism*. To complement the learning experience, we have provided online tools to accompany this edition.

Please consult your local sales representative with any additional questions. You may also e-mail the Academic Sales Team at textbook@elsevier.com.

Qualified adopters and instructors can access valuable material for free by registering at: http://textbooks.elsevier.com/web/manuals.aspx?isbn=9781455731213

1

"Nothing Works" to "What Works"
The History and Social Context of Rehabilitation

Introduction

A number of texts provide excellent overviews of the history of juvenile corrections, correctional treatment, and correctional policy (see Andrews & Bonta, 2010; Bernard & Kurlychek, 2010; Cullen & Gilbert, 2013; Cullen & Jonson, 2012). Several core themes often emerge within these writings. This chapter briefly summarizes many of these common themes as they relate to correctional rehabilitation and the current policies that exist today. By doing so, we hope to provide a historical foundation for understanding the strategies and principles of effective treatment programs for offenders.

The first theme often discussed is the cyclical nature of correctional policy. As with fashion and music, trends often repeat themselves. Unfortunately for corrections (and sometimes fashion), we see repetition of the good but also the bad. We discuss how these trends have emerged and changed over time. Second, the cyclical nature of correctional policy is heavily influenced by social and political context. Consider, for example, the social context of the 1960s. The 1960s were a period of great social upheaval as our society became more invested in the rights of a variety of people including minorities, women, prisoners, and juveniles. In part, these changes (e.g., civil rights movement and women's rights) occurred because the political will and social forces existed to make them possible. The interest in saving those subjected to the correctional system, however, was fairly short-lived as we saw that treatment was abandoned for a punitive approach to crime. In that context, we discuss the third theme, which is the tendency to rely on panaceas as they relate to correctional practice. In that context, we discuss the impact of the get-tough movement on correctional policy.

This chapter focuses on the history of corrections but primarily from a treatment perspective. From that standpoint, we go back in time to quickly review some of the major shifts in policy to understand how the system came to be as it is today. We also discuss the challenges our current set of policies face in the road ahead. Before we begin, however, it should be noted that we do not wish to overemphasize that the American correctional system follows one model or one set of policies. If we count the federal and state systems, our correctional system comprises 51 separate and distinct entities. From there, of course, we have a number of local and regional policies and politics that come into play. Each state and, to a lesser extent, region faces unique issues as it relates to social issues, politics, and budgetary constraints. Thus, although it would be inappropriate to suggest that we have a united system of correctional policy, important themes remain. We begin by discussing the Age of Enlightenment because it represented the first shift toward understanding the role of the individual in criminal behavior.

The Age of Reason/Enlightenment

Make no mistake that the earliest forms of correctional policy were extremely punitive. Prior to the 1700s, the basic philosophy guiding correctional policy (in England and France and eventually in North America) was based on brutality. The retaliatory notion of an "eye for an eye, tooth for a tooth" was seen clearly in the early torture-based punishments and vigilante justice. The shift in philosophy, however, began to take root during the Age of Enlightenment (or sometimes called the Age of Reason). Starting in the mid-1770s, the leading reformers advocated for a benevolent or humanistic approach to guide correctional policy. They argued against the current set of punishments as being too barbaric and having little utility. In particular, they believed that those accused of less serious forms of crime (which were also the most common types, such as theft of property) should be dealt with through a graduated system of punishments rather than such brutal ways.

Interestingly, this notion of utilitarianism is the key concept behind deterrence theory, which developed during this time period. Founded by Cesare Beccaria and Jeremy Bentham, deterrence theory asserts that punishment should be proportionate to the crime. Most people think of deterrence as a punitive or even retributive approach. We often hear politicians and others speak of shaming activities (e.g., pink underwear worn by inmates in Arizona), chain gangs, or even the death penalty in the context of "sending a message" in an effort to deter future crime. In reality, deterrence theory argues that overly harsh and severe punishments can have the reverse effect. For example, **marginal deterrence** can occur if petty crimes are subject to the same harsh punishments as serious crimes. In this circumstance, offenders may choose the more serious crime with the potential of a larger payoff (Stigler, 1970). Deterrence advocates instead argued that the purpose of punishment is prevention of crime, not revenge, and that although the sanctions used must be swift and certain, the degree of severity must simply offset the gains of crime (Devine, 1981; Geis, 1973; for a thorough discussion of deterrence theory, see Paternoster, 2010).

The reason we bring up deterrence theory here is not because we believe it is an effective treatment approach but, rather, to point out that its utilitarian nature is somewhat counterintuitive to the punitive polices of the get-tough movement of the 1980s and 1990s. Boot camps and other harsh punishments were often championed as prevention policies based on deterrence theory. In reality, some question whether the degree and severity of punishments given during the get-tough movement truly met the original principles given the severity was often disproportionate to the crime.

The Penitentiary and Reform

One of the other policy shifts that is important to note is the birth of the penitentiary. We discuss treatment in prison extensively in Chapter 10; however, it bears discussion here that the penitentiary was developed with the goal of reformation (but certainly not rehabilitation, as we advocate for in this text). At this time (early 1800s), treatment as we know it today was not a central focus of prison. Instead, the penitentiary concept was based on the notion of a "workhouse" where inmates were expected to engage in hard labor, reflect on their sins, and eventually see the error of their ways (Hirsch, 1992). The role of the church was significant during this time. The Penitentiary Act of 1779 was based on the notion that criminals were sinners who should be subjected to solitary confinement not simply for the purposes of punishment but also to ask for forgiveness and repent for their sins. Variations on the workhouse concept still exist in prisons throughout the county.

Two models of prison "treatment" came into existence during this time and had a great influence on the types of services we offer inmates in today's prisons. The first model is referred to as the **Pennsylvania system**. The Pennsylvania system followed the basic principles noted previously—that inmates would carry out all of their activities in complete isolation. To that end, prisoners were expected to work, receive religious in-struction, and engage in all activities from their cells with no contact with other inmates (Devereaux, 1999).

This model eventually fell out of favor after inspections of the facilities showed that inmates were subjected to abuse and, by some accounts, that separation led to mental health problems among inmates (Hirsch, 1992). The concept of requiring inmates to work, however, remained popular and carried on in the second model.

The second model, referred to as the Auburn or **New York system**, maintained the work-based component of the Pennsylvania system but instead of requiring inmates to work in solitude, it allowed them to work together during the day. However, in the spirit of the Pennsylvania philosophy, inmates were not allowed to speak or look at one another. The silence was part of a strict system of discipline that was encouraged under this model. Another departure from the Pennsylvania model included having the inmates work on projects within the institution that had direct benefit for the institution, including pro-ducing clothing, furniture, and other marketable goods.

It should be noted that when we examine treatment services with juvenile institutions, there are some historical variations. For example, in early penitentiaries, juveniles, adults, women, and men were housed in the same facilities. However, due to the Child Savers movement (Platt, 1969), by the mid-1800s this began to change. The New York **House of Refuge** is considered to be the nation's first juvenile reformatory and opened January 1, 1825, with nine children (six boys and three girls). Like the adult models discussed previously, the youths were expected to be reformed by spending most of their time working, developing literacy skills, and receiving religious instruction. You can read more at http://www.archives.nysed.gov/a/research/res_topics_ed_reform_history.shtml.

In the end, none of these systems proved to be very successful. Overcrowding, a lack of funding, and abuse were rampant (Conley, 1980). As such, a new set of reforms began to take root. The new reformers argued that prisons should be designed with rehabilitation and eventual release in mind. The **Declaration of Principles** were adopted by the National Prison Association in 1870 with this philosophy in mind.

The principles included the following:

- Punishment should be for reformation.
- Reforming the individual helps protect society.
- Prisoners should gradually progress through the system and receive marks for good behavior (including rewards).
- Special training is required for prison officers.
- Education and religion are important areas that should be addressed.

Visit the following website for more information: http://www.aca.org/pastpresentfuture/principles.asp. These principles represented a departure from previous policies that were focused primarily on punishment via the deterrence philosophy.

One example of an institution that attempted to adopt these principles was the **Elmira Reformatory**. The reformatory was designed for first-time felony offenders ages 16–30 years. The reformatory opened in 1876 and used a system composed of three levels of classification. Offenders would begin at level 2 and were required to progress to level 1 in order to gain release. However, they could be demoted to level 3 for poor behavior. In order to move from level 2 to level 1, inmates were required to follow the rules, attend school, and work for a period of at least 6 months. However, if they refused to follow the rules, the residents were moved from level 2 to level 3. At that point, residents would be required to exhibit positive behavior for at least 3 months before they could progress to level 2 and start the process over again (Pisciotta, 1994).

Although the Elmira Reformatory boasted high success rates, the institution came under criticism due to its harsh conditions and allegations of brutality. As can be seen in our current prison system, the focus of treatment and rehabilitation in a custodial setting is difficult to achieve at best. Although the reformers discussed in the next section did not advocate that prisons should be abolished, they did advocate for the increased use of community-based options such as probation and parole supervision.

Progressive Era

The next major period of reform, at least as it relates to correctional treatment policy, shifted its focus toward understanding why individuals engaged in criminal behavior. The **progressives** believed that understanding each individual's circumstances was the key to reformation. They moved away from a pure free will model and instead blamed social and psychological problems for the offender's behavior. In that vein, they argued that individuals could be rehabilitated if we either changed their social environment or attended to their other needs on a case-by-case basis. Several key reforms were advocated, including the following:

- Probation
- Parole
- Indeterminate sentencing
- Establishment of a separate juvenile court

In this context, the reformers believed that rehabilitation could not occur unless certain conditions existed to allow the state a way to gauge change among inmates. Reformers advocated for a system of probation in which the officer would be able to diagnose and treat offenders. They also believed, based on the principles of the Elmira Reformatory, that release from prison should be based on good behavior. In that context, they advocated for an increased use of indeterminate sentencing to allow the state to assess progress before releasing inmates. For example, indeterminate sentences of varied lengths (e.g., 2–4 years vs. a flat sentence of 3 years) would provide the state the opportunity to assess whether offenders were rehabilitated before they were released (for broader discussion of the progressive movement, see Cullen & Gilbert, 2013).

With regard to juveniles, the creation of a separate juvenile court is a significant shift in the context of rehabilitation and juveniles. The first juvenile court was established in Illinois in 1899. The significance at is relates to rehabilitation is the focus of the juvenile court itself on this very issue—specifically, that the judge would act as a parent or advocate for the child rather than rely simply on punishment. This notion of the judge as an advocate falls under the basic philosophical difference between the juvenile and adult systems: the **parens patriae** doctrine. The *parens patriae* doctrine, which also means "parent of the nation," granted the system the right or authority over children who were seen as in need of its care. In viewing juveniles as "in need of care" rather than "in need of punishment," the juvenile justice system emphasized rehabilitation over punishment. In that context, the juvenile court became informal in nature and the judge became an advocate for the youth rather than simply the enforcer of the law (Sanders, 1970).

In the context of individualized treatment, another shift began to take place in the early 1930s that continued through the 1960s. During this time, the medical model began to take hold as a philosophy guiding the treatment of offenders. Building from the progressive movement, the model emphasized that offenders were in need of therapy and care, much like that which would be provided to those with a medical condition. The field of psychology and psychological testing was gaining prominence during this time, and as a result, the field saw an increase in assessments and different types of therapy. Behavioral approaches such as token economies became popular, as did individual counseling and psychotherapy (for review, see Gendreau, Listwan, & Kuhns, 2011).

The Crime Control Period

As can be seen from this discussion, the notion that offenders were in need of reformation (albeit with varying degrees of success) persisted from the late 1800s into the 1970s. However, we began to see an erosion of the support for rehabilitation for a variety of reasons.

First, there were increases in the crime rate during the late 1960s and 1970s. Drug use among youths was cause for concern at this time. Parents were concerned that marijuana was acting as a gateway drug, and self-report surveys suggested drug use was on the rise among teens (Alberts, Miller-Rassulo, & Hecht, 1991). At the same time, there was a spike in rates of violent crime, particularly gun violence among juveniles (Blumstein & Wallman, 2006). John DiIulio (1995) argued that the system should brace itself for a new kind of juvenile delinquent he termed the "super predator." These juveniles were thought to be gang-involved, intensely violent boys who would roam the streets inflicting mayhem and brutality on the public. All of these concerns proved to be false but were quite persuasive in influencing public opinion.

Second, Robert Martinson (1974) published an article arguing that "nothing works" when it came to rehabilitation. His analysis of programs operating in the late 1960s and 1970s concluded that the programs failed to reduce recidivism among offenders. Although Martinson later indicated that there were some studies that showed certain treatment strategies were effective in reducing recidivism, his "nothing works" statement was championed by those who believed the system coddled the offender rather than focusing on the victim. Even in light of the fact that reviews conducted by researchers on the studies reviewed by Martinson found that some programs worked well to reduce recidivism (Palmer, 1975), it is believed that Martinson's study had the impact it did primarily because it occurred during a social and political time that was ripe for change (Cullen & Gilbert, 2013).

Third, part of this social and political change actually emanated from the civil rights movement. The civil rights movement in the 1960s ushered in civil rights legislation, due process rights for offenders, and rights for inmates in prison. Simultaneously, the Supreme Court put limits on the ways in which youths could be processed through the court system to ensure the *parens patriae* doctrine actually did not lead to the juvenile receiving harsher treatment. Table 1.1 notes several cases in which the court extended due process rights to juveniles. In the context of protecting the offender from state control, a group of reformers referred to as the **justice model liberals** expressed concern that the system's attempt to help the offender was actually leading to their harsher treatment. For example, the use of indeterminate sentencing could lead to longer sentences because the offender was at the mercy of parole boards and other correctional officials who were given the responsibility to decide whether the offender was ready for release but who failed to prove they had reliable measures (assessments) to make this determination. As a result, they argued that the offender's rights should supersede all other concerns. They argued that the discretion of the system (that reached into the community agencies as well) meant that people might be receiving longer sentences, or a longer period of supervision, than was necessary (Cullen & Gilbert, 2013).

The conservatives agreed, not necessarily due to the violation of rights but because they believed the system coddled the offender rather than the victim. Based on the concern for the victim and public safety, they advocated for the increased use of mandatory sentences and arrest policies, the removal of amenities in prison, and punitive strategies such as boot camps and chain gangs in order to deter criminals or, at best, inflict harm (Clear, 1994; Cullen, 1995).

The get-tough movement led to many punitive strategies; however, not surprisingly, it also led to an enormous increase in the use of confinement. An increase in confinement

Table 1.1 Important Supreme Court Decisions Pertaining to the Due Process Rights of Juveniles

Kent v. United States (1966). 383 U.S. 541. A 16-year-old male defendant was arrested for burglary, robbery, and rape. The juvenile court decided to waive the case to the adult system for processing. Kent's attorney requested a hearing on the matter of the waiver; however, the court did not grant the hearing and remanded the case to the adult court. The juvenile was subsequently found guilty of burglary and robbery; however, he was found not guilty by reason of insanity of the rape charge.

- Justices were concerned that juveniles could be remanded to adult court without a hearing. The decision granted juveniles the right to a formal hearing, representation at the hearing, access to the records that would be reviewed by the judge prior to the hearing, and the right to a written justification for the order (Carmen, Parker, & Reddington, 1998).

In re Gault (1967). 387 U.S. 1. A 15-year-old defendant was accused of making a lewd phone call. After a brief hearing before the juvenile court, the defendant was remanded to a state reformatory for delinquents. The lawyers argued that the defendant's rights were violated given that he received a punitive sanction such as incarceration after an informal hearing.

- The *Gault* decision led to four basic rights: the right to a notice of charges, a right to counsel, a right to confront and cross examine witnesses, and a right to remain silent to avoid self-incrimination.

In re Winship (1970). 397 U.S. 358. A 12-year-old defendant stole $112 from a woman's purse. He was subsequently found guilty in juvenile court and sentenced to a state reformatory for a minimum of 18 months that could be extended to his 18th birthday.

- In the *Winship* ruling, the Supreme Court ruled that juvenile court should be required to consider the same standard of evidence required in adult criminal cases.

McKeiver v. Pennsylvania (1971). 403 U.S. 528. In this case, a group of appellants claimed that their request for a jury trial was denied under Pennsylvania law. The Supreme Court was asked to review whether juvenile defendants should have the right to a jury trial similar as was found in the adult court system.

- In this case, the Supreme Court preserved one facet of the informal nature of the juvenile court system. In the *McKeiver* decision, the Supreme Court ruled that juveniles did not have the right to a jury trial because it would alter the inherent nature of the *parens patria* doctrine.

Breed v. Jones (1975). 421 U.S. 519. A 17-year-old male defendant was convicted in juvenile court of a robbery with a weapon. At the dispositional hearing, the case was waived to the adult court system because the judge believed that there were no suitable facilities for the care of this particular defendant. The juvenile was subsequently found guilty in the adult system on the same charges.

- The Supreme Court ruled that juveniles could not be tried in the juvenile court and then be tried again in adult court.

(for both juveniles and adults) was justified on a number of grounds, including public safety, the lack of effectiveness of treatment programs, and selective incapacitation, which would lead to cost-effectiveness. For example, if the system could confine the small portion of offenders who were responsible for a high proportion of criminal behavior, it would significantly reduce the overall crime rate. Finally, in the juvenile justice system, waivers to the adult system increased dramatically. In fact, as noted by Patrick Griffin and colleagues (2011), in the 1970s only 8 states had laws related to transferring juveniles to adult court for particular crimes. By the 1990s, 30 states had enacted such laws. As can be

Table 1.2   Youngest Age a Juvenile Can Be Transferred to the Adult Criminal Court System

Age (years)	State
10	Kansas, Vermont
12	Missouri, Colorado
13	Illinois, Mississippi, North Carolina, Georgia, Wyoming, New Hampshire
14	Alabama, Arkansas, California, Connecticut, Florida, Iowa, Kentucky, Louisiana, Michigan, Minnesota, Nevada, New Jersey, North Dakota, Ohio, Pennsylvania, Texas, Utah, Virginia, Wisconsin

Source: Snyder, H., & Sickmund, M. (2006). *Juvenile offenders and victims: 2006 national report.* Washington, DC: National Center for Juvenile Justice.

seen by Table 1.2, 2 states actually have laws that allow for the transfer of 10-year-olds to the adult system for certain felonies.

The Competing View

It is important to note that even though punishment became the dominant focus during the get-tough movement, many researchers argued against these policies. For example, get-tough policies such as "three strikes and you're out" were based on the idea that the system could utilize selective incapacitation to reduce the crime rate (Zedlewski, 1987), but others countered that the estimates of social cost savings were too high and there was no guarantee that confinement would stop a criminal career in its tracks (Zimring & Hawkins, 1988). Still others were concerned about selective incapacitation on the basis of fairness and ethics. Is it ethical to incarcerate someone for what they might do? Particularly when the person is not given the opportunity to show otherwise? The concern would be to commit a false positive and incapacitate people who are not a threat and thereby deprive them of their freedom. Moreover, Francis Cullen (see Cullen & Gilbert, 2013) predicted that the policies advocated by the justice model liberals would backfire and lead to punitive approaches. Joan Petersilia (1992) and many others expressed concern that incarceration could lead to worse effects because prisons may act as crime schools or that for certain delinquents (particularly drug traffickers), a replacement effect would be likely whereby a new delinquent would be immediately replaced by another.

Finally, scholars such as Todd Clear (2007) predicted that mass incarceration could lead to increases in crime rates.

The most notable research (at least in the context of this book) undertaken during the get-tough movement was performed by a group of Canadian scholars. In particular, Canadian researchers such as Don Andrews, James Bonta, and Paul Gendreau continued to advocate for offender rehabilitation by further examining Martinson's findings that some programs did in fact work to reduce recidivism (for an extensive review, see Chapter 7 of Cullen & Jonson, 2012). Paul Gendreau and colleagues began to publish narrative reviews of studies that found that particular types of treatment programs were successful in reducing recidivism (Gendreau & Ross, 1979, 1987). The literature suggested that certain patterns existed for interventions that were more effective: they were behavioral in nature, they took into account individual differences in delivering treatment, and they focused on factors that could be changed (i.e., dynamic vs. static predictors).

Subsequent research utilizing more sophisticated meta-analytic techniques further uncovered particular strategies that produced higher effects (e.g., reductions in offending) than others. In particular, they found that cognitive and behavioral strategies were most effective, and punishment-oriented programs produced the lowest effects. Moreover, they argued that programs that occur in the offenders' natural environment are multimodal, are sufficiently intensive, encompass rewards for prosocial behavior, target high-risk and high-criminogenic-need individuals, and are matched with the learning styles and abilities of the offender tended to be most likely to reduce recidivism (Andrews et al., 1990; Gendreau, Little, & Goggin, 1996; Lipsey, 1992, 1995; Lipsey & Wilson, 1998). In fact, studies found that if programs relied on these approaches, they could reduce recidivism by as much as 30%. More important, however, were studies that found punishment did not work. In fact, many of the punishments popularized during the get-tough movement (e.g., boot camps, intensive supervision probation, and Scared Straight) actually increased recidivism (MacKenzie & Armstrong, 2004; Petrosino, Turpin-Petrosino, & Finckenauer, 2000).

In an effort to translate these research findings into useful practices, the results were eventually organized into what is now commonly referred to as the **principles of effective intervention** (Gendreau, 1996). These principles and the strong empirical support for treatment-based strategies led the National Institute of Corrections to begin offering training and seminars to agencies on the topic of effective interventions with offenders in the late 1990s. According to Cullen and Jonson (2012), these principles can be summarized into four key themes:

- Treatment should target high-risk offenders (risk principle).
- Treatment should focus on the criminogenic (crime-producing) needs of the offender (needs principle).
- Treatment should be cognitive behavioral in nature (general responsivity).
- Other considerations must be taken into consideration [specific responsivity, training, culture, environment (prison vs. community), etc.].

These principles are ultimately the driving force behind this text, and we will discuss each of them extensively throughout the book.

The Current Landscape

Given the strong effects of treatment and the high cost/low impact of punitive-based strategies on recidivism, we can see that the system appears poised to be softening its approach on crime. However, it is difficult to see change occur quickly within corrections, particularly when the get-tough movement had such strong political support.

If we are to take an optimistic approach, it appears that the system is beginning to take steps back toward a rehabilitative agenda. As noted by Listwan and colleagues (2008), "despite the wildly punitive shift that has occurred in American corrections, ideological and policy space exists to bring about alternative initiatives that emphasize social welfare and challenge the effectiveness of inflicting pain on offenders" (p. 425). To be fair, however, in addition to the empirical literature cited previously with regard to "what works," there are several other reasons why the system may be more amendable to a rehabilitative philosophy.

First, as noted previously, several "get-tough" policies have been shown to be ineffective in reducing recidivism. For example, boot camps were popular primarily due to their punitive nature. What isn't more appealing than making disrespectful youths rise at dawn to engage in "hard work" and discipline? Yet the research found that the boot camps actually led to increases in recidivism (MacKenzie, Brame, McDowall, & Souryal, 1995). If we strip away the yelling and discipline that comprised most boot camps, we are left with no intervention. In other words, the boot camps, as with many of the punitive approaches of the time (e.g., Scared Straight and DARE), do little to intervene in a way that will impact why the youth committed the crime in the first place (e.g., dysfunctional families, communities, and schools).

As noted by Cullen and Gilbert (2013), three reasons explain why these types of harsh penalties have little effect: First, these laws had nothing to do with whether offenders were arrested and sanctioned; rather they sought to increase the harshness of the penalties imposed on lawbreakers. In terms of recidivism, however, offenders appear to respond, if at all, more to the certainty than to the severity of punishment. Second, due to plea-bargaining, the penalties are inconsistently applied, thus undermining their mandatory quality. And third and most important, punitive sanctions do not change the underlying risk factors that create stable propensity to offend (p. 188).

We can also look to the juvenile system and see some movement away from punitive strategies. For example, the Supreme Court recently reversed its stance on the death penalty and in *Roper v. Simmons* (2005) declared it unconstitutional for juveniles younger than 18 years of age. Studies find that transferring juveniles to adult courts is not effective in reducing recidivism through their potentially deterrent effect. In fact, juveniles transferred to adult court were more likely to recidivate, were less likely to have access to treatment services, and were at greater risk for victimization (Applegate, King Davis, & Cullen, 2009).

As we will discuss again in Chapter 11, the sheer number of people incarcerated has strained state budgets past their capacity. It should not be suggested that incarceration has no impact on recidivism. Rather, the question is often, what impact does incarceration have on crime and at what cost? In terms of cost, according to the Pew Center for the States (2008), corrections ranks as the second highest expenditure in the United States. It is estimated that the money spent on corrections by states increased from $12 billion in 1987 to nearly $50 billion in 2007. For some states, this translates into 1 in every 15 state general fund dollars being spent on corrections. Simply put, even if the punitive strategies hold some remaining political or social appeal, state officials simply cannot afford this incarceration binge. Finally, mounting evidence suggests that incarceration can lead to a host of problems, including increases in recidivism, psychological distress, and continues to destabilize already disadvantaged communities (Clear, 2007; Listwan, Sullivan, Agnew, Cullen, & Colvin, 2013).

As already mentioned and in light of the issues discussed previously, we are beginning to see cracks in this penal harm movement. Widescale policy initiatives such as proliferation of problem-solving courts, the passage of the Second Chance Act, the repeal of the Rockefeller drug laws, and an increase in the use of community-based options (including mandatory drug treatment in California) are just a few examples. These policies and the favorable research on rehabilitation illustrate that treatment is not about being soft on offenders or repeating the ineffective programs of the past; rather, it is evidence that we have learned a great deal throughout the years about designing and implementing effective correctional programs. If implemented appropriately, the payoff from effective interventions is potentially far greater than what we have seen the correctional system do in the past.

This text is organized in a way that will allow the reader a more in-depth understanding of the various features of effective programming. The first half of the book discusses the core issues as they relate to effective interventions. We begin by discussing "who" programs should target by reviewing the risk principle and the importance of assessment and screening. Next, we discuss "what" programs should target by identifying the core criminogenic needs that programs should prioritize in treatment. From there, we outline "how" to target the criminogenic needs, particularly how to translate theory into practice with an emphasis on specific components, referred to as core correctional practices. In this context, we also highlight ineffective practices to identify why they are ineffective in reducing recidivism. Then we discuss the specific responsivity principle and identify factors that programs should consider when designing and delivering interventions. Finally, the second half of the book discusses the delivery of effective interventions within particular settings (e.g., drug courts and prison) and to particular subgroups of offenders (women, sex offenders, and parolees) all the while keeping in mind the importance of quality and ensuring fidelity when implementing programs.

Summary

- Correctional policy is cyclical and subject to social and political forces.
- The Age of Enlightenment ushered in a new set of policies that focused attention on the role of the individual in understanding criminal behavior.
- The early history of prisons suggests that they were based on the notion of reformation, although through the ineffective use of punishments.
- By the early 1900s, reformers became committed to reformation and understanding offenders' social and psychological backgrounds.
- The get-tough movement became popular for a variety of reasons, including concern over rising crime rates, evidence unsupportive of treatment, and concern that offenders' rights were being violated.
- Even during the get-tough movement, studies emerged that showed treatment could work and would be most effective if certain principles were followed.
- The principles of effective invention provided the framework for understanding and employing effective treatment strategies to reduce recidivism.
- Although the get-tough movement was very popular for a number of years, studies eventually concluded that its impact was minimal at best and even harmful in some circumstances.
- The system has not fully embraced rehabilitation as a guiding correctional philosophy; however, there is some room for optimism that the system might have begun to soften its punitive approach.

References

Alberts, J. K., Miller-Rassulo, M. A., & Hecht, M. L. (1991). A typology of drug resistance strategies. *Journal of Communication Research, 3*, 129–151.

Andrews, D. A., & Bonta, J. (2010). *The psychology of criminal conduct* (5th ed.). Cincinnati, OH: Anderson.

Andrews, D. A., Zinger, I., Bonta, J., Hoge, R. D., Gendreau, P., & Cullen, F. T. (1990). Does correctional treatment work? A psychologically informed meta-analysis. *Criminology, 28*, 369–404.

Applegate, B. K., King Davis, R., & Cullen, F. T. (2009). Reconsidering child saving: The extent and correlates of public support for excluding youths from the juvenile court. *Crime & Delinquency, 55*, 51–77.

Bernard, T., & Kurlychek, M. C. (2010). *The cycle of juvenile justice* (2nd ed.). New York: Academic Press.

Blumstein, A., & Wallman, J. (2006). Crime drop & beyond. *Annual Review of Law and Social Sciences, 2*, 125–146.

Carmen, R. V., Parker, M., & Reddington, F. P. (1998). *Briefs of leading cases in juvenile justice*. Cincinnati, OH: Anderson.

Clear, T. R. (1994). *Harm in American penology: Offenders, victims, and their communities*. Albany: State University of New York Press.

Clear, T. R. (2007). *Imprisoning communities: How mass incarceration makes disadvantaged neighborhoods worse*. New York: Oxford University Press.

Conley, J. A. (1980). Prison, production, and profit: Reconsidering the importance of prison industries. *Journal of Social History, 14*, 257–275.

Cullen, F. T. (1995). Assessing the penal harm movement. *Journal of Research in Crime and Delinquency, 32*, 338–358.

Cullen, F. T., & Gilbert, K. (2013). *Reaffirming rehabilitation.* Cincinnati, OH: Anderson.

Cullen, F. T., & Jonson, C. L. (2012). *Correctional theory: Costs and consequences.* Thousand Oaks, CA: Sage.

Devereaux, S. (1999). The making of the Penitentiary Act, 1775–1779. *Historical Journal, 42*, 405–433.

Devine, F. E. (1981). Cesare Beccaria and the theoretical foundations of modern penal jurisprudence. *New England Journal of Prison Law, 7*, 8–21.

DiIulio, J. (1995, November 27). The coming of the super predators. *The Weekly Standard*, 23–28.

Geis, G. (1973). Jeremy Bentham. In H. Mannheim (Ed.), *Pioneers in criminology* (pp. 51–68). Montclair, NJ: Patterson Smith.

Gendreau, P. (1996). The principles of effective intervention with offenders. In A. T. Harland (Ed.), *Choosing correctional options that work: Defining the demand and evaluating the supply* (pp. 117–130). Newbury Park, CA: Sage.

Gendreau, P., Listwan, S. J., & Kuhns, J. (2011). *Managing prisons effectively: The potential of contingency management programs.* Corrections Research User Report (2011-04). Ottawa, Ontario, Canada: Public Safety Canada.

Gendrea, P., Little, T., & Goggin, C. (1996). A meta-analysis of the predictors of adult offender recidivism: What works! *Criminology, 34*, 575–607.

Gendreau, P., & Ross, R. R. (1979). Effective correctional treatment: Bibliotherapy for cynics. *Crime and Delinquency, 25*, 463–489.

Gendreau, P., & Ross, R. R. (1987). Revivification of rehabilitation: Evidence from the 1980s. *Justice Quarterly, 4*, 349–407.

Griffin, P., Addie, S., Adams, B., & Firestine, K. (2011). *Trying juveniles as adults: An analysis of state transfer laws and reporting.* Washington DC: Office of Juvenile Justice and Delinquency Prevention, Juvenile Offenders and Victims Bulletin.

Hirsch, A. J. (1992). *The rise of the penitentiary.* New Haven, CT: Yale University Press.

Lipsey, M. W. (1992). Juvenile delinquency treatment: A meta-analytic inquiry into the variability of effects. In T. D. Cook, H. Cooper, D. S. Cordray, et al. (Eds.), *Meta-analysis for explanation: A casebook.* New York: Russell Sage.

Lipsey, M. W. (1995). What do we learn from 400 research studies on the effectiveness of treatment with juvenile delinquents? In J. McGuire (Ed.), *What works? Reducing reoffending* (pp. 63–78) New York: Wiley.

Lipsey, M. W., & Wilson, D. B. (1998). Effective intervention for serious juvenile offenders: A synthesis of research. In R. Loeber, & D. P. Farrington (Eds.), *Serious & violent juvenile offenders: Risk factors and successful interventions* (pp. 313–345). Thousand Oaks, CA: Sage.

Listwan, S. J., Jonson, C. L., Cullen, F. T., & Latessa, E. J. (2008). Cracks in the penal harm movement: Evidence from the field. *Criminology and Public Policy, 7*, 423–465.

Listwan, S. J., Sullivan, C., Agnew, R., Cullen, F. T., & Colvin, M. (2013). The pains of imprisonment revisited: The impact of strain on inmate recidivism. *Justice Quarterly, 30*, 144–168.

MacKenzie, D. L., & Armstrong, G. S. (Eds.), (2004). *Correctional boot camps: Military basic training or a model for corrections?* Thousand Oaks, CA: Sage.

MacKenzie, D. L., Brame, R., McDowall, D., & Souryal, C. (1995). Boot camp prisons and recidivism in eight states. *Criminology, 33*, 327–357.

Martinson, R. (1974). What works? Questions and answers about prison reform. *The Public Interest, 35,* 22–54.

Palmer, T. (1975). Martinson revisited. *Journal of Research in Crime and Delinquency, 12,* 133–152.

Paternoster, R. (2010). How much do we really know about criminal deterrence? *Journal of Criminal Law & Criminology, 100,* 765–824.

Petersilia, J. (1992). California's prison policy: Causes, costs, and consequences. *Prison Journal, 72,* 8–36.

Petrosino, A., Turpin-Petrosino, C., & Finckenauer, J. O. (2000). Well-meaning programs have harmful effects! Lessons from experiments of programs such as Scared Straight. *Crime & Delinquency, 46,* 354–379.

Pew Center on the States. (2008). *One in 100: Behind bars in America 2008.* Washington, DC: Pew Charitable Trusts.

Pisciotta, A. Q. (1994). *Benevolent repression: Social control and the American reformatory-prison movement.* New York: New York University Press.

Platt, R. (1969). *The child savers.* Chicago: University of Chicago Press.

Sanders, W. B. (1970). *Juvenile offenders for a thousand years: Selected readings from Anglo-Saxon times to 1900.* Chapel Hill, NC: University of North Carolina Press.

Stigler, G. J. (1970). The optimum enforcement of laws. *Journal of Political Economy, 78,* 526–528.

Zedlewski, E. W. (1987). *Making confinement decisions.* Washington, DC: National Institute of Justice.

Zimring, F. E., & Hawkins, G. H. (1988). The new mathematics of imprisonment. *Crime & Delinquency, 34,* 425–436.

2

Understanding Risk and Needs and the Importance of Assessment and Screening
Potential Tools and How to Apply Them

Introduction

The assessment of offenders is one of the most important functions in modern corrections. Not only does the assessment of offenders help determine their level of risk of reoffending but also, if done properly, it can assist in identifying those factors of an offender's life that if properly targeted can reduce the likelihood of future criminal behavior. This chapter examines the history and purpose of assessment in corrections. Within that context, the chapter identifies assessment tools for both community and institutional settings, and how those systems should be used for placement, supervision, and treatment decisions. Finally, the chapter identifies measurement and implementation concerns.

Evolution of Classification and Assessment

The first assessment and classification systems for offenders were extremely crude and were based on some readily observable factors: separating males and females or juveniles and adults. For example, in many early penal systems, the penitentiary was reserved for older offenders, whereas the reformatory system was used for young criminals. Although classification is now an integral part of any prison system (maximum security, minimum security, etc.), many systems now use tools that go beyond sorting offenders by risk. These tools can and do provide correctional systems and programs with information that is used to ensure that offenders receive appropriate programs and dosages of treatment. We discuss the application of this process in corrections.

The "first-generation" assessment refers to what is called the "gut feelings" approach: assessment-based intuition, professional judgment, and outright guessing. Decisions based on this approach could be idiosyncratic, subjective, and full of bias. Furthermore, this approach does not yield information that could result in an easy distinction of risk levels. For example, since the development of the indeterminate sentence, parole boards have had to decide "who" to let out. It is natural then that the first formal attempts to develop a risk assessment were done for parole. A parole board member has to make many difficult decisions. Who do you let out and when? Imagine hearing hundreds of cases a month and making this decision with little more than your professional judgment to guide you. Of course, you would have information available, such as prior record, offense, institutional adjustment, and program participation, but no meaningful way to pull it together; even if you could, how do you know what is significantly related to outcome and what is not? This was exactly the problem that the Illinois parole board wanted to solve when they asked Burgess (1928) from the University of Chicago to develop a risk assessment tool based on data rather than intuition. Burgess collected background (criminal record, social history, and institutional information) and outcome (return to prison) information on 3,000 parolees and in 1928 Burgess and associates developed what was the first actuarial instrument used for risk assessment of offenders. The final tool was called the Burgess scale. Table 2.1 shows the factors that were significantly related to outcome. Social type is an interesting factor because it is not clear how they determined if someone was a ne'er-do-well. As you can see, some of the factors were related to characteristics of the offender, whereas others centered on their prison experience. This instrument is considered a first-generation instrument, and although it predicted who would fail and who would not fairly well, it had a number of limitations. Primarily, it was based on what we call static predictors—items that cannot change (criminal history) or cannot be easily influenced (e.g., age or months served prior to parole). These items can change, but only naturally. Dynamic risk factors, also called criminogenic needs, are those indicators that can be influenced to reduce risk, such as substance abuse or employment. We discuss dynamic factors later in the chapter. Following the development of this instrument, most assessment tools took a similar approach and were primarily based on static predictors. Why did static predictors dominate the early risk instruments? Examining the process used to develop these

Table 2.1   Factors in the Burgess Scale

General Type of Offense (e.g., fraud, robbery, sex, homicide)
Parental & Marital Status (parents living, offender married)
Criminal Type (first timer, occasional, habitual, professional)
Social Type (e.g., farm boy, gangster, hobo, drunkard, ne're-do-well)
Community Factor (where resided)
Statement of Trial Judge & Prosecutor (recommend or protest leniency)
Previous Record
Work Record (e.g., no work record, casual, regular work)
Punishment Record in Prison
Months Served Prior to Parole
Intelligence Rating
Age when Paroled
Psychiatric Prognosis
Psychiatric Personality Type (egocentric, socially inadequate, unstable)

Source: Burgess, E. W. 1928. Factors determining success or failure on parole. In A. A. Bruce, A. J. Harno, E. W. Burgess, & J. Landesco (Eds.), *The workings of the indeterminate sentence laws and parole system in Illinois* (pp. 205–249). Springfield, IL: State Board of Parole.

instruments will shed some light on why this occurred, but first let's look at the different types of risk factors.

Dynamic Versus Static Factors

There are two basic types of risk factors: static and dynamic.

- Static factors are those factors that are related to risk and are not changeable. Examples include the number of prior offenses and whether an offender has ever had an alcohol or other drug problem.
- Dynamic factors relate to risk and *can change*. Examples include whether an offender is currently unemployed or currently has an alcohol or other drug problem.

This can be seen in Table 2.2, which shows the risk factors associated with having a first heart attack. The first three are all important factors but are also ones that we cannot change. If your father or grandfather had a heart attack at a young age, you have a family history—important, but you cannot change it. On the other hand, if you do not exercise, are overweight, smoke, and have high blood pressure, your risk increases—these are factors over which we have some control. Of course, you can have them all and still not have a heart attack, but the risk increases considerably. This is at the heart of actuarial prediction: We cannot predict to an individual, but we can predict to a group with similar factors. If we target the dynamic risk factors, we cannot guarantee that we will not have a heart attack, but on the other hand we reduce our risk (based on a similar group) by 20 or 30% or more. Table 2.2 also illustrates another important point: Combining static and dynamic risk factors gives us the best predictors of risk. Remember, just because we cannot change static factors does not lessen their importance. After all, although the dynamic factors are important, are we really concerned about having a heart attack at age 20?

Dynamic factors are those that are usually targeted for change in most correctional programs. However, there are two types of dynamic factors: ones that can change relatively quickly (acute) and ones that require more time and effort to change (stable).

Table 2.2   Risk Factors Associated with a Heart Attack

According to the American Heart Association, there are a number of risk factors that increase your chances of a first heart attack:

Family history of heart attacks
Gender (males)
Age (>50 years)
Inactive lifestyle
Overweight
High blood pressure
Smoking
High cholesterol level

For example, if someone is unemployed, it is conceivable that he or she could interview and get a new job almost immediately. As measured by some tools, the person essentially went from being unemployed (risk factor) to being employed (no risk factor) very quickly. On the other hand, other dynamic factors, many of which will be related to the person's success at employment, such as attitudes about work, lacking self-control, having poor problem-solving or coping skills, and getting along with co-workers, will require more time and effort to change. The mistake that is often made is failing to see the relationship between these factors.

Development of Assessment Tools

The traditional approach to developing a risk assessment tool is identical to the approach used by Burgess and co-workers except now we use computers to analyze the data, whereas they had to calculate all the statistics by hand. You start by identifying a sample of offenders who are representative of your population. Next, you collect all the information you can find in the files related to offender characteristics (age, sex, marital status, criminal history, substance abuse, etc.). Following this, you collect information related to outcome (what you are trying to predict) measures, such as rearrests, program completion, and incarceration. Now you analyze your data to identify those factors that are most strongly correlated with outcome, establish your cutoff scores, and you are in business. Sounds simple, but there are some catches. First, unless you want to wait a couple of years for your sample to have an "at risk" period, you must select offenders who have already been off supervision or out of prison for a couple of years (so you can have outcome data). This means that you have to rely on the background information that is in the file. If the file has information on employment history, peer associations, antisocial attitudes, and so forth, you include it; if it does not, you cannot include it, and therefore it will not show up as a predictor. Most offender files contain a lot of information on offense and criminal history but not much on other important predictors. The result is that you end up with an instrument that predicts risk (it has to because you only use factors in your model that are predictive of outcome) but does not go much beyond that. But isn't that important, you ask? Of course it is, but we can do better. Let's look at a different approach.

Correlates of Criminal Conduct

What factors are correlated with criminal conduct? This is a critical question and one that criminologists have been wrestling with since criminology began. The first person to study criminals scientifically was Cesare Lombroso, who in 1876 wrote *Criminal Man* (1876/2006). Lombroso had personally studied more than 5,000 Italian criminals, and based on his studies believed that approximately one-third of all offenders were "born" criminal, or were what he called atavistic throwbacks. Lombroso believed that the born criminal could be identified through a number of factors: excessive hairiness, sloping foreheads, tattoos, solitary line in the palm of the hand, and other attributes. Despite the popularity at the time of this theory, Lombroso was wrong and his work was flawed. The reason he is important, however, is that he was the first person to try to study criminals scientifically. Since Lombroso, there have been hundreds, if not thousands, of studies. Of course, this is part of the problem. If you start reading this literature, it will take years, and when you are done you will be just as confused as when you started. For every study that says something is a risk factor, there is another that says it is not. So what do we believe? Fortunately, through the use of meta-analysis, researchers have been able to review large numbers of studies and determine effect sizes (how strong factors are in predicting risk). Meta-analysis is a study of studies in which researchers gather and code primary studies. The data is then used to estimate an average effect size on some outcome. Let's review some studies.

Table 2.3 shows a study conducted by Gendreau, Little, and Goggin (1996). Here is how you read this table. The factor is the predictor, the mean *r* is the average correlation, and the last column is the number of studies included in the analysis. The *r* is a value that shows the strength of a correlation between two or more variables: The higher the value, the stronger the relationship. The highest it can be is 1, and the lowest is 0, so a .3 is stronger than a .2, and so forth. Thus, if we look at lower-class origins (the side of the tracks you were born on), we can see that there were 97 studies, which when averaged together produced an *r* of .06. This does not mean you cannot find a study among the 97 that found a stronger relationship between lower-class origins and risk, but when taken all together, it appears that lower-class status is a predictor, but a relatively minor one. On the other hand, the predictor of antisocial attitudes and associates is much stronger.

Table 2.4 is a similar analysis conducted by Simourd (1993). As can be seen in this table, Simourd breaks family into two areas: family structure/parental problems and poor parent–child relations. Although family structure is positively correlated with risk, the relationship is not very strong (.07). Conversely, poor parent–child relations are

Table 2.3   Factors Correlated with Risk

	Mean *r*	No. of studies
Lower class origins	.06	97
Personal distress/ psychopathology	.08	226
Educational/vocational achievement	.12	129
Parental/family factors	.18	334
Temperament/misconduct personality	.21	621
Antisocial attitudes/ associates	.22	168

Source: Gendreau, P., Little, T., & Goggin, C. (1996). A meta-analysis of the predictors of adult offender recidivism: What works! *Criminology, 34*: 575–603. Reanalysis by Andrews and Bonita (1998). *Psychology of criminal conduct.* Cincinnati, OH: Anderson.

Table 2.4   Meta-Analysis of Risk Factors

Risk factor	Adjusted R	No. of studies
Lower social class	.05	38
Personal distress/psychopathy	.07	34
Family structure/parental problems	.07	28
Minor personality variables	.12	18
Poor parent–child relations	.20	82
Personal educational/vocational achievement	.28	68
Temperament/misconduct/ self-control	.38	90
Antisocial attitudes/associates	.48	106

Source: Simourd, L. (1993). Correlates of delinquency: A look at gender differences. *Forum on Correctional Research,* 6:26–31.

approximately three times stronger (.20). This means that although family structure (e.g., coming from a single-parent family) is correlated with delinquency, it is not nearly as important as coming from a "bad" family. The order of factors in her study was very similar to that in Gendreau et al.'s (1996).

A related question concerns the relationship of these factors and gender. There is considerably less research on females than males. Crime has always been a young man's game, and the research has been overwhelmingly devoted to the study of males. However, some studies have attempted to correlate risk factors and gender.

Table 2.5 compares males and females on the same factors shown previously (Simourd & Andrews, 1994). The numbers in parentheses refer to the number of studies.

Table 2.5   Comparison of Risk Factors by Gender

Risk factor	Adjusted R (No. of studies)	
	Females	Males
Lower social class	.07 (19)	.06 (19)
Family structure/parental problems	.07 (17)	.09 (14)
Personal distress/psychopathy	.10 (14)	.09 (17)
Minor personality variables	.18 (9)	.22 (9)
Poor parent–child relations	.20 (41)	.22 (41)
Personal educational/vocational achievement	.24 (24)	.23 (34)
Temperament or misconduct problems	.35 (45)	.36 (45)
Antisocial attitudes/peers	.39 (53)	.40 (53)

Source: Simourd, L., & Andrews, D. A. (1994). Correlates of delinquency: A look at gender differences. *Forum on Correctional Research,* 6:26–31.

Table 2.6 Meta-Analysis of the Predictors of Female Delinquency by Hubbard and Pratt (2002)

Factor	Mean effect size
Socioeconomic status	.03
Anxiety	.06
Self-image	.13
Family relationships	.17
Antisocial attitudes/beliefs	.18
Physical or sexual abuse	.21
Antisocial personality	.21
School relationships	.25
History of antisocial behavior	.48
Antisocial peers	.53

Source: Hubbard, D., & Pratt, T. (2002). A meta-analysis of the predictors of delinquency. *Journal of Offender Rehabilitation, 34*(3):1–13.

These data indicate that there is a very similar correlation between males and females on these risk factors. This is not to say that there are not differences between males and females. For example, females are more likely to be sexually abused than males. Sexual abuse may occur more frequently for females and may be a greater pathway to delinquent behavior (because it is more likely to occur for this group); however, these data indicate that the major risk factors are equally important for males and female. This is discussed further in Chapter 9.

Finally, Table 2.6 shows the results from a meta-analysis study conducted by Hubbard and Pratt (2002) that examined only studies of female delinquents. As you can see from these results, a fairly similar pattern emerges. This is not to say that there has been sufficient research in this area; however, the studies that are available clearly show that the major factors for both males and females are similar.

Major Set of Risk Factors

This and other research led Andrews and Bonta (1996) to identify a major set of risk factors. Table 2.7 shows the eight major risk factors, or correlates, of criminal conduct, starting with antisocial, pro-criminal attitudes, values, and beliefs, and cognitive emotional states (e.g., anger, rage, and criminal identity). This risk factor manifests itself in several important ways: negative expressions about the law, about conventional institutions, about self-management of behavior, and a lack of empathy and sensitivity toward others. In addition, offenders often minimize or neutralize their behavior. Neutralizations are a set of verbalizations, which function to say that in particular situations it is okay to violate the law. Neutralization techniques were first identified by Sykes and Matza (1957) and include the following:

Table 2.7 Major Set of Risk/Need Factors

1. Antisocial/pro-criminal attitudes, values, beliefs, and cognitive emotional states
2. Pro-criminal associates and isolation from anti-criminal others
3. Temperamental and personality factors conducive to criminal activity, including
   - psychopathy
   - weak socialization
   - impulsivity
   - restless/aggressive energy
   - egocentrism
   - below average verbal intelligence
   - a taste for risk
   - weak problem-solving/self-regulation skills
4. A history of antisocial behavior
   - evident from a young age
   - in a variety of settings
   - involving a number and variety of different acts
5. Family factors that include criminality and a variety of psychological programs in the family of origin, including
   - low levels of affection, caring, and cohesiveness
   - poor parental supervision and discipline practices
   - outright neglect and abuse
6. Low levels of personal, educational, vocational, or financial achievement
7. Low levels of involvement in prosocial leisure activities
   - Allows for interaction with antisocial peers
   - Allows for offenders to have idle time
   - Offenders replace prosocial behavior with antisocial behavior
8. Substance abuse
   - It is illegal itself (drugs)
   - Engages with antisocial others
   - Impacts social skills

Source: Andrews, D., & Bonta, J. (1996). *Psychology of criminal conduct.* Cincinnati, OH: Anderson.

Denial of responsibility: Criminal acts are due to factors beyond the control of the individual (e.g., "I was drunk" and "Some dude told me I could borrow his car").
Denial of injury: The offender admits responsibility for the act but minimizes the extent of harm or denies any harm was done (e.g., "Yeah, I beat him up, but they only went to the hospital so they could collect unemployment").
Denial of the victim: Reverses the role of the offender and victim and blames the victim (e.g., "She knows not to nag me" and "I'm really the victim here").
System bashing: Those who disapprove of the offender's act are defined as immoral, hypocritical, or criminal themselves (e.g., "Everyone uses drugs, I just got caught").
Appeal to higher loyalties: Live by a different code; the demands of larger society are sacrificed for the demands of more immediate loyalties (e.g., "Me and my boys have a different set of rules we live by").

The second major risk factor is one that we are all familiar with—having pro-criminal friends and a lack of prosocial friends and acquaintances. As our mothers all knew, whom you hang around with is very important. Friends often act as role models and provide the context and the reinforcement for criminal behavior.

The third major risk factor is one that is often ignored in assessment: temperamental and personality factors. The first two are often associated with offenders who are referred to as psychopaths. Note that egocentrism is correlated with risk. Many offenders are self-centered and have an inflated sense of self rather than the commonly held perception that offenders suffer from low self-esteem. Studies are finding that criminals are more likely to be characterized as negative or hostile in interpersonal relationships, unempathetic, and lacking in self-control. However, personality is most likely working in tandem with other risk factors such as peers and attitudes. Just being egocentric will not make someone high risk for criminal conduct. If that were the case, we would have to lock up most of the judges and professors in this country.

The fourth major risk factor is the one that is most commonly used—history. This of course includes criminal history and other antisocial behavior. Although history is a very strong predictor of future behavior, it has its limitations. The first limitation is that it is not very dynamic, and although it is useful for prediction, it does not provide much direction as to the targets for change. The other limitation of history is that one has to have the history before it can be used in prediction. For example, it is not difficult to predict that someone who has four or five prior driving under the influence (DUI) offenses has a drinking problem and might drink and drive again. At one point, however, this person had his or her first DUI. Undoubtedly, this person probably had a number of other risk factors; however, because he or she had no history of DUI offenses, we would have had little to base prediction if we relied primarily on history. Again, this is not to say that history is not a very strong (if not the strongest) predictor of future behavior. Life-course studies indicate that by age 12 years, up to 40% of later serious offenders have committed their first criminal act, and that by age 14 years, up to 85% have committed their first criminal act.

The fifth major risk factor involves family factors including criminal behavior in the immediate family and a number of other problems, such as low levels of affection, poor parental supervision, and outright neglect and abuse.

The sixth major risk factor is low levels of personal educational, vocational, and financial achievement; essentially work and school achievement are correlated with risk and round out the top six. Getting an offender a job or an education is important for several reasons (it structures time, gets the offender around prosocial people, and helps him or her support family and self), but if one thinks that working is for chumps, shows up late for work all the time, fights with boss or co-workers, and so forth, how long will he or she last on the job? Can you see why attitudes and values are so important to identifying and reducing risk? It is a critical factor in determining how we behave.

Factor seven includes a lack of prosocial leisure activities. This allows for interaction with antisocial peers and idle time (to get into trouble), and the end results is that offenders replace prosocial behavior with antisocial behavior.

Finally, the eighth risk factor is the abuse of alcohol and/or other drugs. This often allows for the interaction with antisocial peers, impacts social skills, and, in the case of illicit drugs, is illegal in and of itself.

A minor set of risk factors include lower-class origins as assessed by adverse neighborhood conditions, and some personal distress factors such as low self-esteem, anxiety, depression, or being officially labeled as mentally disordered. Finally, some biological and neuropsychological indicators have also shown some correlation with criminal conduct. Again, however, these factors are relatively minor and should not be the major focus or targets for changing criminal behavior. For example, making an offender feel better about himself or herself without reducing antisocial attitudes and values will only produce a happier offender. Many researchers believe that most of the secondary risk factors run through what Andrews and Bonta (1996) call the "big" four: attitudes, values, and beliefs; peer associations; personality; and history.

Interestingly, a study of offenders who failed on parole in Pennsylvania by Bucklen and Zajac (2009) illustrates these points. The most important factors centered on attitudes, whether they were about work, behavior, social support systems, or peers. As you can see in Table 2.8, most of the factors were directly related to attitudes, peers and associates, and personality.

Finally, let's review a study that did not involve an offender population. Many years ago, Cullen, Latessa, and Bryne (1990) performed a survey of head football coaches. They surveyed every Division I head football coach in America and asked them about cheating. The coaches told us that they believed that a major reason that there was so much cheating among college athletes was because they had to recruit many players from poor neighborhoods, kids from the inner city, kids without any money, and so on. Their solution to the problem was to have colleges pay athletes to play, believing the result would be less cheating. The National Collegiate Athletic Association (NCAA) saw the study and funded us to conduct another study (Cullen & Latessa, 1996). This time, however, they wanted us to study athletes. So, we surveyed 2,000 Division I football and basketball players randomly selected from every school in America. We were interested in identifying the factors that were significantly correlated with cheating.

Table 2.9 shows the results from our national study. There were five factors that significantly predicted cheating among college athletes. First, we found that the super-stars cheated more. That should not come as a surprise, and there are at least two possible explanations for this finding. First are personality factors, such as egocentrism and a sense of entitlement. Second, of course, is that they had more opportunity to cheat. After all, no one offers the third-string punter a new car. Second, we found that cheaters hung around with other cheaters—birds of a feather, so to speak, or people that would reinforce their own behavior. Third, cheaters had values and attitudes that defined cheating as acceptable. They said things like "Everyone does it," "I'm turning pro anyway," and "The school and coach make a lot of money, why shouldn't I?" Fourth, we found that the cheaters did not have close relationships with their parents or their coaches. Finally,

Table 2.8   Results from Pennsylvania Study of Parole Failures

Social network and living arrangements: Violators were
- More likely to hang around with individuals with criminal backgrounds
- Less likely to live with a spouse
- Less likely to be in a stable supportive relationship
- Less likely to identify someone in their life who served in a mentoring capacity

Employment and financial situation: Violators were
- Slightly more likely to report having difficulty getting a job
- Less likely to have job stability
- Less likely to be satisfied with employment
- Less likely to take low-end jobs and work up
- More likely to have negative attitudes toward employment and unrealistic job expectations
- Less likely to have a bank account
- More likely to report that they were "barely making it" (yet success group reported over double median debt)

Alcohol or drug use: Violators were
- More likely to report use of alcohol or drugs while on parole (but no difference in prior assessment of dependency problem)
- Poor management of stress was a primary contributing factor to relapse

Life on parole: Violators
- Had unrealistic expectations about what life would be like outside of prison
- Had poor problem-solving or coping skills
    Did not anticipate long-term consequences of behavior
- Failed to utilize resources to help them
    Acted impulsively to immediate situations
    Felt they were not in control
- Were more likely to maintain antisocial attitudes
    Viewed violations as an acceptable option to situation
    Maintained general lack of empathy
    Shifted blame or denied responsibility

Successes and failures did not differ in difficulty in finding a place to live after release.
Successes and failures equally likely to report eventually obtaining a job.

Source: Bucklen, K. B., & Zajac, G. (2009). But some of them don't come back (to prison!): Resource deprivation and thinking errors as determinants of parole success and failure. *Prison Journal, 89*:239–264.

cheaters reported prior delinquent behavior—they had a history of breaking the rules. Of course, these are very similar to the risk factors that we see in the criminology literature related to offenders.

We also discovered that there were some factors that were not significantly related to cheating. Recall what the coaches told us: It was the poor kids that cheated. Well, we did not find it. Coming from a poor neighborhood and having a lack of money while in college was unrelated to cheating. Middle-class kids cheated just as much as lower-class kids if they had a history of delinquent behavior, if they hung around with other cheaters, if they thought what they were doing was all right, and if they did not come from strong families. We also looked at organizational context: Did they cheat in some areas of the country more than others? Did some conferences cheat more? Was it the "bad apple" theory that

Table 2.9   University of Cincinnati's Study of NCAA Student Athletes

Results indicated infractions were highest among athletes who
- Were highly recruited
- Associated with fellow athletes who broke rules or saw nothing wrong with cheating
- Personally embraced values defining rule violations as acceptable
- Did not have close relationships with their parents
- Reported prior delinquent behavior

Results indicated that infractions were *not related to*
- Economic deprivation: Coming from an impoverished background and having lack of money while in college do not appear to be a major source of rule infractions.
- Organizational context: How strongly winning was emphasized, success or failure of the program, league, region of the country, were not factors.
- Threats of sanctions: Certainty and severity of punishment for violating rules were not related to infractions.

Source: Cullen, F. T., & Latessa, E. J. (1996). *The extent and sources of NCAA rule infractions: A national self-report study of student athletes. A report to the National Collegiate Athletic Association*. Cincinnati, OH: University of Cincinnati, Division of Criminal Justice.

was often promoted by the NCAA—that it is just some bad coaches or bad schools? We did not find any of these factors to be correlated with cheating. Cheating was widespread. Finally, we examined whether the threat of sanctions had any effect. It did not. You could not scare or threaten higher-risk cheaters out of the behavior. Of course, this is very similar to what we see with higher-risk criminals. Prison, jail, and other sanctions often have little deterrent value for these offenders. What we found in our study of college athletes was very similar to what we see in our review of the meta-analysis of risk factors.

One of the reasons this information is presented is to show that many of the known correlates of criminal conduct have not always worked their way into static risk prediction instruments. To remedy this problem, some researchers have used a more prospective approach to developing risk tools. With this approach, the theoretically important factors identified in the literature are included in data collection efforts and rather than rely solely on existing information (from files), face-to-face interviews are conducted and added to historical data, and then offenders are tracked to see if they recidivate. Of course, this process takes longer because the follow-up periods have to begin after the information is gathered, but the end result is a more complete profile and the inclusion of dynamic risk factors.

Adult Risk/Need Assessment Tools

This problem began to remedy itself in the 1970s with the development of the Wisconsin case management risk/needs classification system. This instrument included three components: a risk assessment tool, a needs assessment tool, and a case management tool that identified offender personality profiles. The third component of the Wisconsin system allowed the probation officer to identify one of four (five in some versions) basic types of offender profiles. A brief summary for the four typologies of offenders identified by the classification system is as follows:

1. Selective intervention: Offenders in this group have led primarily prosocial, stable lives, with little criminal involvement.
2. Environmental structure: This group is characterized by a lack of employment, intellectual, and social skills.
3. Casework/control: These offenders have frequent employment and domestic problems. Alcohol and other drug problems are common.
4. Limit setting: These are the offenders who see criminal activity as a way of life.

For many years, this instrument (mainly the risk tool) was the most widely used classification instrument in probation and parole. The reason is because the National Institute of Corrections promoted it as a model classification system and widely distributed the instruments. Because it was a nonproprietary instrument (free to use), it was widely adopted. Throughout the years, the Wisconsin system has lost some of its luster. There are several reasons for this. First, many departments found the entire case management system too time-consuming to use. As a result, most departments began relying primarily (and often solely) on the risk component to assign offenders to case-loads. This tool consists mainly of static predictors and has limited ability to identify targets for change. Second, over the years the instrument has been bastardized—adjustments made to cutoff scores, items added or deleted, often without new validation studies. Third, newer instruments have been developed that have improved on this tool considerably. There was also a juvenile version of this instrument, but it has not been as widely adopted as the adult version.

In the 1980s, the next generation of risk/need assessment was developed, beginning with the Level of Service Inventory (LSI). The LSI combined dynamic and static risk factors together into one instrument that produced one score. This instrument consists of 54 items in 10 domains: (1) criminal history (2) education and employment, (3) financial, (4) family and marital status, (5) accommodations, (6) leisure and recreation activities, (7) companions, (8) alcohol and drug usage, (9) emotional and personal problems, and (10) attitudes and orientations. The LSI combines risk and need factors into one tool, and the resulting score from the LSI has been found to be highly correlated with recidivism. A more recent version of this tool is called the Level of Service/Case Management Inventory and, as the name implies, includes a case management component.

Recently researchers at the University of Cincinnati developed the Ohio Risk Assessment System (ORAS) (Latessa, Smith, Lemke, Makarios, & Lowenkamp, 2010). Unlike previous tools, the ORAS consists of a series of tools that allows for the assessment of offenders at various stages of their involvement in the criminal justice system. The ORAS consists of four basic tools: Pretrial Assessment (ORAS-PT), which aids courts in making pretrial release decisions; the Community Supervision Tool (ORAS-CST), which is designed for offenders under supervision in the community; the Prison Intake Tool (ORAS-PIT), which is used by prison officials to help determine programs while an offender is incarcerated; and, finally, the Reentry Tool (ORAS-RT), which can aid parole boards in making release decisions. This latter tool is especially important because assessing an offender who has been incarcerated for several years poses a unique problem since many risk factors are not as "dynamic" as they might be in the community. For example, when someone is in prison, he or she does not have as easy access to drugs, employment is more contrived, and so forth. Interestingly, for longer-term inmates (those who served 2 years or longer), the most important areas were criminal history, attitudes and values, personality, and social support.

Figure 2.1 shows the standard cutoff scores for the ORAS-CST and the corresponding recidivism rates. This means that an offender who scores 14 or less has a 9% probability of recidivism. Conversely, an offender who scores 34 or greater has a 69% chance of recidivism. It is important to remember that these probabilities are based on aggregate data. Essentially what this means is that if you have 100 low-risk offenders, approximately 9 out of 100 will recidivate. Unfortunately, you do not know which 9 will recidivate. This is a problem with all prediction devices; prediction is based on a group rather than an individual, but again this is at the heart of actuarial prediction. Figure 2.2 shows a screen shot of the risk determination that is obtained from the ORAS-CST. This tool also allows for staff to reassess and gauge progress over time.

The ORAS, LSI, and the Wisconsin are examples of general risk/need assessment tools that are commonly used in probation, parole, and community corrections. In addition, there are instruments that are designed to measure specific domains, such as substance abuse, distorted thinking patterns, psychopathy, sex offender behavior, and mental health. For example, if you are doing an assessment of an offender with the LSI and were to find that substance abuse was a risk factor for that offender, you might then conduct a more in-depth assessment using one of many assessment tools that are available (e.g., Addiction Severity Index or Offender Profile Index). This assessment will provide you with more detailed and specific information on which to develop a case or treatment plan.

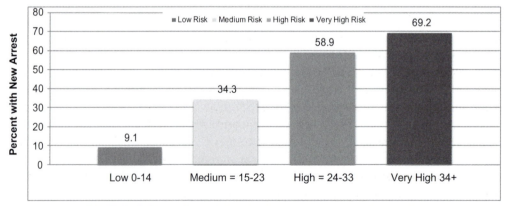

FIGURE 2.1 Risk level by recidivism for the community supervision sample.

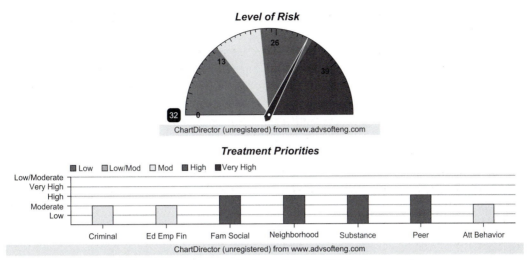

FIGURE 2.2 ORAS-Community Supervision Tool Intake Assessment.

Juvenile Risk/Need Assessment Tools

Traditionally, there have been fewer general risk/need actuarial instruments available for juvenile offenders. Recently, however, we have seen the development of a number of new instruments designed specifically for this population. The Ohio Youth Assessment System (OYAS), the Youthful Level of Service/Case Management Inventory, the Youthful Assessment and Screening Instrument, and the Youthful COMPAS are examples of risk and need assessment tools that have been recently developed for use with the juvenile population. These instruments are very similar in nature to the latest generation of adult instruments.

Reliability and Validity

There are a number of important considerations with any risk/need assessment process that need to be considered. How easy is the instrument to use and score? How long does it take to complete? How much training is involved? Is an interview involved and, if so, how do you verify the information? How much does it cost? These and other questions are important considerations when selecting a risk/need assessment instrument. Of vital importance is the reliability and validity of the instrument. Reliability refers to the consistency of the instrument. For example, if you and I were to use the LSI to assess the same offender, how similar would we score him or her? This is referred to as inter-rater reliability, and it can be a problem with more dynamic instruments. The second important consideration is validity—the accuracy of the instrument in predicting what it is we want it to predict. They are both important. It does not do any good to have an accurate tool if no one can agree on the score. Likewise, we might all agree on the score, but if it does not

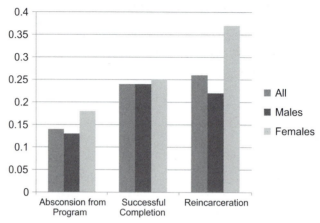

FIGURE 2.3 Correlations between LSI-R and outcome measures by sex. *Source: Lowenkamp, C. T., Holsinger, A., & Latessa, E. J. (2001). Risk/need assessment, offender classification, and the role of childhood abuse.* Criminal Justice and Behavior, *28:543–563.*

predict what we want it to predict, then it does not really matter. As a general rule, most good instruments are approximately 80% accurate. This is determined by validation studies in which we determine the correlation between the score and some outcome (usually some measure of recidivism). The higher the correlation, the stronger the relationship.

Figure 2.3 shows the correlations between the LSI and three important outcome measures: abscovsion, program completion, and subsequent incarceration. These data indicated that the LSI does a reasonably good job predicting all three outcome measures; however, with this sample it worked best predicting incarceration. Noteworthy is that the instrument predicted better for females. Other studies have also found that tools such as the LSI predict well for females (Smith, Cullen, & Latessa, 2009).

Importance of Assessment and Classification

There are a number of reasons why the classification and assessment of offenders is important in corrections. First, it helps guide and structure decision making, and it provides important information that correctional practitioners and officials can use to base decisions such as parole release. Second, it helps reduce bias by eliminating extralegal factors from consideration, such as race and gender. Third, it enhances public safety by allowing us to identify higher-risk offenders. Fourth, it helps manage offenders in a more efficient manner. We can develop caseloads and workloads around risk and needs and conserve scarce resources for those who need them most. Finally, the use of these instruments can aid in legal challenges. Most of us would rather justify a decision based on a structured process that has been validated than on our "gut feeling." Perhaps the most important reason to conduct good assessments of offenders is that it improves the effectiveness of correctional programs. This is best illustrated by examining some principles.

The Principles of Offender Classification

Through the work of Andrews, Bonta, and Hoge (1990) and Gendreau et al. (1996), certain principles have been identified that can help guide the assessment and classification process. Let's now review these principles.

Risk Principle

The risk principle is predicting future criminal behavior and matching interventions and supervision to the risk level of the offender. This principle states that interventions should be focused primarily on higher-risk offenders. The reason is simple: They have the highest risk of reoffending. Besides, why should we devote resources to those offenders who have a low probability of coming back again? Here is another way to think about it. Suppose that half of all offenders who leave prison never return. Are we worried about this group? Well, not as much as the half that will return. This is the group we are most concerned about and the ones on whom we should place most of our efforts. Of course, in order to meet this principle, it is necessary to know who the higher-risk offenders are, and this involves a valid and reliable assessment process. It is not only a question of resources but also an effectiveness question. A number of studies have shown that placing lower-risk offenders into intense programs and higher levels of supervision can actually increase their failure rates. Let's look at some data.

Figure 2.4 shows the results from a study of intensive rehabilitation supervision in Canada (Bonta, Wallace-Capretta, & Rooney, 2000). Risk was assessed using the LSI. The data showed that higher-risk offenders who were placed in the intensive rehabilitation supervision program had a 32% recidivism rate after the 2-year follow-up. Higher-risk offenders who were not placed in the program had a 51% recidivism rate. This is a 19% reduction in recidivism for higher-risk offenders. Not bad. However, low-risk offenders

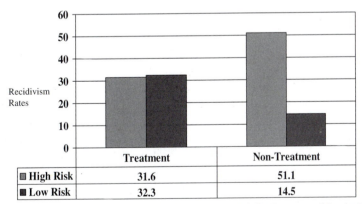

	Treatment	Non-Treatment
■ High Risk	31.6	51.1
■ Low Risk	32.3	14.5

FIGURE 2.4 Example of the risk principle from a study of intensive rehabilitation supervision in Canada.
Source: Bonta, J., Wallace-Capretta, S., & Rooney, J. (2000). A quasi-experimental evaluation of an intensive rehabilitation supervision program. Criminal Justice and Behavior, *27:312–329.*

who were placed in the treatment program reported the same recidivism rate as their high-risk counterparts. Conversely, lower-risk offenders who were not placed in the program reported a recidivism rate almost 20% lower. The intensive rehabilitation supervision program worked for higher-risk offenders but actually increased recidivism rates for lower-risk offenders. How could this happen? Before we answer this question, let's discuss some studies from the United States.

The risk principle can more dramatically be seen in a 2002 study that Lowenkamp and Latessa (2002) conducted in Ohio. At the time it was done, this study was the largest ever conducted of community-based correctional treatment facilities. We tracked a total of 13,221 offenders who were placed in one of 37 halfway houses and 15 community-based correctional facilities throughout the state. A 2-year follow-up was conducted on all offenders, and recidivism measures included new arrests and incarceration in state penal institutions. The experimental groups consisted of more than 3,700 offenders who were released from prison in 1999 and placed in one of 37 halfway houses in Ohio. The second experimental group was more than 3,600 offenders who were directly sentenced to one of 15 community-based correctional facilities. Thus, we had offenders coming out of prison who were sent to a correctional program (halfway house) as well as offenders who were diverted from prison (probationers) who were sent to a program (community-based correctional facility). The comparison group consisted of more than 5,800 offenders released from prison onto parole supervision during the same time. These offenders were not placed in a program but, rather, received straight supervision. Offenders were matched based on offense level and county of sentence. Each offender was given a risk score based on 14 items that predicted outcome. These items were derived from the data in a manner similar to that described previously. That is, we analyzed the data to identify those factors that were significantly correlated with incarceration, and each offender was given a score based on these 14 items. This allowed us to compare low-risk offenders who were placed in a program to low-risk offenders who were not, high-risk offenders placed in a program to high-risk offenders who were not, and so forth. We classified offenders into one of four categories of risk: (1) low risk, who had an 18% recidivism rate; (2) low/moderate risk, who had a 30% recidivism rate; (3) moderate risk, who had a 43% recidivism rate; and (4) high risk, who had a 58% probability of recidivism.

Figure 2.5 shows the effect for low-risk offenders using incarceration as the outcome measure. At the bottom of the figure are all of the programs included in our study. The gray bars or negative numbers show those programs that increased recidivism rates for low-risk offenders. The black and positive numbers show those few programs that actually reduced recidivism for low-risk offenders. As you can see from this figure, the majority of programs in Ohio actually increased the failure rates for low-risk offenders. Only a handful of programs reduced recidivism for this group, and the best was 9%.

Figure 2.6 shows the results for high-risk offenders. Not only did most programs reduce recidivism for this group but also eight programs reduced recidivism more than 20% and three programs reduced it more than 30%. Note that there were a number of

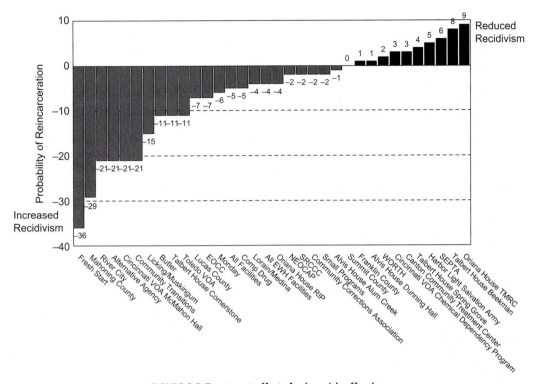

FIGURE 2.5 Treatment effects for low-risk offenders.

programs in Ohio that did not reduce recidivism at any level of risk, but this is more a question of program integrity than the risk principle. We will examine this issue in a later chapter. The best illustration of the risk principle can be seen by looking at the programs that had the most effect for high-risk offenders. If we look at EOCC and Mahoning County, we can see that these two programs reduce recidivism for high-risk offenders more than 30%, yet when we go back and look at their effect for low-risk offenders, we see that EOCC actually increased recidivism for this group by 7% and Mahoning County by 29%. Thus, the same programs that were able to reduce recidivism for higher-risk offenders actually increased it for low-risk offenders.

Recently, we replicated the Ohio study (Latessa, Brusman-Lovins, & Smith, 2010). The new study was even larger, with more than 20,000 offenders: 44 halfway houses and 20 community-based correctional facilities were included in the study. As with the original study, a 2-year follow-up was conducted on all offenders. Some of the results can be found in Figures 2.7 and 2.8. As can be seen from these data, the risk principle was again evident in the results.

The question is why do programs that have such a positive effect on high-risk offenders have such a negative effect on low-risk offenders? There are a couple of explanations. First, placing low-risk and high-risk offenders together is never a good practice.

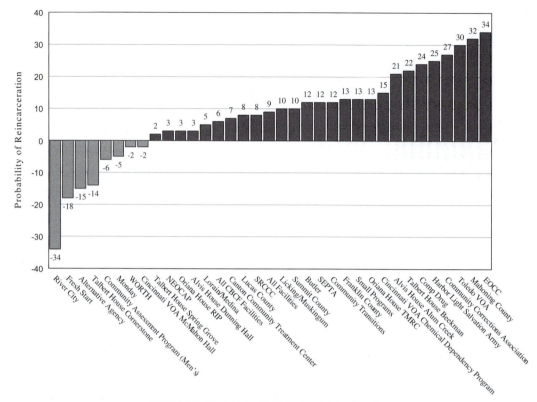

FIGURE 2.6 Treatment effects for high-risk offenders.

For example, if you had a son or daughter who got into some trouble, would you want him or her placed in a group with high-risk kids? Of course not. Second, when we take lower-risk offenders, who by definition are fairly prosocial (if they were not, they would not be low-risk), and place them in a highly structured, restrictive program, we actually disrupt the factors that make them low-risk. For example, if I were to put you in a correctional treatment program for 6 months, how many of you would lose your job? How many would have family disruption? How many think the neighbors would have a "welcome home from the correctional program" party for you when you got out? In other words, you would probably increase your risk, not reduce it. The risk principle is the "who" to target.

How Much Treatment?

Clearly, higher-risk offenders need more intensive supervision and treatment, but the question remains, "What does intensive treatment mean in practice?" Most studies show that the longer someone is in treatment, the greater the effects; however, the effects tend to diminish if treatment goes on too long. We believe that is because if treatment goes on too long, people have a tendency to give up. For example, if your goal was to lose 50 pounds and someone gave you a diet that could help you achieve your goal but it required

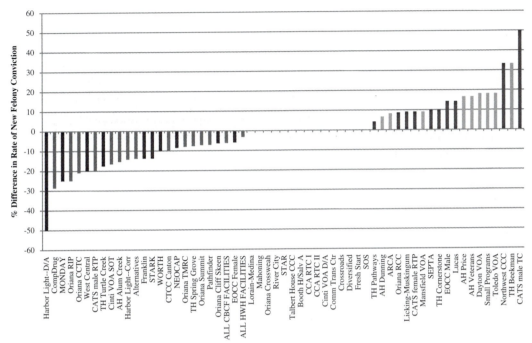

FIGURE 2.7 Treatment effects for low-risk offenders from 2010 Ohio study of residential programs.

you to eat nothing but carrots and alfalfa sprouts for 2 years, some of us might give it a try for a while but would give up well before the time expired. More likely, after a couple months we might say, "I lost 20 pounds, that is good enough."

Researchers have been studying the dosage issue and have found some interesting results. Bourgon and Armstrong (2005) examined treatment dosage and recidivism in a sample of 620 incarcerated adult males and attempted to identify the number of treatment hours required to reduce recidivism at different risk levels. The authors compared the 12-month recidivism rate of 482 offenders who received prison-based treatment to the recidivism rate of 138 untreated offenders. Study results demonstrated that 100 hours of treatment was sufficient to reduce recidivism for offenders deemed to be moderate-risk or to have few needs (defined as three or less). For offenders deemed to be high-risk with fewer needs or moderate-risk with multiple needs (3+), 200 hours of treatment was required to reduce recidivism. For the high-risk and high-need offenders, 300 hours of treatment did not produce reductions in recidivism. In a more recent study, Sperber, Latessa, and Markarios (2013) examined 689 male offenders in a community-based residential program and found that increasing the dosage of treatment for moderate-risk offenders only had modest effects, whereas for high-risk offenders the reduction in recidivism was significant. Figure 2.9 illustrates these results. These findings indicate that we cannot have "one size fits all" programs if we expect to reduce recidivism.

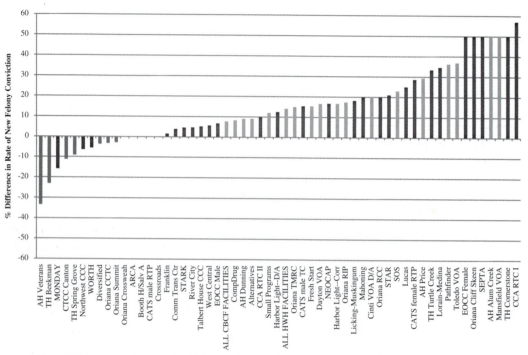

FIGURE 2.8 Treatment effects for high-risk offenders from 2010 Ohio study of residential programs.

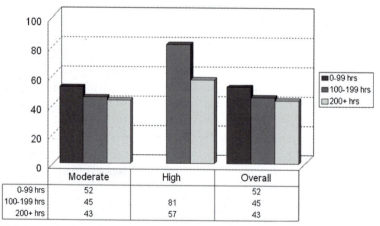

	Moderate	High	Overall
0-99 hrs	52		52
100-199 hrs	45	81	45
200+ hrs	43	57	43

FIGURE 2.9 Recidivism rates by intensity and risk level. *Source: Sperber, K., Latessa, E. J., & Makarios, M. D. (2013). Examining the interaction between level of risk and dosage of treatment.* Criminal Justice and Behavior, *40:338–348.*

Need Principle

The second principle is known as the need principle and is "what to target." The need principle states that interventions and programs should target criminogenic risk factors—those areas highly correlated with criminal behavior. Criminogenic risk factors include those items we have already discussed, such as antisocial attitudes, antisocial peer associations, lack of education, and lack of employment. Noncriminogenic risk factors, such as lack of creative abilities, physical conditioning, medical needs, anxiety, and low self-esteem, are not highly correlated with criminal conduct and should not be the targets for programs.

Figure 2.10 shows the results from a meta-analysis that compares effect sizes from programs that target criminogenic versus noncriminogenic needs (Gendreau, French, & Taylor, 2002). As can be seen by this graph, programs that target at least four to six more criminogenic needs produced a 31% reduction in recidivism, whereas those programs that targeted one to three more noncriminogenic needs essentially showed no effect on recidivism. These data illustrate the importance of assessing and subsequently targeting dynamic risk factors that are highly correlated with criminal conduct. The data also illustrate that the density of criminogenic needs targeted is also important. For example, higher-risk offenders often have multiple risk factors, not just one, and as a result, programs that are limited to focusing on one or two targets for change may not produce much effect. Let's take, for example, employment. For many offenders on probation or parole, being unemployed is a risk factor, but is it a risk factor for you? If you were unemployed, would you start robbing people or selling drugs? Most of us would not. What we would do if we lost our job is to go out and get another one. In other words, just being unemployed is not that major of a risk factor, unless you think working is for fools, you say things like "I can make more money in a day than most can in a month," you hang around others that

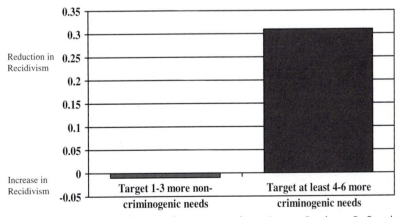

FIGURE 2.10 Targeting criminogenic need: Results from meta-analyses. *Source: Gendreau, P., French, S. A., & Taylor, A (2002). What works (what doesn't work) revised 2002. Invited submission to the International Community Corrections Association Monograph Series Project.*

do not work, and so forth. In this case, being unemployed is a risk factor because you have a number of other critical risk factors, plus you have a lot of time on your hands to do nothing but get into trouble. The problem is that just targeting employment without including the other risk factors (e.g., attitudes) will not produce much effect.

The Responsivity Principle

The third principle is called the responsivity principle, and there are two types: general, which purports that most offenders respond to programs based on structured social learning and cognitive behavioral approaches (discussed in more detail in Chapter 3), and specific—matching offenders to programs and interventions based on learning styles and ability. Responsivity factors include those characteristics of an offender that are related to their learning ability and program engagement. Examples include motivation or readiness to change, social support for change, intelligence, psychological development, maturity, and other factors that can affect an offender's engagement in a program. These factors are often ignored in the assessment process. For example, say you have identified the risk and need levels of an offender, but he or she is low-functioning. The person will not do well in a program that requires normal functioning, so this factor should be taken into consideration when matching him or her to a program, group, or caseworker.

Professional Discretion

The final principle is called professional discretion. Basically this means that the person conducting the assessment—having considered risk, need, and responsivity factors—should now include his or her professional judgment in making a final decision. As a general rule, overrides should not exceed 10% of cases. If assessors are overriding assessments at higher rates, it usually means that they do not trust the tool; if they never override, it means that they are not using their professional discretion even when warranted. Remember that risk and need assessments are designed to help guide decisions, not to make them.

Some Points about "Good" Assessment

There are a number of points about classification and assessment that we should make. First, there is no "one size fits all" approach to assessment. Each agency or jurisdiction has different needs. For example, if operating a pretrial release program, one of the considerations would be "failure to appear." This might not be important to a secure residential program. There is also no one instrument that will provide all the information that is needed for a comprehensive assessment. Assessment often has to be a flexible process that expands as warranted. Second, it is important to validate instruments to ensure accuracy and to determine the degree to which they can predict different outcome measures. For example, if I am interested in predicting violence, I need to make sure that the tools I am using can accurately predict this outcome. Third, classification and assessment are not one-time events. Risk can change over time. An offender who began supervision without a job, drinking, and hanging around with a bad crowd but 6 months later is employed, sober, and attending to family responsibilities will be lower risk than when he or she began supervision. Fourth, statistical prediction is more accurate than clinical prediction. We have known this since 1954 (Meehl, 1954). Instruments specifically designed and validated on offender populations will more accurately predict outcome than the best clinical assessment process. Classification based on standardized factors is also more reliable, easier to make, less time-consuming, and less expensive than clinical assessment. Finally, as mentioned previously, decisions based on objective criteria are less vulnerable to legal challenges.

Some Problems with Assessment

Despite the obvious problems associated with developing, norming, and validating instruments designed to predict human behavior, there are also a number of other problems associated with offender assessment.

Many agencies assess offenders but ignore important factors. An example would be an agency that relies on a static risk assessment instrument that focuses primarily on criminal history. An offender without a long criminal history might be classified as low-risk even though he or she may have a number of other important risk factors. Another example would be an agency that focuses primarily on substance abuse and ignores antisocial attitudes, antisocial friends, and other criminogenic risk factors. Another problem common with offender assessment is processes that assess offenders but do not produce scores or distinguish levels. These processes are usually quasi-clinical in nature. The program or probation department will gather a great deal of information about the offender and write it up in narrative form but when finished will not be able to distinguish levels of risk or needs. A third problem is programs and agencies that assess offenders and then essentially do not use the information; everyone gets the same treatment or intervention regardless of the assessment results. A fourth problem is that some programs begin using an assessment tool without adequately training the staff on the tool's use or interpretation. This can be seen in Figure 2.11 from a study conducted by Flores, Lowenkamp, Holsinger, and Latessa (2006). Needless to say, this affects the instrument's reliability and accuracy, and a host of other problems often emerge when this happens. Finally, many assessment instruments are adopted without being normed or validated on an offender population. Without this information, the accuracy of the instrument is essentially unknown.

Case Planning

Let us now turn our attention to the development of the case plan. Once we have assessed the risk, needs, and responsivity factors of an offender, we know the "who" and "what" to

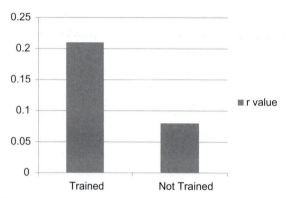

FIGURE 2.11 Predictive ability of assessment tool based on training. *Source: Flores, A., Lowenkamp, C. T., Holsinger, A., & Latessa, E. (2006). Predicting outcome with the Level of Service Inventory-Revised: The importance of implementation integrity.* Journal of Criminal Justice, 34:523–529.

Peer Relations		**Intake Score**	**Reassess Score**

| ***Problems Relating To Treatment*** | 1. Youth stated he has some prosocial friends and acquaintances. However, several close friends and acquaintances are delinquent.
 2. Youth hangs around with delinquent friends mainly on weekends.
 3. Youth is resistant to giving up anti-social friends. | 2 | |

Is youth motivated in area?: __Yes __No

Treatment Goals

1. Youth will understand the importance of associating with individuals who are prosocial and who will support him.
2. Youth will increase association with prosocial associates.
3. Closely monitor whereabouts and associates.

Objectives: Peer Relations	***Duration***	***Responsibility***	***Completed***	***S/U***
1. Youth will provide a list of 3–5 friends who will support him, and who do not have a delinquent or criminal record.	Month 1	Youth		
2. Youth will keep a log of activities and associates.	On-going	Youth		
3. Will work with Mother to assist in monitoring youth during high-risk times.	On-going	Mother/PO		
4. Curfew will be imposed during weekends for one month, after which will be reviewed pending progress.	Month 1	PO		
5. Youth will complete "Thinking for a Change" program.	3 Months	Youth		

Strengths:

Mother is willing to assist, and there are several friends who are very good role models.

FIGURE 2.12 Sample case plan.

target, along with some of the barriers that exist. Now, however, comes the difficult part—how to target these factors for change. Usually, this process starts with the development of a case or treatment plan. Although there are numerous examples of how this is done, they are all similar in that they attempt to identify the problem, the objectives, who is responsible, and the time frame for completion.

Figure 2.12 is an example of how a case plan can be formulated for a specific area of risk (peer associations). Note that in addition to the problem, this form also allows the assessor to identify any strengths or assets that the offenders might have in this domain. Now let's see how we might apply this process to a risk factor.

The area or domain is "peer associations." As we can see, this young man has some "bad" friends. The probation officer has set some goals and identified some activities that, if completed, should help reduce the risk factors in this area. Those responsible have been identified, as has the estimated time. This approach not only provides detailed direction to the probation officer but also gives the officer a number of indicators on which to gauge the offender's progress.

Summary

Offender assessment has been called the engine that drives effective correctional practice and programs. It helps us identify levels of risk and needs and to identify and, it is hoped, target the factors that are related to their criminal conduct. The following points help summarize this chapter:

- First-generation assessment consisted primarily of intuition and professional judgment.
- The first actuarial instrument was developed in 1928 and helped parole boards make release decisions based on valid factors.
- Static predictors are those factors that tend to be historical in nature, whereas dynamic factors are those that can be influenced or changed. Dynamic factors can include those that can change quickly as well as those that require more effort.
- There are two types of dynamic risk factors: acute ones that can change quickly and stable ones that take longer to change.
- The major risk factors include antisocial attitudes, who one hangs around with, personality, criminal history, family, leisure time activities, achievement in education, employment, and substance abuse.
- Instruments such as the LSI and ORAS combined risk and needs factors into one instrument and are considered fourth-generation assessment tools.
- The risk, need, responsivity, and professional discretion principles are the foundation for good offender assessment.
- Treatment effects are strongest when we target higher-risk offenders, and targeting low-risk offenders often increases failure rates.

- New research indicates that higher-risk offenders require a much higher dosage of treatment than low-risk offenders.
- The most effective approach is to target higher-risk offenders, target criminogenic needs factors, and consider responsivity factors that might affect an offender's engagement in programs.
- Good case planning involves hitting the target for change—developing a strategy for reducing the risk factor.

References

Andrews, D., & Bonta, J. (1996). *Psychology of criminal conduct*. Anderson: Cincinnati, OH.

Andrews, D., Bonta, J., & Hoge, R. (1990). Classification for effective rehabilitation: Rediscovering psychology. *Criminal Justice and Behavior, 17*, 19–52.

Bonta, J., Wallace-Capretta, S., & Rooney, J. (2000). A quasi-experimental evaluation of an intensive rehabilitation supervision program. *Criminal Justice and Behavior, 27*, 312–329.

Bourgon, G., & Armstrong, B. (2005). Transferring the principles of effective treatment into a "real world" setting. *Criminal Justice and Behavior, 32*, 3–25.

Bucklen, K. B., & Zajac, G. (2009). But some of them don't come back (to prison!): Resource deprivation and thinking errors as determinants of parole success and failure. *Prison Journal, 89*, 239–264.

Burgess, E. W. (1928). Factors determining success or failure on parole. In A. A. Bruce, A. J. Harno, E. W. Burgess, & J. Landesco (Eds.), *The workings of the indeterminate sentence laws and parole system in Illinois* (pp. 205–249). Springfield, IL: State Board of Parole.

Cullen, F., Latessa, E. J., & Bryne, J. (1990). Scandal and reform in intercollegiate athletics: Implications from a national survey of head football coaches. *Journal of Higher Education, 61*(1), 50–64.

Cullen, F., & Latessa, E. J. (1996). *The extent and sources of NCAA rule infractions: A national self-report study of student athletes*. Cincinnati, OH: Division of Criminal Justice, University of Cincinnati.

Flores, A., Lowenkamp, C. T., Holsinger, A., & Latessa, E. (2006). Predicting outcome with the Level of Service Inventory–Revised: The importance of implementation integrity. *Journal of Criminal Justice, 34*, 523–529.

Gendreau, P., French, S. A., & Taylor, A. (2002). Invited submission to the International Community Corrections Association Monograph Series Project. *What works (what doesn't work) revised, 2002*.

Gendreau, P., Little, T., & Goggin, C. (1996). A meta-analysis of the predictors of adult offender recidivism: What works! *Criminology, 34*, 575–603.

Hubbard, D., & Pratt, T. (2002). A meta-analysis of the predictors of delinquency. *Journal of Offender Rehabilitation, 34*(3), 1–13.

Latessa, E. J., Brusman Lovins, L., & Smith, P. (2010). *Follow-up evaluation of Ohio's community based correctional facility and halfway house programs—Outcome study (2010)*. Cincinnati, OH: University of Cincinnati, Division of Criminal Justice.

Latessa, E. J., Smith, P., Lemke, R., Makarios, M., & Lowenkamp, C. (2010). The creation and validation of the Ohio Risk Assessment System (ORAS). *Federal Probation, 74*(1), 16–22.

Lombroso, C. (2006). Criminal man (Trans.). In M. Gibson, & N. Hahn Rafter (Eds.), London: Duke. Original work published 1876.

Lowenkamp, C. T., Holsinger, A., & Latessa, E. J. (2001). Risk/need assessment, offender classification, and the role of childhood abuse. *Criminal Justice and Behavior, 28*, 543–563.

Lowenkamp, C. T., & Latessa, E. J. (2002). *Evaluation of Ohio's community based correctional facilities and halfway house programs.* Technical report. Cincinnati, OH: University of Cincinnati, Division of Criminal Justice.

Meehl, P. E. (1954). *Clinical versus statistical prediction: A theoretical analysis and a review of the evidence.* Minneapolis, MN: University of Minnesota Press.

Simourd, L. (1993). Correlates of delinquency: A look at gender differences. *Forum on Correctional Research, 6,* 26–31.

Simourd, L., & Andrews, D. A. (1994). Correlates of delinquency: A look at gender differences. *Forum on Correctional Research, 6,* 26–31.

Smith, P., Cullen, F. T., & Latessa, E. J. (2009). Can 14,737 women be wrong? A meta-analysis of the LSI-R and recidivism for female offenders. *Criminology and Public Policy, 8*(1), 183–208.

Sperber, K., Latessa, E. J., & Makarios, M. D. (2013). Examining the interaction between level of risk and dosage of treatment. *Criminal Justice and Behavior, 40,* 338–348.

Sykes, G., & Matza, D. (1957). Techniques of neutralization: A theory of delinquency. *American Sociological Review, 22*(6), 664–670.

3

Putting Theory into Practice
Approaches That Work in Reducing Recidivism

Introduction

Although research is a vital part of the scholarly enterprise, one of the problems with research is that we can often find a study to support just about anything. For example, if we believed every study about what food is bad for us, we would not eat anything; we would just drink a lot of red wine. The problem is that there are often studies that have conflicting findings, and as a result we often do not know what to believe. People often ask, "Do halfway houses reduce recidivism?" "Do prison programs work?" "Do programs for sex offenders work?" and so on. One thing we have learned over the years of studying correctional programs is that there are halfway houses and prison programs that reduce recidivism and some that do not. The same is true for sex offender programs, as well as many of the different types of rehabilitation programs that we operate for offenders. As you also learned, who we place in the program and what the program targets play a major role in reducing recidivism. The third part of this equation is the "how" we target these factors. As it turns out, some approaches are more effective than others. In this chapter, we explore the approaches that are most effective in reducing recidivism.

Understanding a Body of Knowledge

Given all the research that is conducted, and the sometimes contradictory findings, it is difficult to know what to believe. Looking at one study can be a mistake, and besides, there are often limitations to research, especially evaluations that are conducted in the real world (limited sample size, lack of generalizability, lack of adequate control groups, program changes over time, etc.). One of the ways we attempt to address these problems is by looking at a body of knowledge. For example, most of us believe that cigarette smoking is bad for our health. How do we know this? "Research" you say, but don't you think that given the hundreds of studies that have been conducted, there might be studies out there that say that cigarette smoking is not that bad? Well, these few studies may have been funded by the tobacco industry, but if you wanted to justify smoking based on some research, you can probably find these studies out there. The reason why most of us believe that smoking is harmful is because throughout the years there have been many studies, conducted all over the world by independent researchers, most of which have concluded that smoking is harmful. In other words, there is a body of knowledge concerning smoking and health that says that if you smoke, you increase your chances of cancer, heart disease, emphysema, and so forth. Well, guess what, we also have a pretty significant body of knowledge surrounding correctional interventions. The challenge is pulling that research together and summarizing the body of research on correctional interventions.

Ways to Review Research

There are three ways that scholars summarize research: literature reviews, ballot counting, and meta-analysis. You are all familiar with literature reviews: Read all the studies you can find and attempt to summarize the research. This is a common approach, and obviously it has some limitations (studies chosen to review, bias of reviewer, no quantifiable summary statistics, etc.). Ballot counting is where you find all the studies you can on a particular subject and then count the results; if more show negative results than positive ones, then you have a winner. This is the approach that Martinson used in the 1970s to declare that "nothing worked" in correctional rehabilitation. This approach is also problematic for a number of reasons, not the least of which is that it more or less ignores the studies that do show a positive effect. The third approach is called meta-analysis. Meta-analysis is now the favored approach to reviewing large numbers of studies. Some of the advantages and disadvantages of this approach are listed in Table 3.1.

Meta-analysis is very helpful in summarizing the research, and because it yields an "effect size," it can show the relative strength of the intervention or subject under study. An effect size can be positive (i.e., treatment reduces recidivism), negative (treatment increases recidivism), or zero (no effect). The larger the value, the greater the effect. Meta-analysis is a blunt instrument, however, because it cannot correct deficiencies or limitations in original research, but it can point us in the right direction. Thus, for example, let's say you wanted to know if adult drug courts were effective and you reviewed a meta-analysis in which the researchers found that, on average, there was a positive effect (overall reduced recidivism), and the vast majority of the qualified studies showed drug courts to work (whereas one or two studies showed no or negative effects). Most of us would then conclude that as a

Table 3.1   Advantages and Limitations of Meta-Analysis

Advantages
  Easily replicated.
  Identification of range of effect sizes as well as an average.
  Can estimate the changes in magnitude of effects depending on type of offender, type of treatment, quality of research design, etc.
  Allows for organization and summary of large volumes of data.
  Can easily add new studies as they become available.
  From a policy perspective, it provides more definitive conclusions than typical narrative reviews.
Limitations
  Selection of studies—called the file draw problem.
  Inadequacies of individual studies.
  Choice of variables for coding (limited to what is in written reports).
  Coding can be subjective.

strategy, drug courts appear to be effective in reducing recidivism. So without going in too much detail about this technique, let's look at some results.

Criminal Sanctions Versus Correctional Treatment

What is the purpose of corrections? While most would agree that public protection is the primary goal of corrections, disagreements arise as to the best methods to achieve this goal. On one side are advocates for more punitive policies such as increased use of incarceration or simply increasing control and monitoring if the offender is supervised in the community. Those advocating such strategies of crime control often do so on the basis of the often-interrelated goals of punishment: retribution, deterrence, and incapacitation. On the other side are those who argue that we must address the underlying causes of crime and criminal behavior, and we must provide programs and services to address the needs of offenders, especially for those returning to the community. Because most would agree that those who commit serious crimes need to be punished, the question is "Can we achieve the goal of public protection and meet the dual needs for punishment and rehabilitation?"

Punishment is an inherent part of the correctional system, and it is often justified simply because a person has broken the law. Society demands that certain offenders be punished and expects our elected officials to ensure that offenders be held accountable. The problem is the belief that somehow punishment alone will deter offenders from continuing to break the law in the future. The underlying assumption of deterrence is that the offenders are aware of the sanction, they perceive it as unpleasant, they weigh the cost and benefits of their criminal conduct, and they assess the risk and, in turn, make a rational choice to break the law (or not). The problem is that most street-level criminals act impulsively; have a short-term perspective; are often disorganized and have failed in school, jobs, and relationships; have distorted thinking; hang around with others like themselves; use drugs and alcohol; and are not rational actors. In short, deterrence theory collapses.

Incapacitation, which attempts to limit offenders' ability to commit another crime (usually by locking them up), can have some effect, but as many have found out, simply locking up offenders and "throwing away the key" has proven to be a very expensive approach to crime control. This strategy is also limited because the vast majority of offenders return to society. Without treatment, many will return unchanged at best and, at worst, with many more problems and intensified needs for services. Even if one supports incapacitation, one must ask, "What should be done with offenders while incarcerated?" This leads us to rehabilitation. With this approach, the offender chooses to refrain from new crimes rather than being unable to do so. So what works in changing offender behavior?

When we examine the body of research on the effects of official punishment alone (custody, mandatory arrests, increased surveillance, etc.), we see no consistent evidence of reduced recidivism. On the other hand, at least 40% and up to 60% of the studies of correctional treatment services reported reduced recidivism rates relative to various comparison conditions, in every published review. Of course, this is published research,

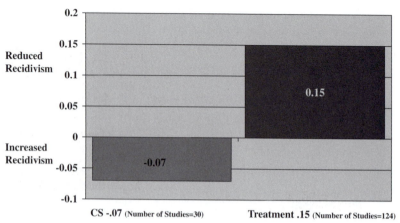

FIGURE 3.1 Meta-analysis: Criminal sanctions versus treatment. *Source: Andrews, D. A. (1994). An overview of treatment effectiveness: Research and clinical principles. Ottawa, Ontario, Canada: Department of Psychology, Carleton University.*

and we know that what are often published are studies that show some effect. So let's look more closely at the research.

Perhaps the best illustration of the overall effects of sanctions versus treatment can be seen in Figure 3.1, which is a meta-analysis by Andrews (1994) that shows the overall effect size of criminal sanctions (official punishment, such as jail time and mandatory arrests) and treatment. As you can see, just punishing offenders produces a slightly negative effect size, whereas treatment shows a modest reduction in recidivism with a positive effect size of .15. This means that the average reduction in recidivism for the correctional treatment programs in this study was approximately 15%. Dowden and Andrews (1999) found similar results when they examined programs for juveniles: Criminal sanctions produced slight negative effects and treatment reduced recidivism (Figure 3.2). These results are similar to what other scholars have found in studies from Europe and North America. So what do these meta-analyses tell us?

First, they indicate that punishment alone does not appear to be an effective strategy in reducing recidivism. This does not mean that we are not going to punish offenders, nor does it mean that they do not deserve punishment or that punishment does not work on some people. It also does not mean that you cannot find a study that shows some effect. What it does show is that when we look at this body of research, we do not see any positive effect from punishment alone, but that treatment does have some modest effect on recidivism. Research has also shown that punishment appears to be least effective with psychopathic risk takers, those using alcohol and other drugs, and those with a history of punishment. Unfortunately, these are common attributes of many higher-risk offenders. In other words, punishment appears to work least with the group we want it to work most—the higher-risk offenders.

Most researchers who study correctional interventions have concluded that without some form of human intervention or services, there is unlikely to be much effect on

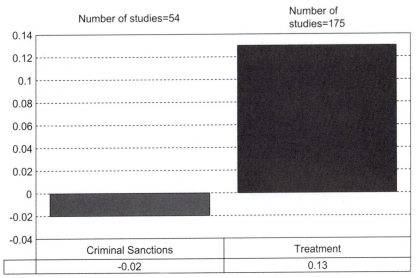

FIGURE 3.2 Meta-analysis: Criminal sanctions versus treatment for youthful offenders. *Source: Adapted from Dowden, C., & Andrews, D. A. (1999). What works in young offender treatment: A meta-analysis.* Forum on Correctional Research, 11(2), 21–24.

recidivism from punishment alone. If you do not believe that, just look at the number of offenders who have been incarcerated in our jails over and over again. As Einstein said, "The sign of insanity is doing something over and over again and expecting a different outcome." Although treatment may be more effective in reducing recidivism from punishment alone, unfortunately, not all correctional treatment programs are equally effective.

Nonbehavioral Versus Behavioral Treatment

The essential question is "How do we change an offender's behavior?" We must first recognize that is not easy to change behavior. If you think it is, just try changing your own. Losing weight, quitting smoking, or stopping other bad habits is not easy, but of course we know it can be done. So how might we go about it? One way might be to educate offenders about the behavior, teach them that drug use is harmful, or teach them the wheel of violence. Another approach might be to try and scare them out of their behavior: "If you don't change, all these bad things will happen to you." We could always help them develop some insight or go back to their childhood and talk about how they were raised. Another approach would be to actually teach them new ways to behave by challenging their thinking, modeling new behaviors, and having them practice and rehearse new ways to act and behave in risky situations. So which approach do you think would work best with higher-risk offenders? If you picked the last one, go to the head of the class. So let's look at some research.

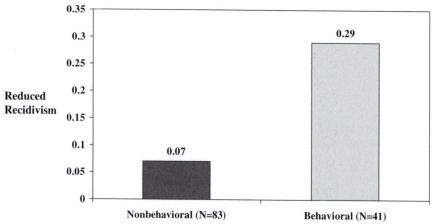

FIGURE 3.3 Meta-analysis: Behavioral versus nonbehavioral programs. *N* refers to the number of studies. *Source: Andrews, D. A. (1994). An overview of treatment effectiveness: Research and clinical principles. Ottawa, Ontario, Canada: Department of Psychology, Carleton University.*

When researchers have more closely examined the treatment data, they have found that there is a great deal of difference based on the type of treatment. Figure 3.3 shows what happened when Andrews (1994) divided treatment into two basic types: nonbehavioral and behavioral. The effect size of nonbehavioral treatment is .07, but it jumps to .29 for behavioral programming. In other words, behavioral treatment programs on average reduce recidivism approximately 30%. Again, similar results are found in Figure 3.4, which shows the effects for programs for juveniles (Dowden & Andrews, 1999).

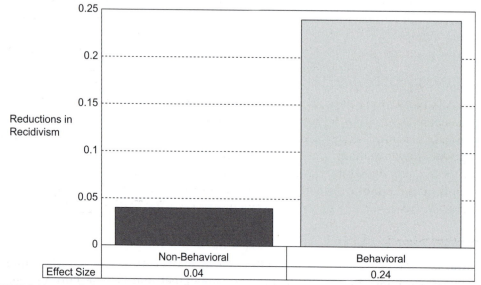

FIGURE 3.4 Meta-analysis: Type of treatment and effect sizes for youthful offenders. *Source: Adapted from Dowden, C., & Andrews, D. A. (1999). What works in young offender treatment: A meta-analysis. Forum on Correctional Research, 11(2), 21–24.*

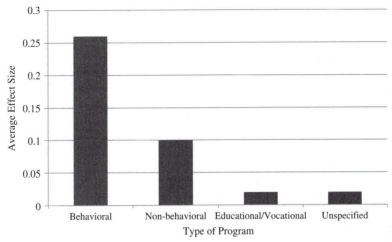

FIGURE 3.5 Meta-analysis: Effects of type of programming on prison and jail misconducts. *Source: Adopted from French, S., & Gendreau, P. (2006). Reducing prison misconducts: what works!* Criminal Justice and Behavior, 33, *185–218.*

Depending on the setting, recidivism may not always be the primary outcome. For example, prisons and jails are most often concerned about inmate behavior and keeping the facility safe for staff and offenders. Programming is often used as a way to keep inmates busy and occupied and thus out of trouble. In a 2006 meta-analysis by French and Gendreau, they looked at the effects of programs on prison and jail misconduct, including violent and nonviolent misconduct and institutional adjustment. This analysis included 68 studies involving more than 21,000 offenders. Male, female, and coed facilities were included as well as adult and juvenile. Figure 3.5 shows the results. On average, when a prison or jail offered behavioral programming, the average reduction in misconducts was 26%, compared to 10% of nonbehavioral programming and even less for educational, vocational, and unspecified programs. These findings should not come as a surprise because by their very nature, behavioral programs are designed to teach people new ways to behave differently.

Behavioral interventions are clearly the direction we want to head when we develop correctional intervention programs. Unfortunately, many of the programs we operate in corrections are nonbehavioral and produce minimal effects. Some examples of nonbehavioral programming include educational-type programs (e.g., drug education), talk therapy, and targeting noncriminogenic factors. These approaches are discussed in more detail in Chapter 5 when we examine ineffective approaches.

Characteristics of Behavioral Programs

So, what are behavioral programs? Well, behavioral programs have several important characteristics. First, they focus on the present—target and change current risk factors that influence behavior—not the past. Current risk factors might include hanging around with the wrong crowd, abusing substances, not having a job, minimizing one's behavior and not accepting responsibility, and so forth. Remember, sometimes the past can help explain current behavior or even be a barrier, but we cannot change the past. Second, effective programs are *action*-oriented rather than talk-oriented. In other words, offenders do something about their difficulties rather than just talk about them. These types of programs teach offenders new prosocial skills to replace the antisocial ones (e.g., stealing, cheating, and lying) they often possess. Interventions based on these approaches are very structured and emphasize the importance of modeling and behavioral rehearsal techniques that engender self-efficacy, challenge cognitive distortions, and assist offenders in developing new prosocial skills. Third, they include techniques to model and reinforce appropriate behavior and extinguish (punish) inappropriate behavior. So, should we hold offenders accountable for their behavior? Absolutely. However, punishment and treatment need not be incompatible, and doing one without the other is not likely to achieve long-term public safety.

What have we learned up to this point? First, it is myth that nothing works—we have clear evidence to the contrary. Second, there is a large body of knowledge that says that treatment is more effective in reducing recidivism than punishment alone but that not all correctional treatment programs are equally effective—the most effective programs are behavioral in nature. Now let's turn our attention to leaning more about the types of behavioral models commonly used in corrections.

Behavioral Approaches Used in Corrections

The most common behavioral models used in corrections include the following:

1. Structured social learning—programs in which new skills are taught, and behavior and attitudes are modeled and reinforced.
2. Cognitive behavioral programs that attempt to change the attitudes, values, and beliefs that offenders have about who they associate with, substance use, anger, employment, and other criminogenic areas.
3. Family-based interventions that train family on appropriate behavioral techniques so that they can assist the offender in making prosocial choices.

Although there are other behavioral approaches, such as radical behavioral (sometimes used with sex offenders), they are less commonly used in traditional correctional programs and will not be discussed here.[1]

Social Learning Models

One of the pioneers of social learning is Bandura (1965, 1973, 1977), who demonstrated that most learning by human beings occurs through observation, with role models and

---

[1]For an excellent discussion of radical behavioral approaches, see Van Voorhis, P., & Salisbury, E. (2013). *Correctional counseling and rehabilitation*, 8th ed. Boston: Elsevier/Anderson.

modeling instrumental in the process. Social learning refers to several processes through which individuals acquire attitudes, behavior, or knowledge from the persons around them. Both modeling and instrumental conditioning appear to play a role in such learning. For example, although most of us do not like to admit it, when we have children, we often become our parents, saying and doing things we never thought we would when we were kids. If you do not believe me, just wait until you have teenagers. This is social learning. Of course, as we also know, some of what is learned through social learning includes inappropriate behavior. This is why all staff need to be modeling and practicing appropriate behavior. If not, it can undermine the effectiveness of the program. Social learning models are becoming more common in correctional treatment programs and are often combined with cognitive behavioral approaches.

Cognitive Behavioral Treatment

Cognitive behavioral strategies often include cognitive self-control, anger management, social perspective taking, moral reasoning, social problem solving, and attitudinal change. Cognitive behavioral programs that include multiple components appear to have the greatest potential for reducing antisocial and violent behavior. The four principles of cognitive intervention are as follows:

1. Thinking affects behavior.
2. Antisocial, distorted, unproductive irrational thinking causes antisocial and unproductive behavior.
3. Thinking can be influenced and changed.
4. We can change how we feel and behave by changing what we think.

An example of how our thinking affects our behavior can be taken from driving too fast. Let's say that the speed limit on the interstate is 55 miles per hour and you are driving 65, or 10 miles over the limit. What are some of the thoughts that we have that allow us to break the law? "Everyone is doing it," "I'm within the 10-mile-per-hour limit," "I'm a good driver," "I'm in a hurry," "It's actually safer," "I won't get caught," and so forth. Now suppose there is a state highway patrol car in the median as you speed by. What thoughts do you have? "I hope he doesn't see me," "I hope he gets the other guy," "What excuses can I come up with?," and so on. You get the picture, and by the way, no one is thinking "I'm within the 10-mile-per-hour limit." Now you are not so certain there is a limit. Ok, so he pulls you over and is writing the ticket. What are some of you thinking now? "He's a jerk," "Why me?" "It's not my lucky day," "Didn't he see the other guy going faster than me?" "I'm going to fight this," "I'm the victim here," "What is it going to cost me?" By the way, don't you think that offenders often think like this when they get into trouble? Sure they do; the behavior is just more serious than speeding. Ok, so you have your ticket and you are 30 miles down the road when you look down and see that you are doing 65 again. What are some of the thoughts that allow you to speed again? "I can't get caught twice," "There aren't any more police," "Now I am really late," "I will be more careful and will pay attention more so that I see the police before they see me" (this is our favorite one: I will be a smarter criminal). If it is not 30 miles later, it will be the next day. So much for punishment, since you have not even paid the ticket yet! Finally, what are some possible thoughts that might get us to slow down? How about "It cost too much," "I didn't save any time," "It is the law," "I want to be a good role model for my kids," "It is too stressful," "I hate telling my family," "I can't afford the points on my license, increased insurance, etc." Any one of these thoughts might get us to slow down. This is called a cognitive restricting problem because it really does not take any skill to slow down; anyone can back off the pedal. All it takes to get us to slow down is to change some of our thoughts. Of course, not all problems are this easy. Some require us to change our thinking *and* learn new skills. This is why combining cognitive restructuring and behavioral skill development often produces the strongest effects.

Results from studies of cognitive behavioral therapy (CBT) with offenders have generally been positive. For example, a study of the effectiveness of one commonly used curriculum developed by the National Institute of Corrections, Thinking for a Change (Lowenkamp, Hubbard, Makarios, & Latessa, 2009), found strong results. Figure 3.6 shows that probationers who completed the program had almost 50% lower recidivism rates than those who did not participate. In a meta-analysis of studies of cognitive behavioral therapy, Landenberger and Lipsey (2005) found that, on average, CBT reduced recidivism by 25%; however, when certain conditions were met, the effects were 50%. Table 3.2 shows a summary of their findings. As can be seen, the effects were stronger when dosage was increased, when staff were trained and monitored, when completion rates were high, when the program targeted higher-risk offenders, and when other needs were met. In other words, the effects were strongest when the principles of risk, need, treatment, and responsivity were met. Among the factors that were not significant were

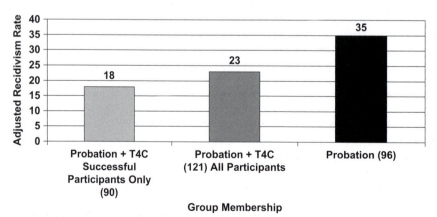

FIGURE 3.6 Effectiveness of Thinking for a Change: Recidivism rates of treatment versus comparison group.
Source: Lowenkamp, C., Hubbard, D., Makarios, M., & Latessa, E. J. (2009). A quasi-experimental evaluation of Thinking for a Change: A "real world" application. Criminal Justice and Behavior, 36(2), 137–146.

Table 3.2 Summary of Findings from Meta-Analysis of CBT Programs

Significant findings (effects were stronger if)

Sessions per week (2 or more)—Risk
Implementation monitored—Fidelity
Staff trained on CBT—Fidelity
Higher proportion of treatment completers—Responsivity
Higher-risk offenders—Risk
Higher if CBT is combined with other services—Need

Source: Adapted from Landenberger, N. A., & Lipsey, M. W. (2005). The positive effects of cognitive-behavioral programs for offenders: A meta-analysis of factors associated with effective treatment. *Journal of Experimental Criminology, 1,* 451–476.

the setting, juveniles versus adults, minorities or females, or the brand name of the curriculum. These findings not only give some direction on maximizing the effectiveness of CBT but also tell us that it has wide generalization.

Today, there are a number of cognitive curricula that have been developed to target or change antisocial attitudes and behavior. The following are some of the more common curricula that are in use today with offenders:

- Thinking for a Change (T4C is a curriculum developed by the National Institute of Corrections).
- Cognitive Behavioral Interventions for Substance Abuse (this is a nonproprietary curriculum developed by the Corrections Institute at the University of Cincinnati).
- Aggression Replacement Training (ART™) targets anger and was developed originally for adolescents but also has been validated with adults.
- Strategies for Self-Improvement and Change (also called Criminal Conduct and Substance Abuse Treatment). The curriculum targets substance abuse and includes motivation to change and cognitive restructuring and social skills.
- Moving On (this curriculum was designed specifically for female offenders).
- Reasoning and Rehabilitation (R&R).
- Controlling Anger and Learning to Manage It (CALM and CALMER)

There are several reasons why CBT can be effective in reducing recidivism:

1. Based on scientific evidence (cognitive and behavioral theories)
2. Based on active learning (not talk therapy)
3. Focus on the *present* (how offenders currently think and behave)
4. Based on learning (most crime is learned)
5. Target major criminogenic needs (e.g., attitudes, values, and beliefs)

Cognitive behavioral programs have several advantages. First, they can be used in almost any setting. They are used in secure settings such as prisons, detention centers, and jails; in community settings by probation and parole officers; in schools; in day reporting

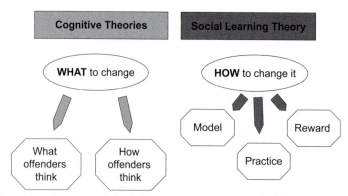

FIGURE 3.7 Social learning and cognitive behavioral treatment. Cognitive theory and social learning theory work together to form the "cognitive–behavioral" approach. Together, they dictate (1) what about offenders should be targeted in order to change their behaviors and (2) how to go about making the changes.

centers; and in residential and outpatient programs. Second, they provide structure for a program by providing the facilitators with a set format, which includes specific targets for change as well as activities that allow the offender to rehearse and practice new skills. Third, almost any staff member can be trained to deliver the program. Fourth, they are relatively cheap to deliver, especially because there are a number of nonproprietary (free) curricula. Finally, research has demonstrated that if implemented properly, these approaches can reduce recidivism.

Social Learning and CBT

A cognitive behavioral approach based on social learning theory includes three components: (1) cognitive restructuring, which is "what" we think or the content of thought; (2) cognitive skill development, which involves "how" we think or the process of thought; and (3) behavioral strategies, which include reinforcement and modeling of prosocial behavior. Effective cognitive behavioral programs include all three components. Figure 3.7 illustrates this model.

In 2007, researchers from the University of Cincinnati used a structured social learning model with cognitive behavioral treatment to develop a program for youths who had parole revoked and were returned to an institution. The program targeted higher-risk youths and provided more than 200 hours of structured treatment. There were three primary goals:

1. Shorten the length of stay
2. Reduce misconducts in the institution
3. Reduce recidivism

The results from the evaluation (Brusman-Lovins & Latessa, 2010) showed that all three goals were met: The average length of stay was reduced from approximately 130 to 90

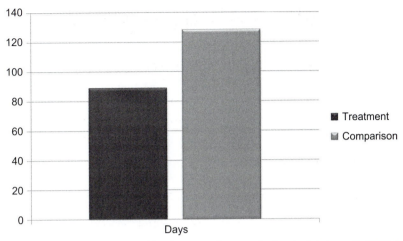

FIGURE 3.8 Revocation center length of stay (days). *Source: Brusman-Lovins, L., & Latessa, E. (2010). Revocation center analysis. Cincinnati, OH: Center for Criminal Justice Research, University of Cincinnati.*

days; institutional misconduct was reduced; and most important, postrelease recidivism was reduced from 34 to 19% (Figures 3.8–3.10).

By creating a structured social learning environment and incorporating cognitive behavioral curricula, youths were allowed to learn and practice new skills and behaviors that translated into a safer environment for them and staff, saved the state money by reducing the length of stay, and ultimately increased public safety by reducing recidivism.

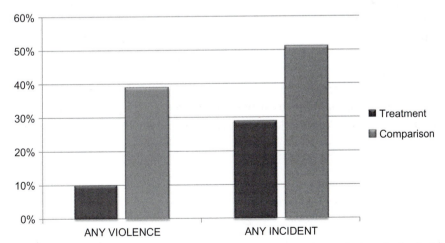

FIGURE 3.9 Institutional misconduct for treatment versus comparison groups. *Source: Brusman-Lovins, L., & Latessa, E. (2010). Revocation center analysis. Cincinnati, OH: Center for Criminal Justice Research, University of Cincinnati.*

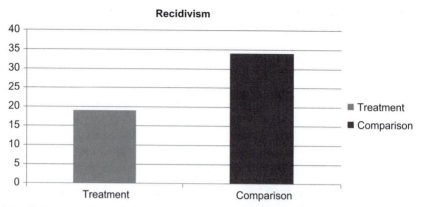

FIGURE 3.10 Recidivism rates 12 months later for treatment versus comparison group. *Source: Brusman-Lovins, L., & Latessa, E. (2010). Revocation center analysis. Cincinnati, OH: Center for Criminal Justice Research, University of Cincinnati.*

Family-Based Approaches

Behaviorally based family-based interventions are essentially social learning and cognitive behavioral approaches directed at the family. These interventions are most widely used with juvenile offenders and include a number of interventions and curricula. Table 3.3 gives some examples of family-based programs that have been found to be effective in reducing recidivism. Some, such as functional family therapy and multisystemic therapy, involve highly trained caseworkers working with family and other committed caregivers to target and change antisocial behavior in youths. Others, such as Common Sense Parenting and Parenting Wisely, are curriculum-based. Whereas these programs are often used with troubled youths, a program focused on youths more deeply involved in the juvenile justice system is Family EPICS (Effective Practices for Correctional Supervision), developed by researchers at the University of Cincinnati and based on some core correctional practices (Dowden & Andrews, 2004). These practices are discussed in more detail in Chapter 4.

Family EPICS is designed to target high-risk youths who have been released from a state facility by training the youth's parole officer on the model so that the officer can use

Table 3.3   Family-Based Interventions Designed to Train Family on Behavioral Approaches

Functional family therapy
Multisystemic therapy
Teaching-Family model
Strengthening Families Program
Common Sense Parenting
Parenting Wisely
Family EPICS (Effective Practices for Correctional Supervision)

it when he or she conducts home visits.[2] With the EPICS model, each visit with the youth and his or her family is structured around four steps:

1. Check-in, in which the officer determines if the offender has any crises or acute needs, builds rapport, and discusses compliance issues.
2. Review, which focuses on the skills discussed in the prior session, the application of those skills, and continued troubleshooting in the use of those skills.
3. Intervention, in which the officer identifies continued areas of need and trends in problems the offender experiences, teaches relevant skills, and targets problematic thinking.
4. Rehearsal and homework, in which the offender is given additional opportunity to see the model of a skill previously learned and to role-play the application of that skill in increasingly difficult scenarios; homework is assigned on the intervention.

Officers are taught how to use behavioral approaches to work with family and youth. Some of the core skills in which officers are trained include the following:

• Use of authority
• Relationship skills
• Cognitive restructuring
• Structured skill building
• Problem solving
• Reinforcement
• Disapproval and punishment

Essentially, FAMILY EPICS uses a structured social learning model with cognitive behavioral treatment; the parole officer becomes the role model for the youth and his or her family and then teaches and practices concrete skills that can help keep the youth out of trouble. It expands the role of the parole officers from authority figure there to do surveillance to someone there to also help in a very specific and focused way.

In a 2003 meta-analysis of family-based interventions, Dowden and Andrews examined 38 primary studies and found that the average reduction in recidivism was 21%. However, they also noted that there was a great deal of variability in the results. When they examined the data through the lens of risk, need, and responsivity, they found that the effects were very strong, provided the programs targeted higher-risk families, focused on criminogenic needs, and utilized behavioral models. Figure 3.11 shows these results.

Working with families has often been common with juveniles but often overlooked in adult corrections, but we are starting to see some changes. For example, one jail-based substance abuse program in Oregon requires family to attend a 2-hour group prior to visitation. If they do not attend, they are not allowed to visit the offender. Other programs

---

[2]EPICS is widely used with adults and follows a similar structure. What is unique about the family version is that it is often done in the home and training includes a caseworker accompanying the parole officer until they master the model.

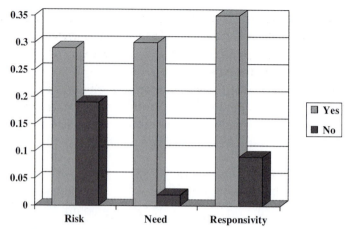

FIGURE 3.11 Meta-analysis: Average recidivism rates for family intervention based on adherence to risk, need, and responsivity. *Source: Dowden, C., & Andrews, D. A. (2003, July). Does family intervention work for delinquents? Results of a meta-analysis.* Canadian Journal of Criminology and Criminal Justice, *327–342.*

require family to attend groups before passes are issued. In one juvenile probation department in Virginia, family intervention specialists are assigned to each probation unit and are available to provide services as needed.

Summary

Changing behavior is never easy, but clearly some approaches are more effective than others. This chapter focused on the "how" of reducing recidivism by summarizing the body of knowledge on correctional interventions. The following summarizes the major points of this chapter:

- There is a significant body of research on the effectiveness of correctional interventions.
- There are three ways that research is reviewed: (1) literature review, (2) ballot counting, and (3) meta-analysis, which is now the preferred way to summarize large numbers of studies.
- Although there are strengths and limitations to meta-analysis, it helps point policymakers in the right direction.
- Although punishment is an important part of the correctional system, overall the effects on recidivism appear to be minimal.
- Correctional treatment programs are more effective than punishment alone; however, not all correctional programs are equally effective. Nonbehavioral programs are considerably less effective than behavioral programs.
- Behavioral programs have some important attributes: They focus on current risk factors, are action-oriented, and use reinforcement and other behavioral techniques to help shape behavior.

- Structured social learning, cognitive behavioral treatment, and family interventions are the most commonly used behavioral interventions in corrections.
- Using curricula helps give a program structure. There are a wide range of cognitive behavioral treatment curricula available.
- Research has demonstrated that the effectiveness of behavioral programs is enhanced when they meet the principles of risk, need, and responsivity.

References

Andrews, D. A. (1994). *An overview of treatment effectiveness: Research and clinical principles.* Ottawa, Ontario, Canada: Department of Psychology, Carleton University.

Bandura, A. (1965). Influence of model's reinforcement contingencies on the acquisition of imitative responses. *Journal of Personality and Social Psychology, 1,* 589–595.

Bandura, A. (1973). *Aggression: A social learning analysis.* Englewood Cliffs, NJ: Prentice Hall.

Bandura, A. (1977). Self-efficacy: Toward a unifying theory of behavioral change. *Psychological Review, 94,* 191–215.

Brusman-Lovins, L., & Latessa, E. (2010). *Revocation center analysis.* Cincinnati, OH: Center for Criminal Justice Research, University of Cincinnati.

Dowden, C., & Andrews, D. A. (1999). What works in young offender treatment: A meta-analysis. *Forum on Correctional Research, 11*(2), 21–24.

Dowden, C., & Andrews, D. A. (2003, July). Does family intervention work for delinquents? Results of a meta-analysis. *Canadian Journal of Criminology and Criminal Justice,* 327–342.

Dowden, C., & Andrews, D. A. (2004). The Importance of staff practice in delivering effective correctional treatment: A meta-analytic review of core correctional practice. *International Journal of Offender Therapy and Comparative Criminology, 48,* 203–214.

French, S., & Gendreau, P. (2006). Reducing prison misconducts: What works! *Criminal Justice and Behavior, 33,* 185–218.

Landenberger, N. A., & Lipsey, M. W. (2005). The positive effects of cognitive-behavioral programs for offenders: A meta-analysis of factors associated with effective treatment. *Journal of Experimental Criminology, 1,* 451–476.

Lowenkamp, C., Hubbard, D., Makarios, M., & Latessa, E. J. (2009). A quasi-experimental evaluation of Thinking for a Change: A "real world" application. *Criminal Justice and Behavior, 36*(2), 137–146.

4

Changing Behavior Long Term
Behavioral Techniques and Using Core Correctional Practices

Introduction

In the previous chapter, we learned that when it comes to reducing recidivism, behavioral models are the most effective approaches—the "how" of changing behavior. These models are based on social learning and cognitive behavioral theories and form the foundation that effective correctional programs use for targeting criminogenic risk and need factors and teaching offenders new skills and behaviors. In this chapter, we learn about some of the core correctional practices that accompany these approaches, why they are important, and how they can enhance the effectiveness of correctional programs. These techniques are part of behavioral strategies and should be used in group setting as well as one–one interactions with offenders.

Core Correctional Practices

Andrews and Kiessling (1980) first introduced five core correctional practices (effective use of authority, anti-criminal modeling and reinforcement, problem solving, use of community resources, and interpersonal relationships) that were later expanded into a training curriculum (Andrews & Carvell, 1998). In 1989, Gendreau and Andrews added to this list of practices with the development of the Correctional Program Assessment Inventory (CPAI), which is discussed in Chapter 12. Table 4.1 briefly defines the expanded list of core correctional practices (CCPs).

Necessary Ingredients for Change

The factors that affect whether change will take place can be organized into four areas. Of greatest impact are facilitator qualities. Program participants are most likely to experience change when they develop a therapeutic alliance—or helping alliance—with program staff. This happens when facilitators demonstrate respect for participants, are genuine, have appropriate boundaries, and are consistent. In other words, relationship skills matters. Participant characteristics also affect whether they will benefit from treatment. This includes such factors as risk to reoffend, specific criminogenic needs, and barriers to treatment. Our approach to treatment also matters because some treatment approaches are more effective at enacting offender change than others. For example, we know that cognitive behavioral approaches are more effective at reducing recidivism than

Table 4.1 Core Correctional Practices

Anti-criminal modeling—Staff serve as an anti-criminal model for offenders by engaging in prosocial behaviors and reinforcing them when they do the same.

Effective reinforcement—Staff use effective reinforcement to reinforce a specific behavior that includes immediate statements of approval and support and the reasons why this behavior is desirable followed by consideration of the short- and long-term benefits associated with continued use of the behavior.

Effective disapproval—Staff use effective disapproval to communicate disapproval for a specific behavior that includes immediate statements of disapproval and the reasons why this behavior is undesirable followed by consideration of the short- and long-term costs associated with continued use of the behavior and a clear demonstration of an alternate, prosocial behavior.

Effective use of authority—Staff make effective use of their authority by guiding offenders toward compliance, which includes focusing their message on the behavior exhibited, being direct and specific concerning their demands, and specifying the offender's choices and attendant consequences.

Problem solving—Problem solving is a specific social skill that is taught to offenders to address a variety of high-risk situations.

Relationship skills—Effective staff possess several critical relationship skills, including warm, open, nonjudgmental, empathetic, flexible, engaging, solution-focused, and directive.

Cognitive restructuring—Staff need to help offenders understand the link between their thoughts and their behavior: What they think (e.g., attitudes, thoughts, and beliefs) affects how someone emotionally and behaviorally responds to a given situation, as opposed to situations directly dictating a person's response.

Skill building—In order for an offender to learn ways to behave, staff need to teach and practice new skills with offenders. There are cognitive skills (e.g., how well people solve problems, experience empathy toward others, and rationally assess situations) that affect how a person behaves.

Motivational enhancement—Effective staff help motivate offenders to change by increasing intrinsic motivation (getting them to want to change). Techniques include motivational interviewing, weighing the pros and cons, and goal setting.

are some other approaches. The fourth ingredient for change is the expectancies of both staff and clients. If staff and clients think that the clients can change, it is more likely that they will change.

Staff Characteristics and Developing Relationship Skills

Let's take a look at some of the personal characteristics or attributes of effective staff. There are a number of qualities on this list, such as the following:

- Being open and warm with the clients.
- Being genuine: Clients know when staff are being fake or disingenuous with them. When they perceive staff as being fake, they are less apt to learn from staff.
- Showing respect for the clients.
- Having empathy: People often confuse sympathy (or feeling sorry for someone) with empathy. Empathy is the ability to understand someone else's view or circumstance. Another way of saying this is that you have the ability to put yourself in someone else's shoes. This does not necessarily mean that you agree with or

condone the other person's view or circumstance. For example, we may look at an offender's family and life circumstances and have some level of understanding of how he or she came to be involved in criminal and delinquent behavior without condoning that behavior.

- Caring and demonstrating sensitivity.
- Demonstrating trust.
- Being understanding.
- Being highly motivated.
- Being prosocial.
- Having realistic goals for the client.
- Demonstrating acceptance of the client: Effective staff can distinguish between the person and the behavior.
- Believing that offenders can change: Obviously, staff who do not believe that the offender can change will be far less effective at helping him or her to change.
- Being firm but fair.
- Being enthusiastic about their work.
- Being knowledgeable about offender behavior and attitudes.

These attributes also serve as a reminder of what we should be looking for when assessing, teaching, and evaluating staff for effectiveness. These skills apply to all staff who are responsible for direct service, not just clinical staff, but can also include security staff.

Introduction to Effective Behavior Change

Ultimately, the public expects that offenders will not commit more crime. Therefore, the main goal of correctional treatment programs is to teach offenders new, more responsible ways of thinking and behaving. By doing so, those served in correctional programs will be more successful in the community. Often, correctional programs are focused on compliance rather than long-term change. It is important to remember that the long-term goal is to help clients *change* by gaining self-control, regulating emotions, and managing risky situations in a prosocial way. We are striving for the change to occur in unsupervised situations, sustained across environment and time.

Correctional treatment staff have a unique opportunity to do some very focused work with offenders in a structured setting to teach them the skills they need to be successful upon release from correctional settings. However, to be effective, staff must utilize those teaching techniques that have been shown to work. Probably the easiest way to think about behavior models, then, is simply as a package of specific teaching techniques that staff use to help offenders change their behaviors.

Shea and Bauer (2007) define behavior management as "all of the actions and conscious inactions to enhance the probability that people, individually and in groups, choose behaviors which are personally fulfilling, productive, and socially acceptable."

Take a moment to think about what this definition means to you. Now, let's break this definition into two parts:

1. All of the actions and conscious inactions to enhance the probability; and
2. People, individually and in groups, choose behaviors which are personally fulfilling, productive, and socially acceptable.

The first part of this definition is focusing on the action of staff. In other words, what is it that staff do—whether through action or purposeful inaction—to impact the likelihood that the offender will make decisions to engage in certain types of behaviors? This implies that staff should be using very purposeful strategies to affect the choices of the offender. The second part of the definition talks about influencing the extent to which the offender chooses to engage in certain types of behaviors—those that are fulfilling, productive, and socially acceptable. It is important to note that the definition acknowledges that offenders have to choose their behaviors. Even in controlled environments, offenders choose their behaviors. This is important to acknowledge because staff sometime think it is their job to control the behavior of offenders, so we need to distinguish between trying to control offender behavior and helping to manage and change offender behavior.

We can expect to achieve a number of outcomes if we are effective at behavior change. First, we should be able to help offenders stop engaging in inappropriate behaviors. If we want them to stop engaging in these behaviors for the long term, however, we will need to teach them some new behaviors to use to replace the old ones. This is also a goal of behavior change systems—teaching appropriate replacement behaviors. As just mentioned, we also have long-term behavior change as a goal. It is not sufficient for offenders to simply change their behaviors while in a program or under supervision. Most programs can achieve short-term rule compliance. Only effective programs can bring about long-term behavior change in offenders. Finally, we want to use behavior management techniques to help offenders learn how to manage their own behaviors across a variety of settings. Consequently, the skills we teach them should be helpful not just for staying out of crime but for other things as well, such as staying out of trouble with friends and demonstrating achievement in work, at home, and other settings.

Social Learning Theory

The primary theory underlying behavior management models is social learning theory. Although social learning theory is considered its own theory, it is actually a combination of theories that work to explain how people learn behaviors. Social learning theory integrates cognitive theories and behaviorist theories to explain how cognitive factors (i.e., factors that involve the thinking process), behavioral factors, and environmental factors interact to influence behavior. It is important to remember as we go forward that this theory explains how we *all* learn, not just how offenders learn. It also explains how we learn any new behavior, not just criminal behavior.

Key Components of Social Learning Theory

One of the primary components of social learning theory is the assertion that people learn behaviors by observing the behaviors of others and the outcomes of those behaviors. In other words, if we see someone engage in a behavior and experience some sort of positive outcome, we are likely to try the behavior ourselves.

Social learning theory also tells us that the likelihood that we will repeat the behavior depends on the extent to which we are either reinforced or punished for that behavior. In other words, if we receive some sort of reward or positive outcome as a result of the behavior, then we are more likely to repeat that same behavior again. However, if we experience some sort of punishment or negative outcome as a result of that behavior, we are less likely to repeat that behavior. This is the behavioral part of learning.

Finally, social learning theory states that people form expectations about the consequences of future behaviors based on these past experiences. In other words, if I have experienced a positive outcome the last few times that I have engaged in a specific behavior, then I will come to expect a positive outcome from that behavior in the future. This expectation will now also influence my decision to engage in the behavior. This is the cognitive part of learning behaviors.

Environmental Influences

The most direct method of reinforcement of a behavior that we engage in is to personally experience a positive outcome or consequence of our behavior. However, there are other ways in which a behavior can be reinforced—or punished—by others in our environment. The examples we discuss here focus on reinforcement, but they all hold true for punishment as well.

One way in which the environment can influence our behavior is when our behavior is reinforced by the person who we modeled our behavior after. Let's take delinquency as an example to see how the youths we serve are often reinforced for their criminal behaviors. Let's say Johnny sees his friend Steve shoplift some CDs and get away with it. Based on Steve's successful outcome of getting away with the theft and then getting to listen to the CDs, Johnny decides to shoplift some CDs as well. After Johnny successfully shoplifts the CDs, Steve high-fives him and tells him how cool he is. This serves to reinforce the shoplifting behavior of Johnny. Another way that Johnny might be reinforced for shoplifting is through a third person. Maybe after Johnny shoplifts the CDs, he tells his friend Tyler about the theft, and Tyler also congratulates him for getting away with it and tells Johnny how cool he is for stealing the CDs. A third way that Johnny might be reinforced for shoplifting is through what we call vicarious reinforcement. This is when Johnny sees his model (Steve) being reinforced for shoplifting. An example of this is when Johnny sees Steve getting respect from other friends in their peer group as a result of shoplifting the CDs.

Components of Effective Behavior Change Systems

Now that we have an understanding of how people learn new behaviors and the goals for utilizing behavior management techniques within correctional treatment programs, we need to identify the specific strategies that staff should use to bring about positive behavior to change offender behavior:

- Use of reinforcers
- Use of effective praise
- Use of punishers
- Use of effective disapproval
- Effective use of authority

Use of Reinforcers

There are two types of reinforcers: positive reinforcement and negative reinforcement. Regardless of whether the reinforcement is positive or negative, the goal of reinforcement is always to *increase* specific behaviors.

Positive Reinforcement

Positive reinforcement involves the application of a stimulus to increase behavior. This means that you are going to introduce something positive into the environment in order to increase the chance the behavior will be repeated.

Let's discuss a couple of examples. In the first example, an offender actively participates in group so he earns two extra positive peer points (this is based on a point system in which the offender can later redeem the points for material goods). The positive peer points are the stimulus that was introduced or applied. The target behavior that we are trying to increase is group participation. In the second example, an offender goes 3 days with no rule infractions, so she earns an additional hour of free time. Here, the stimulus that is applied or introduced is the extra free time. The target behavior is program rule compliance.

Negative Reinforcement

As discussed previously, any form of reinforcement is meant to increase behavior. Sometimes people confuse negative reinforcement with the concept of punishment. This is because of the word "negative." Negative simply means that rather than introducing a positive stimulus into the environment to reinforce good behavior, we are going to remove or *subtract* something unpleasant from the environment. If we remove something unpleasant from the environment, this still serves as a reinforcer.

Here are a couple of examples to illustrate this point. The first is a youth who stays awake in class so she earns a later bedtime. In this scenario, the bedtime restriction was removed or lessened. This is what makes this type of reinforcement a negative reinforcement. The target behavior in this scenario is staying awake in class. In the second example, a youth improves his grades so he earns no chores for a week. This example is similar to the first in that we are removing or subtracting something unpleasant (i.e., chores) in order to reward or reinforce good behavior. The target behavior in this scenario is improving school performance.

Types of Reinforcers

There are four types of reinforcers that we can use. The first is tangible reinforcers. These are material objects that can be given to an offender in exchange for appropriate behaviors. An example of a tangible reinforcer is food. For example, some programs provide extra snacks as tangible reinforcers for prosocial behavior. The second type of reinforcer is token reinforcers. These are symbolic items given to the offender that are then later exchanged for something of value. The most common example of this is a point system in which youths earn points for demonstrating appropriate behaviors. Once they earn a certain number of points, they can exchange those points or "purchase" something of value. The types of things they purchase may be tangible, such as food items, toiletries, CDs, and DVDs. They may also use the points to purchase the next type of reinforcer—a reinforcing activity. Reinforcing activities are extra activities that the person finds enjoyable, such as extra free time, extra rec time, and extra phone time. The final type of reinforcer is social reinforcement. This includes praise, acknowledgment, attention, and approval.

Benefits of Social Reinforcers

Although all types of reinforcers are effective, it is worth highlighting some of the specific benefits of social reinforcers. First, social reinforcers are the easiest to use of the types of reinforcers that we discussed. This technique simply involves telling someone that you noticed and liked what he or she did. Second, there is an endless supply of social reinforcers—we cannot run out of words. Third, they are available for immediate use. In other words, there are no barriers that prevent us from telling an offender that we liked or appreciated the behavior that we just witnessed. Fourth, they do not cost money to implement. Finally, and perhaps most important, they are a more natural form of reinforcement and more likely to be experienced outside of the program. In other words, few of us receive tangible items, special activities, or points for engaging in prosocial behavior in our everyday lives. This is true of the offenders as well. Outside of a program, they are not likely to experience those things either, yet many of us do hear nice words from other people acknowledging good deeds or hard work.

Effective Social Reinforcement

Although social reinforcement is one of the easiest forms of reinforcement to use, it is not as easy as simply telling someone "good job." There are some ground rules for utilizing effective social reinforcement, sometimes referred to as effective praise. To be most effective, social reinforcement—or praise—should be used immediately following the positive behavior. In other words, staff should tell the offender that they liked the behavior as soon as reasonably possible upon witnessing the behavior. When doing so, staff should make sure to use concrete, behavioral language as much as possible. For example, instead of telling an offender that you liked that he was able to "control his anger," you might want to describe exactly what you saw him do, such as "I noticed that instead of yelling you used a normal tone of voice and told Jim that you needed some time to calm down before continuing your conversation because you didn't want to get into a fight." This language specifies exactly what the person did (i.e., the behaviors he engaged in) that you liked. This makes it easier for him to replicate this behavior in the future. If we simply tell him we liked that he calmed down, he might not know how to replicate that because it is an abstract concept and we all use different strategies to "calm down."

The next step is to explain to the offender why you liked the behavior. In the previous example, you might tell the offender that you liked what he did because it meant that he did not get into a fight like he might have in the past. When discussing this with the offender, you should provide more emphasis to the approved behavior than the type of support normally given to the offender. We want to make sure that this conversation stands out from everyday conversation to elevate its importance and to increase the chance that the offender will remember it in the future. During the conversation, the staff person should also encourage the offender to identify for himself or herself why this target behavior is desirable—in our example, the ability to calm down and avoid a fight. We do this by asking the offender if he can identify how this behavior will meet his short-term and long-term goals. You may have to help him identify his short-term and long-term goals first, however. A common example of a short-term goal is simply to get out of the program. A sample long-term goal might be to avoid future arrests or to get along better with his significant other or family members. Ideally, through guided questioning by staff, he should be able to identify examples of how being able to calm down will help him with these types of goals— for example, that being able to calm down means he gets into less fights while in the program so he gets written up less and might get out earlier or that being able to calm down means he will get into fewer fights with his spouse or will not get arrested for fighting.

As with all types of reinforcers, we want to make sure that we use a variety of social reinforcers, and we want to pair social reinforcers with other types of reinforcers, such as tangible reinforcers or token reinforcers. Typically, social reinforcement is used while explaining to an offender why he or she has earned the tangible or token reinforcer.

Examples of Reinforcers

The following are examples of reinforcers that can be used in correctional treatment programs. As you go through the list, think of those that you already use or that you could possibly add:

- Specific praise or feedback on performance
- Indirect praise: For example, saying something positive about the offender's performance to the offender's probation officer in front of the offender so that the offender hears it.

- Group recognition: This involves recognizing an offender in front of a group, such as recognizing him or her in front of peers. This should be used with caution, however, because not all people are comfortable with public recognition. Examples of this include resident of the month or public award ceremonies.
- Field trips
- Extra visits or phone calls
- Items from the commissary
- Game room privileges
- Private room or choosing a specific desk or bed: Some programs also utilize an honors room or dorm that comes with greater privileges attached.
- Free time
- Television or radio privileges: This might include more time spent or simply being the one to choose that night's station or show.
- Playing host for visitors: For example, an offender may lead a tour of the facility for a visitor. In addition to being a potential reinforcer, this type of activity also has other benefits in that it can teach additional skills such as introducing oneself, leadership, and public speaking.
- Lunch with a staff member
- Badges, ribbons, certificates: These are often very appreciated because many offenders never received these types of things in school.
- Extra recreation time

Guidelines for Selecting Reinforcers

Remember, not everyone responds to the same reinforcement. So how do you know which reinforcer to use with which offender? There are a number of guidelines to help you make that decision.

First, you should consider the interests of the offender who you are trying to reinforce. For example, what types of activities or hobbies does he or she like? This may serve as a source of ideas for reinforcers. You should also consider the type of behavior that you are trying to target through reinforcement so that you can match the reinforcer to the complexity of the behavior. For example, offering a small reward for a very complex behavior or skill may not serve as a strong reinforcer, especially when that behavior/skill is still new for the offender and difficult to achieve.

Consider asking the offender what he or she finds reinforcing or is interested in. Often what we think is reinforcing for someone is not at all. For example, if you tell a shy introverted person that she can spend more time at the gym playing sports with the others, she may not find this appealing. In fact, she may find this to be a punishment. Maybe for her, a reinforcer would be to get an extra hour alone in her room reading a book. The program could consider allowing the offender to select from a menu of reinforcers. For example, an offender may be able to choose whether he would like an extra phone call, extra free time, or extra recreation time. Having a say in the reinforcer should serve to make the reward more potent for the offender.

Observing the offender's routine behaviors can provide staff with ideas for what would appeal to a specific offender and therefore serve as a strong reinforcer. Staff should also use a variety of reinforcers. This is because when used too much, a reinforcer starts to lose its potency. In other words, it is less likely to increase the chance that someone will repeat the rewarded behavior in the future. Finally, consider using generalized reinforcers that are pleasant or reinforcing for most people, such as praise.

Administering Reinforcers

There are a number of rules for administering reinforcers in order to be most effective. First and most important is that the reinforcement must be contingent on performing the desired behavior. For example, if staff tell all of the offenders in the facility that they can watch a movie if they all remain infraction-free for the week, then only the offenders who remain infraction-free actually get to watch the movie. If everyone but one offender accomplishes this, that one offender should not be allowed to watch the movie.

The reinforcer should be administered immediately following the behavior in order to ensure that the offender connects the reward to that behavior. Similarly, the offender should be aware that the reinforcer is a consequence of performing the target behavior. This means that staff need to explain why the offender has earned the reinforcer. As mentioned previously, staff should utilize the techniques of effective social reinforcement when doing this.

Reinforcers should be administered consistently. This means that *all* staff administer reinforcements for the target behaviors identified by the program. Continuous reinforcement is most effective when first strengthening a behavior. Once the offender demonstrates a fairly consistent ability to engage in the behavior, then an intermittent schedule of reinforcement is most effective to maintain the behavior. Why is this? Because as mentioned previously, overuse of reinforcement results in a satiation effect and the reward begins to lose its power—it is no longer potent. What is intermittent reinforcement? This means that the reinforcement only happens sometimes rather than every time. A noncorrectional example of intermittent reinforcement is a slot machine. Finally, we should always assess whether the reinforcer is effective at increasing the target behavior. If it does not appear to be working, we should experiment with a different reinforcer.

Widahl, Garland, Culhane, and McCarty (2011) demonstrated how even an intensive supervision program can dramatically improve success when the ratio of rewards to punisher increases. Figure 4.1 shows that the completion rates of offenders on intensive supervision increased dramatically when the ratio of rewards reached a ratio of 4:1. Table 4.2 shows the list of rewards and punishers developed and used by the probation staff.

Potential Barriers

There are a couple of barriers that staff commonly face when trying to use reinforcement. Some offenders are simply more difficult to reinforce than others. One reason might be

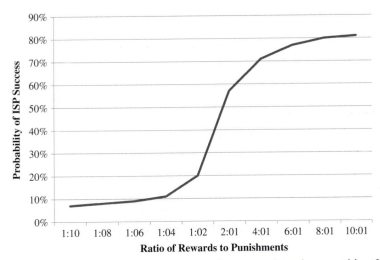

FIGURE 4.1 Ratio of rewards to punishments and probability of success on intensive supervision. *Source: Widahl, E. J., Garland, B., Culhane, S. E., & McCarty, W. P. (2011). Utilizing behavioral interventions to improve supervision outcomes in community-based corrections.* Criminal Justice and Behavior, 38(4), 386–405. *Reprinted by permission of SAGE Publications.*

due to the severity of their behavior problems. So, what if you do not have anything to reinforce? There are two primary strategies for dealing with this situation:

1. Watch very carefully for *any* evidence that the offender is engaging in the behavior. When you see the behavior occur, even at the lowest level, begin giving systematic reinforcement. For example, an offender who chronically fails to participate in group activities joins in the group. This should be reinforced.
2. Model and prompt the behavior for the offender. If it appears as though the offender is not using the target behavior at all, you may have to show the offender how to use

Table 4.2 List of Rewards and Sanctions

Sanctions	Rewards
Verbal reprimand	Verbal praise and reinforcement
Written assignment	Remove from electronic monitoring
Modify curfew hours	Level advancement
Community service hours	Increased personal time
Restrict visitation	Approved special activity
Program extension or regression	Fees reduced
Electronic monitoring	Approval of extended special visitation
Inpatient or outpatient treatment	
Detention time	

Source: Widahl, E. J., Garland, B., Culhane, S. E., & McCarty, W. P. (2011). Utilizing behavioral interventions to improve supervision outcomes in community-based corrections. *Criminal Justice and Behavior, 38*(4), 386-405. Reprinted by permission of SAGE Publications.

the skill and then purposefully provide him or her opportunities to use the skill, even if it means that staff instruct him or her to use the skill in that situation. If the offender does so, reinforce that behavior.

Some people simply do not like attention. What if the offender seems to reject or dislike direct attention and approval? In this case, you can try indirect approval—for example, praising the offender to others in front of the offender for performing desired behaviors.

Punishers

Just as there are two types of reinforcers, there are two types of punishment: positive punishment and negative punishment. Regardless of whether the punishment is considered positive or negative, the goal of punishment is always to decrease certain behaviors. The term most often used by programs to think of punishment is *sanction*.

Positive Punishment

The phrase "positive punishment" does not imply that the punishment is somehow "good." Positive punishment, like positive reinforcement, simply involves the application or introduction of a stimulus into the environment. The difference here, however, is that positive reinforcement is meant to increase a behavior, whereas positive punishment is meant to decrease a behavior. This means that you are going to introduce something into the environment in order to decrease the chance the behavior will be repeated.

Let's look at a couple of examples. In the first example, an offender is given community service hours for failing to report. The community service hours are the stimulus that was introduced or applied. The target behavior that we are trying to decrease is failure to report. In the second example, an offender is given extra chores for failing to complete her group assignments. Here, the stimulus that is applied or introduced is the extra chores. The target behavior is failure to complete group assignments.

Negative Punishment

With negative punishment, we are going to remove or *subtract* something from the environment in order to decrease the chance that someone will repeat a behavior. A couple of examples illustrate this point. In the first scenario, an offender loses his free time when he refuses to attend group that day. In this scenario, the free time was removed. This is what makes this type of punishment a negative punishment. The target behavior in this scenario is skipping group. In the second example, an offender gets put on electronic monitoring for 1 week for violating her itinerary. This example is similar to the first in that we are removing or subtracting a privilege in order to reduce inappropriate behavior. The target behavior in this scenario is failing to follow her itinerary.

Administering Punishments

The rules for effectively administering punishments are much the same as those for administering reinforcements. For example, the punishment should be administered immediately following the behavior in order to ensure that the offender connects the punishment to that behavior. Similarly, the offender should be aware that the punishment is a consequence of performing the undesirable behavior. This means that staff need to explain why the offender has earned the punishment. Also, the punishment should be preceded by a warning cue. The offender should not be taken totally by surprise by the punishment.

Just like reinforcers, punishments should be administered consistently. This means that *all* staff administer punishments for rule violations identified by the program every time. Finally, we should always assess whether the punishment is effective at decreasing the target behavior. If it does not appear to be working, we should experiment with a different punishment.

Potential Barriers

There are a number of potential barriers to effectively using punishments to change behavior. The first is that after administering a punishment, you may actually see the unwanted behavior increase at first. This is often temporary and an initial rebellion against structure because many of these offenders have never experienced consistent consequences for their behaviors. Remaining consistent with the punishment (and reinforcement) process typically resolves this issue.

A related problem is that the unwanted behavior may spontaneously recover. In other words, you may see the undesirable behavior stop after administering punishments a few times and then seem to spontaneously reappear after a period of time. This is also normal and to be expected on occasion. The most effective way to avoid this is to ensure that while you are trying to extinguish certain undesirable behaviors, you are also teaching the offender acceptable replacement behaviors.

If punishment is used alone, another maladaptive behavior is likely to replace the old one. Again, this is related to a failure to teach the offender alternative acceptable behaviors that are consistently reinforced. Finally, punishment can produce a number of potential side effects, including emotional reactions (e.g., angry outbursts), avoidance/withdrawal, and perpetuation effects. Therefore, staff should be trained to watch for, identify, and resolve any unwanted side effects of punishment.

Limitations of Punishment

When used correctly, punishment can be an effective technique for stopping undesirable behaviors. However, it does have its limitations, including the following:

- Punishment only stops behavior in the short term. Used alone, it does not teach alternative behaviors; yet, alternative behaviors are what is needed to bring about long-term behavior change.

- What staff think is a punishment for an offender may in fact be a reinforcer. For example, sending an offender into some form of isolation may be reinforcement for some who would prefer to be alone and away from the other offenders.
- Overreliance on punishment provides no incentive for behavior change. In other words, if we take everything away from someone, what does he or she have left to lose? Often when people get to this point, they simply give up and may act out even more.
- Positive reinforcement is a more powerful teaching tool than punishment. Although punishment certainly has its place in the behavior change process (as we have already outlined), reinforcement has been shown to be a more effective teaching tool. This is why the use of reinforcers should outweigh the use of punishers by at least 4:1.

Response Cost

Finally, when learning about punishment techniques, we often discuss the use of response costs. A response cost refers to a specific punishment technique that involves the removal of something pleasant. It involves the removal of a reinforcer—or the loss of some quantity of positive reinforcement that is contingent upon an identified behavior (e.g., the loss of privileges or tokens).

Effective Disapproval

Just as we covered ground rules for how to talk with an offender when delivering effective praise, we now cover the rules or steps for using effective disapproval when delivering punishments. These should seem very familiar because they are much the same as those we discussed for effective social reinforcement or effective praise.

First, you should immediately tell the offender that you did not like the type of behavior or speech he or she just exhibited. Again, we want to be behaviorally specific in our language. For example, rather than tell an offender that she is "out of control," we might say, "I see you had a dispute with a staff member and you raised your voice." This is so the offender knows the exact behaviors that she needs to avoid in the future.

Next, you should explain why you did not like what the offender said or did. In this scenario, you could tell the offender that when she gets into a dispute and raises her voice, it can be interpreted as threatening and she is more likely to get in trouble.

As previously discussed, you should provide more emphasis to this conversation than to the type of support normally given to the offender. We want to ensure that this conversation stands out from everyday conversation to elevate its importance and to increase the chance that the offender will remember it in the future. During the conversation, the staff person should also encourage the offender to identify for himself or herself why this target behavior is undesirable—in our example, arguing with staff and raising her voice when angry. We do this by asking the offender if she can identify how this behavior will interfere with her meeting her short-term and long-term goals. You may have to help the offender identify her short-term and long-term goals first, however. An example of a short-term goal might be to obtain extra recreation time. A sample long-term goal might be to get a job. Ideally, through guided questioning by staff, she should be able to identify examples of how arguing with staff and raising one's voice when angry can interfere with achieving these specific goals. For example, this behavior might lead to her getting into a fight with the person at whom she is yelling, which could result in her getting written up for a rule infraction. If this happens, she could lose privileges. If she continues to engage in this behavior at work, she could end up getting fired, which could have a negative impact on her ability to get another job.

Behavior Contracts

Another tool that can be helpful with behavior change in offenders is a behavior contract. A behavior contract is simply an agreement between two or more persons that lists specific behaviors that the parties will perform and the consequences that will result. As it sounds, this is a formal process that is documented between the two parties. It is most often used with offenders who are demonstrating chronic behavior problems within the program.

Effective Use of Authority

It is common in correctional treatment environments for staff to have to intervene with offenders who are not following rules or who are being disruptive. During these times when staff have to utilize their authority to redirect the offender, there are some strategies that can be used to make this a more effective process, including the following:

- Focus your message on the behavior and not the person. For example, we would not tell an offender that he is "out of control" or that he is "being histrionic." Rather than label the offender or utilize judgment statements, we simply focus on the behavior, and we describe that behavior to the offender in very concrete terms.
- Be direct and specific concerning your demands. Rather than simply tell an offender that you need for him to follow the rules, you should tell him exactly what behaviors he is expected to engage in to be in compliance with those rules. For example, "You need to lower your voice."
- Use a normal voice when utilizing authority. Do not yell. Yelling only escalates the situation.
- Always specify to the offender what his or her choices are and the consequences of those choices. For example, you can do A and this will happen, or you can do B and this will happen. This reinforces for the offender that he or she always has choices and helps the offender link his or her choices to their consequences. Make sure that any consequences are realistic, however. For example, do not tell an offender that he or she will be kicked out of the program if that is not really within your control to do.

Other techniques include the following:

- Giving encouraging messages: When trying to guide an offender to compliance, we should be making statements that we acknowledge that it is within the ability of the offenders to engage in the desired behavior and that we are confident in their abilities.

- Supporting words with actions: Follow through. For example, if we tell an offender that a certain outcome will result from his or her behavior, we must be sure to implement that outcome, whether positive or negative.
- Providing respectful guidance toward compliance: Making overt demands on the offender or threatening the offender into compliance is often ineffective.
- Looking for good things, too: Do not just monitor compliance.
- Rewarding or praising compliance.
- Staff should use respectful communication.
- Staff should be nonblaming, empathic, and genuine.
- Staff should be flexible, use humor, and be engaging.
- Staff should be enthusiastic and express optimism.
- Staff should avoid argumentation and support self-efficacy.

Showing concern and developing a good relationship does not mean we condone what they have done or that we want to become friends. We should also remember to establish boundaries and use ethical approaches when dealing with offenders. We want you to have professional relationships, set appropriate limits, and enforce sanctions. Remember, it is how you say it, not whether you say it.

Implementing a Behavior Management System

It is one thing to have a strong conceptual understanding of behavior management techniques. It is another to implement a behavior management model in a real-world setting. To be most effective, a program's implementation efforts should, at a minimum, address the following:

- System design
- Selection of reinforcements and sanctions
- Policies and procedures
- Documentation and tracking
- Staff training

We know from research and experience that programs that implement purposeful, systematic systems of reinforcements and sanctions are more effective at changing offender behavior. Therefore, one of the first decisions a program has to make when implementing a behavior management system is to decide what it will look like. For example, will the program use a somewhat generic model of reinforcements and sanctions in which the offenders are simply reinforced or sanctioned for each individual behavior without tying the reinforcement and sanctions model to treatment progress? Although these types of models do not tie reinforcers and sanctions directly to progression through treatment, they should still utilize a basic system of graduated reinforcers and sanctions. This means that more complex positive behaviors garner larger reinforcements, whereas more serious rule violations bring more serious sanctions.

How These Systems Go Awry

One way in which these systems are rendered less effective is when staff are inconsistent with applying sanctions for inappropriate behaviors. Let's consider a scenario in which the staff on first shift are stricter about sanctioning offenders for not following the rules than are the staff on second shift. In other words, the offenders have a higher likelihood of getting away with rule violations on first shift than on second shift. What does this teach the offenders? This teaches them to manipulate the rules. They make decisions about whether to break the rules based on whether they think they can get away with it. This is something they already know how to do before they get to us and is what got them into trouble with the law in the first place. Thus, it is critical that our behavior management practices do not further reinforce this type of behavior.

Another way in which these systems can go awry is when staff focus reinforcement on behaviors not related to criminal conduct. The example provided here is focusing re-inforcements on such behaviors as making beds and doing chores without being asked. Although residential facilities do have a need to keep things orderly and to have the offenders manage their own living spaces, these types of behaviors have no relationship to criminal conduct. In other words, those of us who chronically fail to make our beds every day are not at higher risk for criminal behavior. Thus, it is not that these behaviors cannot be part of the reinforcement system, but they should not dominate the list of target behaviors. More appropriate target behaviors should focus on things related to treatment progress (e.g., group attendance, group participation, completion of treatment home-work, and participation in role plays) and to skill demonstration (e.g., evidence of sobriety, fewer rule infractions and disturbances on the unit, improved work perfor-mance, and building positive peer associations).

A third way that these systems can go awry is when staff utilize group reinforcements inappropriately. For example, staff tell the offenders that if everyone completes their homework assignments from group for an entire week they can get extra privileges, and then two of the offenders do not comply but the staff give them all extra privileges. What is the impact on the offenders who did not complete their homework assignments? Remember that reinforcement is used as a learning tool. What did these offenders learn from this process? They learned that they can deliberately fail to perform and still get a reward; therefore, there is no motivation to perform in the future. We have set the expectation that they will receive a reward regardless of whether they perform or not. We have also shown them that staff do not follow through with consequences.

Finally, yet another way that these systems go awry is when staff utilize group punishment inappropriately. For example, someone sneaks contraband into the facility and staff cannot determine who did it. Staff then take that evening's free time away from everyone and restrict them to their rooms. This is typically due to a belief that *someone* needs to be punished and that if there is no punishment at all, then the offender will think it is okay to bring in contraband. But what is the impact on the offenders who did not sneak contraband into the facility? What is the impact on their thought processes? They might think something along the lines of "If I am going to get punished for it, I may as well do it." Staff are also possibly judged as unfair. This can also make it less likely that staff will be effective at teaching new behaviors to these offenders in the future.

Translating CCPs into Practice: The EPICS Model

In contrast with "traditional" community supervision—which has underscored the importance of monitoring compliance with court-ordered conditions and making referrals to service providers—some recent initiatives have attempted to teach probation and parole officers how to structure their face-to-face interactions with offenders using evidence-based practices and CCPs.

The research on the principles of effective intervention, coupled with the most recent research on community supervision, provided the impetus for the development of a new model by the University of Cincinnati: Effective Practices for Correctional Supervision (EPICS). Based on the work of Bonta and colleagues (Bonta, Rugge, Scott, Bourgon, & Yessine, 2008) and Trotter (2006), EPICS is designed to teach probation and parole officers and case managers how to apply the principles of effective intervention and CCPs specifically, including relationship skills, cognitive restructuring, structured skill building, problem solving, reinforcement, and use of authority to correctional supervision practices. The CCPs (or competencies) are organized into an overall framework to assist with the application of specific skills within the context of community supervision. This overall framework, or "Action Plan," assists with the development and implementation of case management plans to target the criminogenic needs of higher-risk offenders. With the EPICS model, probation officers follow a structured approach to their interactions with their offenders. Specifically, each session includes four components:

1. Check-in, in which the officer determines if the offender has any crises or acute needs, builds rapport, and discusses compliance issues.
2. Review, which focuses on the skills discussed in the prior session, the application of those skills, and troubleshooting continued problems in the use of those skills.
3. Intervention, in which the probation officer identifies continued areas of need, trends in problems the offender experiences, teaches relevant skills, and targets problematic thinking.
4. Homework and rehearsal, in which the offender is given an opportunity to see the model that the probation officer is talking about, and the officer provides opportunities to role play, assigns homework, and gives instructions that the offender should follow before the next visit.

The EPICS model is designed to use a combination of monitoring, referrals, and face-to-face interactions to provide the offender with a sufficient "dosage" of treatment interventions and to make the best possible use of time to develop a collaborative working relationship. Furthermore, the model helps translate the risk, needs, and responsivity principles into practice. Probation officers are taught to increase dosage to higher-risk offenders; stay focused on criminogenic needs, especially the thought–behavior link; and use a social learning, cognitive behavioral approach to their interactions. The EPICS model is not intended to replace other programming and services but, rather, is an attempt to more fully utilize probation officers as agents of change.

Preliminary research has demonstrated that teaching probation officers how to restructure their interactions with offenders and to use CCPs to target criminogenic needs can reduce recidivism. Results from several studies suggest that the use of CCPs within the context of community supervision has been associated with meaningful reductions in offender recidivism. Figure 4.2 shows the results from a Canadian study (Bourgon et al., 2010). Reconviction was 25% for offenders supervised by trained officers and 40% for those supervised by untrained officers. Figure 4.3 shows the importance of fidelity (Latessa, Smith, Schweitzer, & Labrecque, 2013): Officers who adhered to the EPICS model significantly reduced recidivism for high-risk offenders, whereas high-risk offenders supervised by officers who did not adhere to the model failed at higher rates. This work affirms the role of probation and parole officers as agents of behavioral change, and it provides empirical support for the notion that community supervision can be effective in reducing recidivism.

The use of CCPs with offenders allows us to structure our interventions, teach and model new skills, allow the offender to practice with graduated difficulty, and reinforces the behavior. Finally, Figure 4.4 shows the results from a meta-analysis that examined studies on the use of some CCPs with offenders (Gendreau, 2003). These results show consistent evidence that these techniques are more effective than traditional practices.

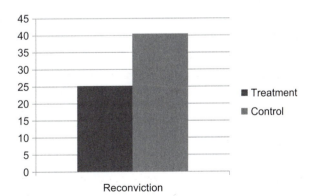

FIGURE 4.2 **Two-year recidivism results from a Canadian study.** *Source: Bonta, J., et al. (2010). The Strategic Training Initiative in Community Supervision: Risk–need–responsivity in the real world. Ottawa, Ontario, Canada: Public Safety Canada.*

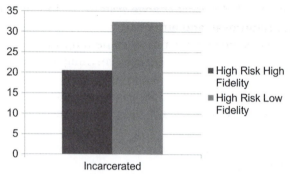

FIGURE 4.3 Recidivism results from EPICS looking at fidelity and high-risk offenders. *Source: Latessa, E., Smith, P., Schweitzer, M., & Labrecque, R. (2013). Evaluation of the Effective Practices in Community Supervision Model (EPICS) in Ohio. Cincinnati, OH: School of Criminal Justice, University of Cincinnati.*

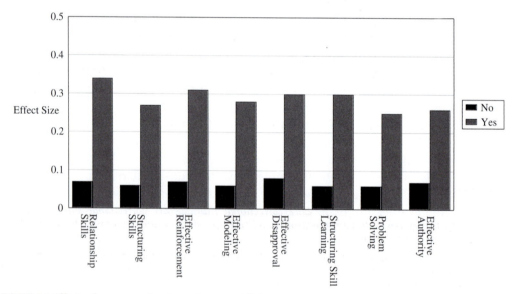

FIGURE 4.4 Effects of core correctional practices on recidivism. *Source: Gendreau, P. (2003). Invited Address, Division 18, APA annual convention, Toronto, Canada.*

Summary

This chapter reviewed behavioral techniques and CCPs that are used by effective correctional programs as interventions to help shape and change offender behavior. The following are some of the takeaways from this chapter:

- The necessary ingredients for change include facilitator qualities, participant characteristics, our approach to treatment, and expectancies of both staff and clients.
- The primary goal of correctional treatment and intervention programs is to change behavior in the long term.

- Components of effective behavioral change systems include the use of reinforcers, praise, punishers, disapproval, and authority.
- Positive reinforcement is the introduction of something positive to increase behavior.
- Negative reinforcement is when we remove something unpleasant from the environment to increase behavior.
- The basic types of reinforcers include tangible, token, activities, and social.
- Social reinforcers are easiest to use, cost-free, natural, and there is an endless supply of them.
- The rules for reinforcers include being contingent on the performance of the behavior, immediacy, and consistency.
- Punishers include positive (introduction of stimulus) and negative (remove something from the environment) punishers.
- Punishment alone often results in another maladaptive behavior unless the offender is taught an acceptable alternative behavior.
- Successfully implementing a behavioral management system includes system design, selection of reinforcers and sanctions, policies and procedures, documentation, and staff training.
- Behavioral management systems go awry for several reasons: inconsistency, focus on behaviors not related to criminal conduct, and inappropriate use of group reinforcers and punishers.
- Recent attempts to teach probation and parole officers how to use CCPs have shown success in reducing recidivism.

References

Andrews, D. A., & Carvell, C. (1998). *Core correctional training–core correctional supervision and counseling: Theory, research, assessment and practice.* Unpublished training manual. Ottawa, Ontario, Canada: Carleton University.

Andrews, D. A., & Kiessling, J. J. (1980). Program structure and effective correctional practices: A summary of the CaVic research. In R. R. Ross, & P. Gendreau (Eds.), *Effective correctional treatment* (pp. 441–463). Toronto: Butterworths.

Bourgon, G., Bonta, J., Rugge, T., Scott, T., Yessine, A. K., Gutierrez, L., et al. (2010). *The strategic training initiative in community supervision: Risk-need-responsivity in the real world (User Report 2010-01).* Ottawa, Ontario, Canada: Public Safety and Emergency Preparedness Canada.

Bonta, J., Rugge, T., Scott, T., Bourgon, G., & Yessine, A. K. (2008). Exploring the black box of community supervision. *Journal of Offender Rehabilitation, 47,* 248–270.

Bourgon, G., Bonta, J., Rugge, T., Scott, T., & Yessine, A. K. (2010). The role of program design, implementation, and evaluation in evidence-based "real world" community supervision. *Federal Probation, 74*(1), 2–15.

Gendreau, P. (2003). *Invited Address, Division 18, APA annual convention.* Toronto.

Gendreau, P., & Andrews, D. A. (1989). *Correctional Program Assessment Inventory. Saint John.* Canada: University of New Brunswick.

Latessa, E., Smith, P., Schweitzer, M., & Labrecque, R. (2013). *Evaluation of the Effective Practices in Community Supervision Model (EPICS) in Ohio.* Cincinnati, OH: School of Criminal Justice, University of Cincinnati.

Shea, T. M., & Bauer, A. M. (2007). *Behavioral management: A practical approach for educators.* Boston: Pearson.

Trotter, C. (2006). *Working with involuntary clients: A guide to practice* (2nd ed.). Thousand Oaks, CA: Sage.

Widahl, E. J., Garland, B., Culhane, S. E., & McCarty, W. P. (2011). Utilizing behavioral interventions to improve supervision outcomes in community-based corrections. *Criminal Justice and Behavior, 38*(4), 386–405.

5

What Doesn't Work
Ineffective Approaches and Correctional Quackery

Introduction

In Chapter 3, we learned that punishment alone is not very effective in reducing recidivism, and that treatment, especially behavioral treatment, yields the strongest effects. In this chapter, we further explore this issue by examining what doesn't work in reducing recidivism with offenders. Included in this list are so-called "punishing smarter" approaches that are designed to get tough with offenders, as well as so-called therapeutic approaches, some of which are outright quackery. Let's start with examining some common risk management strategies, often called intermediate sanctions.

Intermediate Sanctions

Many of the sanctions and programs that are referred to today as intermediate sanctions have actually been used in community corrections for many years. In the 1980s, however, the dramatic increase in the prison population led to a renewed interest in the development and expansion of programs that fall between regular probation and prison or jail. Some of these programs were designed to provide more services and treatment to offenders, whereas others were part of the "get-tough" movement that swept the country during this period. The two major issues facing intermediate sanctions are offender diversion and public safety. These two issues are often conflicting because if your goal is to reduce the prison population, you are often required to divert higher-risk offenders to community supervision, thus potentially increasing the risk to public safety. Let's explore some of the more widely used intermediate sanctions.

Intensive Supervision

Although the vast majority of offenders who are on probation receive what is usually referred to as regular supervision, it is not uncommon to find a probation department, especially one that supervises felons, that does not include an intensive supervision unit or component. Let's start by looking at intensive supervision and its history.

The first experiments in intensive supervision were conducted during the 1950s and early 1960s in California. These studies were designed to examine whether there was a relationship between caseload size and probation effectiveness. The theory was similar to the one found in education, in which there have been attempts to find the magic number or ideal class size. These early experiments theorized that by reducing caseload size, we could increase contacts, improve treatment and service delivery, and thus reduce recidivism. Unfortunately, the research did not support this contention. Although caseloads were reduced and more contacts and services were provided, there were no significant differences in outcome between those who received intensive supervision and those who received regular supervision.

In the late 1970s and early 1980s, a new form of intensive supervision was developed. This new generation also incorporated smaller caseloads and more contacts; however, instead of more services and treatment, the emphasis was on surveillance and control, with the goal of reducing the prison population by diverting higher-risk offenders to probation. Many also believed that probation needed to toughen its image, and what better way to "get tougher" with offenders than adding more restrictive conditions? Some even claimed that offenders would prefer prison to intensive supervision!

The most widely emulated version was found in Georgia, which had caseloads as small as 10 assigned to two probation officers, whose primary role was to increase surveillance and control. Frequent contact, curfews, late-night checks, frequent drug testing, and other strategies designed to increase supervision were used. Early reviews lauded this attempt at prison diversion; however, as research grew, we learned that increasing surveillance and control often led to higher rates of failure, particularly with regard to technical violations and revocations. With the advance of drug testing and electronic monitoring, surveillance and control techniques became even more rigorous and, as one would expect, led to even higher violation rates. Numerous studies of intensive supervision have been performed throughout the years. In one of the largest studies conducted of intensive supervision, Petersilia and Turner (1993) examined 14 sites throughout the country. What made this study so valuable was that offenders were randomly placed into intensive supervision or regular supervision. Findings from this study confirmed that more surveillance and control led to higher failure rates. This study is considered the most comprehensive ever done on intensive supervision.

The other major issues surrounding the expansion and use of intensive supervision programs concerns their ability to reduce prison populations. Few studies have concluded that they are diverting offenders from prison, and most have concluded that intensive supervision programs often are simply widening the net. Undoubtedly, the increase in technical violation rates is counterproductive to the goal of diverting offenders from prison. Some have argued that by identifying offenders who cannot follow the rules and conditions of supervision, we are actually reducing crime (by catching them early). Unfortunately, the research does not support this. Clear, Harris, and Baird (1992) found that technical violations often involved minor offenses and that the majority of violators did not engage in future violations.

A number of years ago, the American Probation and Parole Association advocated the development of a more balanced approach to intensive supervision. This model called for an increased level of supervision commensurate with the services and interventions provided the offender. In an attempt to test this model, the University of Cincinnati and the American Probation and Parole Association received a grant from the National Institute of Justice. Two sites were selected for this study: the Seventh Judicial District in Iowa and Hartford, Connecticut. Offenders were randomly assigned to either intensive or regular supervision. The intensive supervision programs (ISPs) were based on a balanced supervision model in which services and treatment were substantially increased along with contacts. In order to determine the quality of the services, we visited each site and assessed those service providers in each of the two jurisdictions that were working with offenders. We found that offenders in Connecticut received more services than the offenders in Iowa; however, the services in Iowa were of higher quality (Latessa, Travis, Fulton, & Stichman, 1998).

There were two important findings from this study. First, intensive supervision, even when more services were provided, did not reduce recidivism rates. Second, our study did indicate that the quality of treatment and services was more important than the quantity of services, even when controlling for differences between the offenders. In other words, the programs in Iowa that provided higher-quality treatment were more beneficial than those programs in Connecticut, despite the fact that more services were given the Connecticut offenders.

A summary of the research on ISPs is provided by Fulton, Latessa, Stichman, and Travis (1997, p. 72):

- ISPs have failed to alleviate prison crowding.
- Most ISP studies have found no significant differences between recidivism rates of ISP offenders and those of offenders in comparison groups.
- There appears to be a relationship between greater participation in treatment and employment programs and lower recidivism rates.
- ISPs appear to be more effective than regular supervision or prison in meeting offenders' needs.
- ISPs that reflect certain principles of effective intervention are associated with lower rates of recidivism.
- ISPs do provide an intermediate punishment.
- Although ISPs are less expensive than prison, they are more expensive than originally thought.

Day Reporting Centers

Whereas some programs and sanctions have been around for a long time, others, such as day reporting centers, are a more recent invention. The first day reporting center in the United States was opened in Massachusetts in 1986, with the concept having originated in England. Day reporting, like other correctional innovations, quickly spread across the United States. The day reporting center concept is relatively simple: Have those offenders who require increased supervision and services report daily to an identified location at which they will receive closer surveillance and a wide range of services. The idea of the day reporting center is to have the offender report much more frequently and to offer programming such as job skills, drug abuse education, treatment, group and individual counseling, adult education, life skills, drug treatment, and other services designed to help the offender remain crime-free. Unfortunately, some day reporting centers are simply reporting stations, where offenders sign in, perhaps take a drug test, and leave. Day reporting centers usually involve a central location, such as an old house, storefront, or even the probation department; however, unlike residential programs, the offender does not live on site but, rather, reports on a regular basis (sometimes daily).

There has not been a great deal of research on the effectiveness of day reporting centers, but one multisite study was conducted in Ohio. In the late 1990s, the state of Ohio decided to create five pilot day reporting centers throughout the state. As part of this initiative, the state decided to conduct an evaluation (Latessa, Travis, Holsinger, & Hartman, 1998). Here is a summary of the findings from the evaluation:

1. Most of the offenders selected were appropriate, reported prior involvement with the criminal justice system, and reported a host of needs across a wide range of areas. Day reporting programs in Ohio did not widen the net.
2. None of the pilot day reporting programs exhibited high-quality correctional programming, nor did researchers find much evidence that the day reporting centers provided a substantial level of services to offenders.
3. The time spent in day reporting centers lasted on average approximately 2 months, with the range from 60 to 180 days.
4. In terms of recidivism measures, offenders in day reporting programs were slightly more likely to be arrested than the comparison groups (probation, ISP, and prison), and they reported incarceration rates slightly lower than those in every group except for probation.
5. The day reporting centers did not lead to higher technical violations.
6. The cost of Ohio's day reporting centers compared favorably with that of other correctional options, and it was significantly lower than the cost of imprisonment.

Not all day reporting centers were as poorly designed and implemented as the ones in Ohio. However, as mentioned previously, to date there has not been a great deal of research on this type of programming. Day reporting centers are cheaper to operate than traditional residential programming because they do not involve the housing and feeding of offenders. It is important to remember that day reporting centers can be a place to deliver quality programming and service; if they do, there is little doubt that they can be effective in reducing recidivism, provided they follow the principles of effective intervention.

Home Detention and Electronic Monitoring

We discuss these two concepts together, although as you will see, the idea of home detention predates electronic monitoring (EM) by centuries. Today, they are so closely linked as to be considered synonymous.

Home detention (or house arrest, as it is commonly referred to) has traditionally been associated with political prisoners, disposed government officials, and others who are restricted to their homes pending some action. In this country, it has become a popular alternative to incarceration—that is, a way to restrict offenders to their premises except for work or school. Although house arrest has been used for many years in the United States, particularly with juveniles, in recent years its use has spread dramatically, especially since the development of EM devices that can be used around-the-clock to monitor the offender.

The concept of EM dates back to 1964 when a professor named Schwitzgebel first conceptualized the idea for mentally ill patients (Schwitzgebel, Schwitzgebel, Pahnke, & Hurd, 1964). By the 1980s, the technology allowed his idea to be put into practice. With EM, the offender is restricted to a specified area except during certain times (work, doctor's appointments, school, grocery store, etc.). If the offender leaves during restricted times, he or she is considered in violation of probation. The arguments for EM have been that it is a cheaper alternative than incarceration, allows the offender to remain at home and support his or her family, and can reduce jail crowding. The arguments against home detention primarily have centered on the net-widening issue, in which low-risk and petty offenders are brought under correctional control when other less restrictive alternatives are available.

Electronic monitoring is big business in the United States. Some local jurisdictions routinely use this alternative to aid with jail crowding. Despite its popularity, however, there are several important considerations regarding its use. First, who is appropriate for EM? Should it be used for serious offenders? Or for those who do not pose a serious threat to the community? Deciding who is appropriate for EM is not easy The problem is that if we are going to reduce jail crowding, then we need to take people who would be in jail. If not, then just give them probation and be done with it. The other problem centers on the effectiveness of EM. The question is, Why would we expect it to have an effect on someone's behavior in the long term? After all, what risk factors is it targeting? As a correctional intervention, it serves as a risk management tool, but as a risk reduction strategy there is little substance to it besides a short period of incapacitation. So, who should it be used for?

Given what we know from the research concerning offender risk factors and effective correctional programming, there is little reason to expect that EM offers anything more than short-term and limited control of offenders. Simply stated, placing an offender on EM neither targets nor reduces the risk factors that are correlated with offender recidivism.

So what are the arguments for using EM? One certainly can make the argument that EM allows offenders who might otherwise be incarcerated to stay with their families, continue to work, and participate in prosocial activities that might not be possible if they were incarcerated. The counterargument to this is that EM targets lower-risk offenders and thus widens the net. There is also the often-made argument that EM is cheaper than jail; however, this assumes that jail would be the alternative, and that recidivism rates are not higher than one would achieve without the sanction. Because jails and detention facilities are often filled to capacity, EM is probably adding costs rather than savings. Likewise, the research also seems to indicate that, at best, EM has no effect on recidivism and, at worst, increases it, which makes it difficult to justify EM on the basis of costs alone.

Shock Incarceration

Shock incarceration programs, also known as "boot camps," came of age in the 1980s. Georgia and Oklahoma were the first states to introduce this concept, and it quickly became popular throughout the country, used for adults and juveniles, males and females. Federal funding by the Clinton Administration's Justice Department led to the rapid growth of this "punishing smarter" alternative. The early boot camps were modeled after the old military-style programs of the same name. Drill and ceremony, physical conditioning, and breaking down of the individual followed by building him or her back up were the hallmarks of these programs. Some were designed as an alternative to long-term incarceration (upon completion, offenders received shorter sentences), some were part of "jails," some were weekend programs, and some were simply alternatives to other forms of residential programs. Boot camps have been extremely popular with politicians and the public, who, unfortunately, believe that getting tough with offenders is the most effective way to change offender behavior. Unfortunately, as we will see, getting tough often makes offenders worse.

Let's discuss some studies. In the late 1990s, the Cuyahoga County Juvenile Court (Cleveland) started a large boot camp for juveniles. The program was designed as an alternative to a commitment to the Department of Youth Services. The program was operated by a private provider under contract with the county. In 1997, the first study was completed on this and two other juvenile boot camps. The results are shown in Figure 5.1.

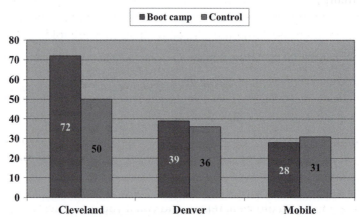

FIGURE 5.1 Juvenile boot camp rates of recidivism following release from confinement. Recidivism was defined as a court adjudicated new offense from time of release to cutoff date. *Source: Peters, M., Thomas, D., & Zamberian, C. (1997).* Boot camps for juvenile offenders program summary. *Washington, DC: Office of Juvenile Justice and Delinquency Prevention, U.S. Department of Justice.*

The recidivism rate for the Cleveland boot camp participants was 72%, and it was only 50% for the control group. The Denver boot camp reported slightly higher recidivism rates, whereas the Mobile program had slightly reduced rates.

Subsequent to this study, researchers from the University of Cincinnati were asked to visit the Cleveland boot camp and conduct assessment as part of a larger study that was being conducting for the state. When the program director was asked what she believed was the most effective treatment offered at the camp, she replied, "When they can climb the big rope." Is this a skill that we really want delinquents to acquire? She was referring to the obstacle course; when the youths could climb the 40-foot rope, they felt extremely good about themselves. Undoubtedly they did, but increasing one's self-esteem—and, by the way, most studies indicate that boot camps do increase self-esteem—has little to do with reducing risk because increasing self-esteem without reducing antisocial attitudes simply makes one feel good about being bad. In a more comprehensive review, Wilson, MacKenzie, and Mitchel (2008) conducted a meta-analysis of 32 research studies of boot camps and found no effect in reducing recidivism. The researchers concluded that militaristic boot camps were not effective in reducing recidivism.

Why don't boot camps reduce recidivism? There are a number of reasons. First, boot camps attempt to bond delinquent and criminal groups together. After all, that is one of the goals of military-style boot camps—to take a group of young recruits and establish esprit de corps. The problem is that we do not want to bond delinquents and criminals together; we call those "gangs." Second, boot camps target non-crime-producing needs, such as physical conditioning, drill, and ceremony. What does getting an offender in better shape have to do with reducing criminal behavior? The third major problem with boot camps is that the selection criteria are usually minimal. If you are in good physical condition, you can usually get into a boot camp. The result is we end up mixing low-, medium-, and high-risk offenders together, and then we bond them together. Finally, boot camps actually model aggressive behavior. When offenders get off the bus, someone bigger, stronger, and tougher than them gets in their faces and tells them that he or she is going to "straighten them out" and they "need to do as they are told or else." Remember, these are antisocial people, and they learn very quickly that if they want to get someone to do as they are told, they just have to get in their face. Now I know some of you will ask, "Doesn't the military do a great job of taking young people and molding them into productive citizens?" Yes it does, but studies conducted by the military in the 1940s and 1950s of men who were drafted and had prior records indicated that they were less likely to complete military duty and more likely to receive dishonorable discharge. That is one of the reasons why the military does not take recruits with serious criminal records. Let us ask those of you who have been in the military, when you finished your boot camp training, did the military give you a job and housing allowance, put someone in charge of the unit, promote you if you did well, reprimand you if you broke the rules, and give you a paycheck every month? That is why the military does structured social learning as well as any large organization. Unfortunately, most offender boot camps simply toughen them up and send them home. Fortunately, we are starting to see some changes in boot camps as a result of the research. Most have abandoned the focus on drill and ceremony and physical conditioning, and many now incorporate treatment as part of the program. Only time will tell if these changes can produce any positive results.

Scared Straight Programs

One of the more popular sanctions throughout the years has been the use of "Scared Straight" approaches designed to frighten offenders into changing their behavior. Although the concept has been around a long time, it became popularized when Peter Falk (Columbo, to those of you old enough to remember the show) hosted a documentary on television demonstrating a program operated by the New Jersey Department of Corrections using inmates from Rahway State Prison. During the documentary, lifers from the prison yelled and screamed at young delinquents and told them all the bad things that would happen to them if they kept on the path to criminal behavior. Through the power of TV, many came to believe that this could be an effective way to steer youthful offenders from a life of crime. What a great concept. It is cheap to do because almost every community has a jail, and there is also a large supply of offenders more than willing to scare some kids. Add some delinquents and you are in business. Unfortunately, the research has not been as kind to the idea. Table 5.1 shows the results from seven experimental studies of Scared Straight programs. As you can see, beginning in 1967 in Michigan, there have been a number of studies, none of which showed reductions in recidivism. In fact, the most famous of the programs, New Jersey's, led to a 30% increase in recidivism for the youths who participated in the program. Why is this the case? The research found that instead of scaring the kids straight, most of the kids actually received reinforcement for their delinquent behavior. Rather than shame, they achieved status and standing from their peers. Rather than fear, they were emboldened by the experience. A subsequent meta-analysis by Petrosino, Turpin-Petrosino, and Buehler (2004, p. 8) concluded that Scared Straight programs were more harmful than doing nothing.

Table 5.1   Review of Seven Studies of "Scared Straight" Programs

Year	Site	Measure	% change
1967	Michigan	% delinquent	+26% increase in failure
1979	Illinois	% contact by police	+5% increase in failure
1979	Michigan	% new offense	+1% increase in failure
1981	Virginia	% new court intakes	+2% increase in failure
1981	Texas	% official delinquency	+11% increase in failure
1982	New Jersey	% new offense	+30% increase in failure
1982	California	% new arrests	+1% increase in failure
1986	Kansas	Crime outcomes	No difference
1992	Mississippi	Crime outcomes	No difference

Source: Petrosino, A., Turpin-Petrosino, C., & Finkenauer, J. O. (2000). Well-meaning programs can have harmful effects! Lessons from experiments of programs such as Scared Straight. *Crime and Delinquency, 46,* 354–371.

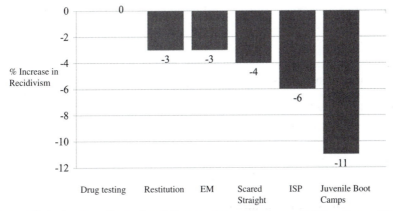

FIGURE 5.2 Meta-analysis: Average effects of punishing smarter programs on recidivism. *Source: Gendreau, P. (2000). The effects of community sanctions and incarceration on recidivism.* Forum on Corrections Research, 12, *10–13; and Aos, S., Phipps, P., Barnoski, R., & Lieb, R. (1999).* The comparative costs and benefits of programs to reduce crime. *Olympia, WA: Washington State Institute for Public Policy.*

Finally, Figure 5.2 shows the average effects of some of the so-called "punishing smarter" approaches to dealing with offenders. Although some techniques, such as drug testing, can be useful in supporting treatment efforts, alone they do not appear to have much effect on recidivism. Others, such as Scared Straight, are actually harmful.

Correctional Quackery

Although many of the intermediate sanctions or punishing smarter approaches are not effective in reducing recidivism, some are used to divert offenders from prison and jails and possibly save some money, and others, such as EM or drug testing, are often used in conjunction with treatment programs. Quackery, on the other hand, often occurs when we are dismissive of scientific knowledge (Latessa, Cullen, & Gendreau, 2002). Throughout the years, we have assessed hundreds of correctional programs[1] and have seen just about every theory and idea you can imagine. Table 5.2 shows some of the so-called "theories" we have come across. These include the "it worked for me theory," where the staff believe that because they shared common experiences (prior substance abuse, gang membership, ex-offenders, etc.), they can somehow change the behavior of the current offenders. The "offenders lack creativity" theory states that if we can just get offenders interested in exploring their creative side, we can set them on the right track. We once assessed a halfway house program in California for parolees in which the primary activity was art therapy. When asked why all the program time was spent on

---

[1]The Correctional Program Assessment Inventory and the Correctional Program Checklist are designed to assess correctional programs and the degree to which they meet the principles of effective intervention. Researchers at the University of Cincinnati have assessed more than 600 correctional programs. These tools are discussed in more detail in Chapter 12.

Table 5.2   Some So-Called "Theories" We Have Come Across

"It worked for me" theory
"Offenders lack creativity" theory
"Offenders need to get back to nature" theory
"Offenders lack discipline" theory
"Offenders have low self-esteem" theory
" Offenders lack organizational skills" theory
"Offenders need to have a pet in prison" theory
"Offenders need to change their diet" theory
"Treat them as babies and dress them in diapers" theory
"We just want them to be happy" theory
"Offenders (females) need to learn to put on makeup and dress better" theory
"Male offenders need to get in touch with their feminine side" theory

these activities, the program director said that "it reduced stress." They must have had the most relaxed offenders in California. In one therapeutic program, the program director would have the men wear diapers if they acted up, which is a shaming technique—"If you are going to act like a baby, I am going to treat you that way." The problem is that this is not a very effective way to change someone's behavior, especially that of an offender. After all, how many of us like to be shamed and humiliated in front of others? So what do you think you get when you shame an antisocial offender? One mental health program we assessed just wanted them to be happy, so that was their target—happy offenders. A favorite has always been "have them get in touch with their feminine side" theory. This one goes something like this: "The reason men are aggressive brutes is because they just aren't sensitive enough." One halfway house we visited in New Jersey had the men attend groups dressed in drag. If you are ever mugged in New Jersey by a guy dressed in drag, it may be one of their graduates. Table 5.3 shows other forms of correctional quackery.

Table 5.3   Correctional Quackery

Acupuncture
Aura focus
Drama therapy
Dance programs
Heart mapping
Sage smudging
Horticulture therapy
Plastic surgery
Yoga
Pet therapy
Dog sledding as wilderness training
Hand writing formation

Ineffective Treatment Approaches

Let's now discuss some of the so-called therapeutic approaches that are not effective. These include some widely used interventions and techniques.

First, take a minute and think of three speeches you have heard that have changed your life. My guess is that most of you cannot do it. Now think of three people who have changed your life. That should be much easier. Most of us can identify the people who have influenced us and whom we tried to be like: spouse, parents, grandparents, aunts, uncles, teachers, friends, siblings, ministers, mentors, bosses—the list goes on. The point is that most of us do not remember what we hear; in fact, we retain only approximately 20% of what is told to us. On the other hand, we can all think of the people we modeled after and who had a significant influence on our lives. This brief exercise helps demonstrate how much more effective social learning is than "talking" cures. The problem is that many correctional programs still think they can "talk" offenders into changing. Table 5.4 shows some of the ineffective approaches often used with offenders.

Included in the list in Table 5.4 are techniques such as client-centered approaches, in which offenders often get to talk about what they want to. We have seen groups in which offenders sit in a circle and the facilitator asks, "So what do you think the problem is?" or "What do you want to talk about today." Psychotherapy and psychodynamic approaches

Table 5.4 Ineffective Approaches in Changing Offender Behavior

Drug prevention focused on fear and other emotional appeals
Drug education
Client-centered, nondirective approaches
Bibliotherapy (reading books)
Lectures
Self-help
Psychotherapy and Freudian approaches
Increasing the cohesiveness of delinquent/criminal groups
Good relationship with the offender as the primary goal
Self-actualization through self-discovery
Medical model approaches
Radical nonintervention
Vague unstructured rehabilitation programs
   "Counseling" for everyone
   Life skills
   Case management
   Good relationships with the offender as the primary goal
Targeting non-crime-producing needs
   Self-esteem
   Anxiety
   Vague emotional and physical complaints
   Diet
   Lack of creative abilities
   Physical conditioning

are talk therapies that often focus on the past and help the client develop "insight." These approaches are ineffective with offenders and can sometimes be harmful in their effects. We also see vague, ill-defined approaches, such as "counseling" or "life skills." These terms tell us little about the approach used or the target for change. As we have learned previously, targeting non-crime-producing needs will also be ineffective. In the end, we will have offenders that feel better about themselves, are in good shape, and can draw a picture. Unfortunately, prisons are filled with good artists. Because many offenders abuse substances and many of these approaches are used in substance abuse treatment, let's discuss some examples from the substance abuse literature.

Substance Abuse Treatment

Because substance abuse is so prevalent with offenders, let's examine some of the reviews of research. Table 5.5 is from a review of the literature conducted by Lightfoot (1999). As you see, the most effective approaches were social learning, cognitive behavioral, and behavioral. On the other hand, the approaches in which there was no clear evidence of effectiveness included many of the techniques that are commonly used with offenders. Table 5.6 is a review by Taxman (2000). Again, we see the same pattern.

Some of you might say, " But I see Alcoholics Anonymous and 12-step programs on these lists. Haven't these programs saved millions of people from alcohol abuse?" Our response is, "Yes, they have, but remember, we are often dealing with offenders who happened to abuse substances, not prosocial people who drink too much." Look at how Alcoholics Anonymous (AA) and the 12-step program developed. The founders—Bill W., a stockbroker, and Dr. Bob S., a surgeon—were both highly successful individuals who,

Table 5.5   Review of Drug Treatment Effectiveness by Lightfoot

What treatment types showed no clear evidence of effectiveness from controlled studies?
Acupuncture
Education
Lectures
Bibliotherapy
Self-help
Alcoholics Anonymous
Narcotics Anonymous
Adult Children of Alcoholics
Psychotherapy
Supportive
Confrontational
Pharmacotherapies
Al-Anon

Source: Lightfoot, L. (1999). Treating substance abuse and dependence in offenders: A review of methods and outcomes. In E. Latessa (Ed.), *What works strategic solutions: The International Community Corrections Association examines substance abuse*. Lanham, MD: American Correctional Association.

Table 5.6   Review of Drug Treatment Effectiveness by Taxman

What treatment types showed no clear evidence of effectiveness of reduced recidivism?
Nondirective counseling
Reality therapy
Psychosocial education
12 Step or other self-help groups
Psychoanalytical

Source: Taxman, F. S. (2000). Unraveling "what works" for offenders in substance abuse treatment services. *National Drug Court Institute Review, 2,* 2.

over the course of many years, lost all they had achieved because of their addiction to alcohol. Their addiction developed over an extended period of time—decades, in fact. It makes sense that for these two men, the concepts central to the 12 steps would be extremely powerful:

- They felt they were powerless over their use of alcohol.
- Their lives had become unmanageable.
- A power greater than themselves—and we can assume these were two individuals with very strong egos—was needed for them to gain back order in their lives.
- It also makes sense that these two individuals would respond to a spiritual path to recovery. After all, AA evolved from the Oxford Group, which was an Episcopal self-help movement in the 1920s and 1930s. Both Bill W. and Dr. Bob S. had been involved in the Oxford Group prior to getting sober.

Now think about a criminal population: What have they achieved in their lives? Most often, very little. Unfortunately, for many, drugs is their achievement. Drugs are what made them successful. Drugs gave them money, status, power, and sex. What have they lost because of their alcohol or other drug use? For many, their actual drug use has not progressed to the point that it has cost them much other than their freedom. Consequently, they believe that is it the government, and not their use of drugs, that is their problem. If they can get out from under community control or prison, they believe their problems will be solved.

What skills do they bring to the table to take advantage of the fellowship of AA? Most act out of short-term hedonistic, self-centered concerns. They lack the ability to form lasting empathic relationships with others, and the relationships they form are often based on short-term self-gratification. They often do not understand the needs of regulating their behavior to accommodate the needs of others. So you tell them they are powerless over their substance use, their lives are unmanageable, and they need to submit their will to a higher power and use the fellowship of AA. The typical response:

- I'm not powerless.
- Drugs and crime are my power.
- My life is not unmanageable. My life is fine, except I am under community control, or incarcerated. As soon as I am free, my life will be quite manageable.

- I will not submit my will to anyone. I've got it all figured out. You're the confused one.
- Sure I'll go to AA meetings. It will get the judge off my back.

Remember, the AA and 12-step model was developed by successful upper-middle-class men who lost everything to their addiction. Many offenders simply do not connect to this model. The other major issue is that the AA and 12-step model was never designed for an offender population. The fact is that most higher-risk offenders have a number of risk factors, of which substance abuse may be one, but it often is not at the top of the list when it comes to why someone is engaged in criminal conduct. AA and 12-step programs were designed as anonymous and voluntary programs; they are often required for offenders, which means that most are not willingly seeking help and are often not ready for change. Finally, because the only "quality assurance" we have with AA programs is the requirement that offenders get a signature that they attended, we know little about their actual participation or involvement.

So, what does the research tell us? First, drug abuse and addiction is a chronic relapsing condition. As we have learned, applying short-term, education-based treatment services will not effectively reduce it. Second, traditional models used by substance abuse programs, such as drug/alcohol education and 12-step models, have not been found as effective as cognitive behavioral models. Third, most offenders have several risk factors that need to be addressed through interventions; substance may be one, but it is rarely the only one contributing to their behavior. Finally, criminality is an independent factor that independently affects a treatment outcome.

Targeting Noncriminogenic Needs

There are a number of reasons why correction programs are not always effective. Sometimes it is because the techniques they use to attempt to change behavior are not effective—for example, trying to talk offenders into behaving differently or educating them about their problems. Sometimes even well-designed programs are not effective because the program is not being delivered with integrity (more on this later). Another reason is because the program may be targeting noncriminogenic needs—those needs that have little, if any, correlation with criminal behavior. Figure 5.3 shows the results from juvenile programs based on the target. Fear of punishment (Scared Straight-type programs), bonding antisocial peers together (e.g., boot camps), making offenders feel better about themselves without reducing antisocial thinking, working on vague emotional problems, showing respect for antisocial thinking, or getting offenders in good shape all increase recidivism rates. Again, we see that targeting criminogenic needs is positively correlated with significant reductions in recidivism.

Treatment programs that use ineffective approaches or even outright quackery have the potential to do harm in several ways. First is the obvious: failing to help offenders stay out of trouble. A second way in which ineffective treatment programs are harmful is that

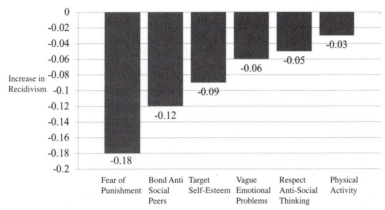

FIGURE 5.3 Needs targets and correlation with effect size for youthful offenders. *Source: Dowden, C., & Andrews, D. (1999). What works in young offenders treatment: A meta-analysis. Forum on Correctional Research, 11, 21–24.*

they undermine confidence and support for treatment for offenders. Latessa and Holsinger (1998, pp. 6–7) summarized the harm that can be done:

> *When faced with the existence of ineffective correctional treatment strategies, judges, legislators, and the public lose confidence in treatment efforts, which in turn undermines support for effective programs. Another result is that when we use programs that are not effective, the offender received the blame, not the program. Too often we hear judges say that they have already sent the offender to some program and that they have failed. This "failure" is then used to justify even harsher punishments. Blaming the offender absolves us from designing and operating high-quality and effective intervention programs.*

We end this chapter by showing the results from a National Institute of Justice study (Sherman et al., 1998) (Table 5.7). Although the methodology used by the authors was not

Table 5.7   Review from the National Institute of Justice

What doesn't work?
  Correctional boot camps using traditional military basic training
  Drug prevention classes focused on fear and other emotional appeals including self-esteem
  D.A.R.E.
  School-based leisure-time enrichment programs
  "Scared Straight" programs in which juvenile offenders visit adult prisons
  Shock probation, shock parole, and split sentences adding time to probation and parole
  Home detention with electronic monitoring
  Intensive supervision
  Rehabilitation programs using vague, unstructured counseling
  Residential programs for juvenile offenders using challenging experiences in rural settings

Source: Sherman, L. W., Gottfredson, D. C., MacKenzie, D. L., Eck, J., Reuter, P., & Bushway, S. D. (1998). *Preventing crime: What works, what doesn't, what's promising* [Research in Brief]. Washington, DC: National Institute of Justice.

a meta-analysis, the findings are the same that others have found using that technique. What this and the other studies confirm is that there are many approaches and interventions that are not effective in changing offender behavior and that may actually lead to increases in recidivism.

Summary

- During the 1980s, there was a dramatic increase in the prison population that led to an increase in intermediate sanctions between probation and prison.
- Intensive supervision is one of the most widely used intermediate sanctions; it involves increasing the supervision and surveillance of higher-risk offenders. Most studies have demonstrated that just increasing supervision can lead to higher technical violation rates and increased recidivism.
- Day reporting centers became popular in the late 1980s and 1990s, and they require offenders to report to a central location on a regular basis to participate in services. Few studies have been conducted on this alternative.
- Electronic monitoring and house arrest have become almost synonymous and involve restricting the offender to his or her home. Issues facing electronic monitoring include selection criteria, net widening, and risk reduction.
- Boot camps are very popular; however, most research has shown that they are not effective in reducing recidivism.
- Scared Straight programs, which usually involve juveniles, often do anything but scare them, with most studies showing increased failure rates for those who participate in the program.
- Correctional quackery includes a wide range of programs and interventions. Most are based on flawed theories of criminal behavior and can actually lead to increased recidivism.
- Many of the treatment approaches used in corrections are not effective. This includes talking cures, client-centered approaches, psychotherapy, vague and ill-defined approaches, and those that do not target criminogenic needs.
- Many of the traditional approaches used in substance abuse treatment are not effective with an offender population. AA and 12-step approaches were never designed for an offender population and show little, if any, effect in reducing recidivism.
- There is a great deal of consensus in the academic community about the research on what does not work in reducing recidivism.

References

Clear, T. R., Harris, P. M., & Baird, C. S. (1992). Probationer violations and officer response. *Journal of Criminal Justice, 20,* 1–12.

Fulton, B., Latessa, E. J., Stichman, A., & Travis, L. F. (1997). The state of ISP: Research and policy implications. *Federal Probation, 61*(4), 65–75.

Latessa, E. J., Cullen, F. T., & Gendreau, P. (2002). Correctional quackery: Professional responsibility for evidence-based practice. *Federal Probation, 66*(2).

Latessa, E. J., & Holsinger, A. (1998). The importance of evaluating correctional programs: Assessing outcome and quality. *Corrections Management Quarterly, 2*(4), 22–29.

Latessa, E. J., Travis, L. F., Fulton, B., & Stichman, A. (1998). *Evaluating the prototypical ISP final report.* Cincinnati, OH: Division of Criminal Justice, University of Cincinnati.

Latessa, E. J., Travis, L. F., Holsinger, A., & Hartman, J. (1998). *Evaluation of Ohio's Pilot Day reporting programs.* Cincinnati, OH: Division of Criminal Justice, University of Cincinnati.

Lightfoot, L. (1999). Treating substance abuse and dependence in offenders: A review of methods and outcomes. In E. Latessa (Ed.), *What works strategic solutions: The International Community Corrections Association examines substance abuse.* Lanham, MD: American Correctional Association.

Peters, M., Thomas, D., & Zamberian, C. (1997). *Boot camps for juvenile offenders program summary.* Washington, DC: Office of Juvenile Justice and Delinquency Prevention, U.S. Department of Justice.

Petersilia, J., & Turner, S. (1993). *Evaluating intensive supervision probation/parole: Results of a nationwide experiment.* Washington, DC: U.S. Department of Justice, National Institute of Justice.

Petrosino, A., Turpin-Petrosino, C., & Buehler, J. (2004). *"Scared Straight" and other juvenile awareness programs for preventing juvenile delinquency.* Campbell Systematic Reviews, 2. http://dx.doi.org/10.4073/csr.2004.2.

Petrosino, A., Turpin-Petrosino, C., & Finkenauer, J. O. (2000). Well-meaning programs can have harmful effects! Lessons from experiments of programs such as Scared Straight. *Crime and Delinquency, 46,* 354–371.

Schwitzgebel, R. K., Schwitzgebel, R. L., Pahnke, W. N., & Hurd, W. S. (1964). A program of research in behavioral electronics. *Behavioral Science, 9*(3), 233–238.

Sherman, L. W., Gottfredson, D. C., MacKenzie, D. L., Eck, J., Reuter, P., & Bushway, S. D. (1998). *Preventing crime: What works, what doesn't, what's promising* [Research in Brief]. Washington, DC: National Institute of Justice.

Taxman, F. S. (2000). Unraveling "what works" for offenders in substance abuse treatment services. *National Drug Court Institute Review, 2,* 2.

Wilson, D. B., MacKenzie, D. L., & Mitchel, F. N. (2008). Effects of correctional boot camps on offending. *Campbell Systematic Reviews, 2003,* 1. http://dx.doi.org/10.4073/csr/2003, 1.

Zamble, E., & Porporino, F. J. (1988). *Coping, behavior, and adaptation in prison inmates.* New York: Springer-Verlag.

6

Responsivity
What Is It, and Why Is It Important?

Introduction

The responsivity principle is considered the third component of the risk–need–responsivity (RNR) model. The responsivity principle may actually be the least understood or, at best, the most neglected of the three principles. At its core, the responsivity principle recommends that treatment programs "maximize the offender's ability to learn from a rehabilitative intervention by providing cognitive behavioral treatment and tailoring the intervention to the learning style, motivation, abilities, and strengths of the offender" (Bonta & Andrews, 2007, p. 1). In other words, treatment effectiveness can be enhanced if the program staff takes into consideration the characteristics of the clients.

The two key components of the responsivity principle include the delivery of a particular type of approach and a recognition that individuals respond differently to staff, interventions, and environments. These two issues are referred to as the general responsivity and specific responsivity principles:

> **General responsivity**: Structured social learning and cognitive behavioral approaches are the most effective way to teach people new behaviors.
> **Specific responsivity**: Treatment should be tailored to individual characteristics that may impact its success.

The topic of general responsivity is left primarily to the other chapters pertaining to the core correctional practices and what works with offenders. This chapter instead focuses primarily on the specific responsivity component and why it is imperative that programs take these issues into consideration when providing treatment.

Why Is It Important?

Correctional counselors are keenly aware that some clients are easier to manage than others. At the same time, some staff members are better equipped at dealing with certain clients. For example, some staff may be skilled at handling resistant clients compared to others who have more success with those who are highly withdrawn or anxious. These individual styles and interactions can impact even the most effective approaches.

Studies suggest that certain therapeutic styles among staff are more effective than others. For example, Marshall (2005) found that therapists' characteristics impacted the effectiveness of sex offender treatment. In particular, those who were warm, non-confrontational, empathetic, and directive were more effective. Similarly, Andrews and

Kiessling (1980) found that probation officers who showed sensitivity in their dealings with clients were more likely to receive positive reviews and use behavioral strategies during their meetings. Finally, a number of studies find that the strength of the relationship between staff and client impacts retention and criminal behavior post-treatment (Joe, Simpson, Danserau, & Rowan-Szal, 2001; Simpson, Joe, Greener, & Rowan-Szal, 2000). Attrition is of particular concern given that dropouts tend to have significantly higher recidivism rates compared to those who complete treatment. In fact, high program attrition rates among certain populations (e.g., younger clients, those with mental illnesses, and minority clients) confirm that responsivity factors can interfere with the treatment process (Olver, Stockdale, & Wormith, 2011).

Risk, need, and responsivity are often intertwined. Antisocial personality is a good example of how these factors are interrelated. James Bonta (1995, p. 36) summarized this issue well in his discussion of dealing with psychopaths:

> *Many of the responsivity factors frequently found among offenders do, however, also function as risk factors. A diagnosis of antisocial personality or psychopathy are examples of the ways risk, criminogenic needs, and responsivity may operate together. Not only are such individuals more likely to recidivate (risk), but therapists may attempt to target aspects of the antisocial personality, such as impulsivity (criminogenic need). Further, research suggests that group work may not be the best approach for treating psychopaths (responsivity).*

In this example, responsivity includes planning for the potential impact that individual characteristics (i.e., psychopathic traits) can have on the dynamics of a treatment group. In another example, we can see that family can act as both a risk and responsivity principle. The literature suggests that the dysfunctional family environments are a risk factor for both juveniles and adults (Patterson & Yoerger, 1993). The family can influence criminal behavior in a variety of ways, including providing youth with reinforcement for certain behaviors, modeling prospects for learning new behaviors, and providing opportunities for committing deviance. The family may also act as a barrier to youth when they start treatment. For example, the family may not be willing to drive the youth to attend treatment sessions or a court hearing. If clients cannot get to treatment or court review hearings because of transportation, they are more likely to receive a technical violation. Taking the approach of "tough love" in this circumstance and simply telling the youth to figure out a way to attend is short-sighted. Although it may be that transportation needs to be the responsibility of the client, the reality is that the client's transportation issues may be tied to family dysfunction.

Understanding that individual differences can impact treatment is one thing, but determining the entire set of issues that can impact treatment might be quite another, especially if we conceive that responsivity factors can range from individual-level characteristics such as motivation and cognitive ability/intelligence to external factors such as transportation, child care, and homelessness. These responsivity factors are likely to change throughout the course of treatment, necessitating continuing adaptation of the treatment plan and treatment services. Assessment of these issues should occur before deciding placement in treatment or assignment to staff caseloads. The assessment process should also be comprehensive so as to provide staff with a level of detail regarding the client's circumstance and allow for a reassessment of needs during the course of treatment.

Although it is impossible to determine an exhaustive list of specific responsivity factors, there are issues that are more likely to occur within offending populations and impact the rehabilitative process. These responsivity factors are often categorized into two groups: individual or client-centered characteristics and external characteristics. Individual-level responsivity factors are likely to include motivation, cognitive ability, mental health, personality, and demographic characteristics (age, gender, race, and ethnicity). We are also providing a discussion of trauma as a responsivity consideration given the growing interest regarding trauma informed care models. In addition, there are a myriad of external factors that could have an impact, including the client's life circumstances (e.g., homelessness, lack of transportation, or child care). As we will see throughout this chapter, many of the internal and external factors intersect in a variety of ways. We begin by focusing on the client's willingness or motivation to change his or her behavior.

Motivation to Change

Motivation to change is a commonly discussed topic in the substance abuse literature. It was once thought that coerced treatment was ineffective and individuals needed to hit "rock bottom" before they were ready to change their addictive behaviors. Although it is now believed that coerced treatment can be effective with offenders, the client's level of motivation does have the potential to impact the effectiveness of services. Motivation to change exists on a continuum, with those who are actively taking steps to change on one end and those who fail to recognize they even have a problem on the other. In the 1980s, two researchers developed categories to capture the different levels of motivation through which people progress when deciding whether to change their behavior. They referred to these levels as the **"stages of change"** model (Prochaska & DiClemente, 1983). As shown in Figure 6.1, there are five stages. In the first stage, referred to as *precontemplation*, individuals are not actively seeking to change their behaviors. They may be unaware that the behavior needs to be changed or simply do not see their "problem" as something to be addressed. Examples include clients who believe that the benefits of their criminal behavior outweigh the problems that it creates or gang members who feel so strongly about adhering to the gang culture that they do not care whether they are arrested or even sentenced to prison. This antisocial attitude can influence how motivated they are for treatment (another reason why cognitive behavioral treatment is so important).

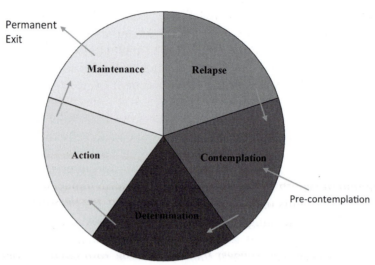

FIGURE 6.1 **Stages of readiness for change.** *Source: Prochaska, J. O., & DiClemente, C. C. (1983). Stages and processes of self-change of smoking: Toward an integrative model of change.* Journal of Consulting and Clinical Psychology, 51, 390–395.

In the next stage, *contemplation,* clients may be willing to recognize that the problem exists, but they have yet to commit to a change. In this stage, drug users may see the downside of their addiction but feel powerless to stop using. This stage is sometimes referred to as a "teeter-totter" stage in which clients feel ambivalent and may go back and forth in their desire to change.

In the third stage, *determination,* the clients may begin to seek out resources and think seriously about how they might change their behaviors. In this stage, individuals may decide that change is needed, and they begin to think about other activities that would help keep them busy during the times that drug use typically occurs (e.g., after school and on weekends).

In the fourth stage, *action,* clients commit to change and begin to modify the behavior(s) in question. In this stage, clients stop engaging in the problem behavior (e.g., using alcohol or other drugs or associating with antisocial peers). In the final stage, *maintenance,* clients develop clear steps to maintain the behavioral change. The maintenance stage includes relapse prevention strategies such as avoiding high-risk situations (e.g., bars) and friends that could trigger a lapse. It is important to meet clients where they are at on the wheel. For some, motivation can take some time, whereas others are fully motivated at the beginning.

Program staff should assess the client's level of motivation to determine whether services in this area are needed. There are a number of assessment tools to measure a client's motivation to change. One tool, developed by researchers at the University of Rhode Island, is referred to as the University of Rhode Island Change Assessment Scale (URICA). The 32-item questionnaire assesses how the client feels about entering treatment. The tool can be utilized as a barometer for the staff as well as the clients

(McConnaughy, Prochaska, & Velicer, 1983). Another tool, created by Texas Christian University, is referred to as the TCU-ENG (Engagement) form (Table 6.1). This assessment captures a client's willingness to engage in treatment throughout the process and can be used to reassess the client at various intervals.

Once motivation level is established, staff may choose to use the **motivational interviewing** (MI) techniques (Miller & Rollnick, 2012) to transition the client through the various stages. Motivational interviewing is an interview-based technique that is designed to reduce an individual's resistance to engaging in treatment. Staff members should begin by working with clients to have them see why the behavior is a problem. For example, if a youth does not want to attend school, the interviewer can discuss the reasoning behind the youth's resistance and the long-term impact of truancy. By helping the youth see the problems that the behavior is creating, the person may be more likely to see the benefits of changing the behavior. Techniques used in MI include being nonconfrontational, rolling with resistance, and supporting the client's self-efficacy. Proponents of this approach suggest that by working with clients rather than simply relying on coercion increases the likelihood of sustained behavioral change (Miller & Rollnick, 2012).

Keeping clients motivated can be difficult in the face of relapse. Although expecting and anticipating relapse is considered a "best practice" within substance abuse treatment, there is a potential downside. When explaining this issue of relapse to a client, the program staff may tell the client that relapse is an expected part of the recovery process. If we begin treatment by telling a client that he or she will likely relapse, however, there is a risk that the client will see this as a justification or reason to have a relapse. On the other hand, it is important to intervene when clients do relapse to help them understand that a small mistake does not need to turn into a full blown relapse. In effect, staff members must be prepared to help clients through relapse should it happen, however, but should be aware that telling clients to expect relapse may have unintended consequences.

Cognitive Ability

Another responsivity factor is the client's ability to understand the content of treatment. This is of particular concern for cognitive restructuring programs that rely on abstract empathy building. Cognitive ability can be measured in a number of ways, but it is often associated with intelligence (IQ). Much of the literature on intelligence in criminology focuses on whether it is a risk factor for crime. In the controversial book, *Bell Curve*, Herrnstein and Murray (1996) argue that IQ is a significant predictor of criminal behavior. Other studies, however, refute the notion that there is a direct relationship between IQ and crime. Instead, scholars argue that IQ works indirectly through school performance. In other words, low IQ could impact an individual's school achievement and could eventually influence other factors related to crime (e.g., truancy, dropping out of school) (Andrews & Bonta, 2010a, 2010b; Cullen, Gendreau, Jajoura, & Wright, 1997; Ward & Tittle, 1994).

Table 6.1 The TCU(ENG) Engagement Form

Scoring Instructions. Items shown below from this assessment are *re-grouped by scales*, and response categories are 1 = Strongly Disagree to 5 = Strongly Agree. Scores for *each scale* are calculated as follows (and no more than half of the items for any scale can be missing).

TREATMENT ENGAGEMENT PROCESS DOMAINS

A. Treatment Participation (TP)

You are willing to talk about your feelings during counseling.
You have made progress with your drug/alcohol problems.
You have learned to analyze and plan ways to solve your problems.
You have made progress toward your treatment program goals.
You always attend the counseling sessions scheduled for you.
You have stopped or greatly reduced your drug use while in this program.
You always participate actively in your counseling sessions.
You have made progress in understanding your feelings and behavior.
You have improved your relations with other people because of this treatment.
You have made progress with your emotional or psychological issues.
You give honest feedback during counseling.
You are following your counselor's guidance.

B. Treatment Satisfaction (TS)

Time schedules for counseling sessions at this program are convenient for you.
This program expects you to learn responsibility and self-discipline.
This program is organized and run well.
You are satisfied with this program.
The staff here are efficient at doing their job.
You can get plenty of personal counseling at this program.
This program location is convenient for you.

C. Counseling Rapport (CR)

You trust your counselor.
It's always easy to follow or understand what your counselor is trying to tell you.
Your counselor is easy to talk to.
You are motivated and encouraged by your counselor.
Your counselor recognizes the progress you make in treatment.
Your counselor is well organized and prepared for each counseling session.
Your counselor is sensitive to your situation and problems.
Your treatment plan has reasonable objectives.
Your counselor views your problems and situations realistically.
Your counselor helps you develop confidence in yourself.
Your counselor respects you and your opinions.
You can depend on your counselor's understanding.

D. Peer Support (PS)

Other clients at this program care about you and your problems.
Other clients at this program are helpful to you.
You are similar to (or like) other clients of this program.
You have developed positive trusting friendships while at this program.
There is a sense of family (or community) in this program.

Whereas intelligence may not be a core risk factor, cognitive functioning can be an important responsivity factor. For example, an individual who is low functioning may not be able to understand empathy exercises that include taking another's perspective. In addition, a person with a mental disorder such as autism may have a higher IQ and be able to handle specific complex tasks but not able to handle the general scope of cognitive reasoning. Thus, teaching social skills may be too difficult for them to learn, or they may not be able to understand why a certain thinking error is problematic.

Assessment of cognitive functioning can be difficult. However, there are certain tools, such as the *Culture Fair IQ* test, can be administered fairly quickly. Programs may also find it useful to utilize educational achievement as a proxy for cognitive functioning. For example, clients with less than an eighth-grade reading level or who are not verbally skilled may need additional groups and services before they are ready to attend certain groups.

Although caution may be in order when placing those who are low functioning into cognitive groups, it not suggested here that these interventions would not work for this population. In fact, John Taylor and colleagues (2008, p. 725) assert that

> *the suggestion that mature and complete cognitive capacity is necessary for good outcomes in CBT is however debatable. There is no evidence in the intellectual disabilities field that deficits in particular cognitive abilities result in poorer outcomes, and studies involving children show that it is not necessary to have mature adult cognitive apparatus to benefit from CBT.*

Moreover, Cullen et al. (1997) assert that those with low IQ may do quite well in highly structured behavioral programs (e.g., token economies). Programs simply need to be responsive to clients with these issues when assigning clients to groups. Another possible solution is to offer separate groups for those with cognitive delays where the pace of the curriculum is delayed. In a circumstance in which that is not possible, the client may be better served in a one-on-one session with a counselor rather than a group setting.

Mental Health

Another issue that could impact treatment is the existence of mental illness. The term *mental health* is used in a variety of contexts. On the one hand, those who experience situational anxiety or bouts of depression are often said to be experiencing mental health problems. Alternatively, others think of the term mental illness in the context of serious disorders such as schizophrenia or antisocial personality disorder. Within this context, professionals rely on the ***Diagnostic and Statistical Manual of Mental Disorders***, fourth edition–text revision (*DSM-IV-TR*; American Psychiatric Association, 2000). The *DSM-IV-TR* is considered the bible among mental health professionals for diagnosing individual mental disorders. The disorders are classified into Axis 1–Axis 5 categories. For many disorders, a person must be experiencing symptoms over a period of time that leads to impairment in functioning (e.g., life, school, and work).

To understand mental illness from a responsivity perspective, we first need to consider the debate surrounding whether mental illness is a risk factor for criminal behavior. There is no doubt that those with **serious and persistent mental illnesses** (SPMI) are over-represented in the criminal justice system[1] given the rate of mental illness is significantly higher than the rate found in the general community (Steadman, Osher, Robbins, Case, & Samuels, 2009).

The role of mental illness in predicting criminal behavior, however, is an issue of debate. On one side of the debate are those who argue that mental illness is a predictor or risk factor for crime. Jennifer Skeem and colleagues (2011) refer to this philosophy as a one-dimensional model of understanding the relationship between mental illness and crime. The one-dimensional model suggests that the symptoms of the mental illness are the driving force behind criminal behavior. As a result, the system developed a number of policies and interventions centered on the individual's mental illness. One popular intervention is mental health courts. As noted in Box 6.1, mental health courts are becoming an increasingly popular option for dealing with those with SPMI diagnoses.

Mental health courts often focus services around increasing the self-sufficiency of the client through a targeted case management approach. The focus on case management makes sense if we take the one-dimensional model into consideration. Logically, if we believe that an individual's mental illness is the driver behind the criminal behavior, then we should be able to fix the criminality issue by fixing the mental illness issue. Most often, the strategies utilized include medication management and stabilization in the community (e.g., housing and support services). One of the main tasks of case managers in the mental health court model is to ensure that clients take their medications, keep doctor's appointments, assist them with insurance or Medicaid paperwork, etc. Stabilization centered on the client's mental health maintenance should have the positive consequence of reducing criminality if that was the driving cause.

On the other side of the debate, however, are those who suggest that mental illness is more likely a responsivity issue for treatment. There is a body of research that suggests that the one-dimensional perspective is ill-informed. For example, a meta-analysis by James Bonta and colleagues (1998) finds that mental illness is a weak predictor of criminal behavior. Moreover, others find that mental illness is likely the driver for criminal behavior in only 10% of the cases involving those with mental illnesses (Skeem et al., 2011). Perhaps more compelling are studies that find those with mental illnesses, including those with SPMIs such as schizophrenia and bipolar, held the same level of antisocial views or attitudes as those without mental illness (Morgan, Fisher, Duan, Mandracchia, & Murray, 2010; Wolf, Frueh, Shi, & Schumann, 2012).

This debate notwithstanding, if we consider the core risk factors for criminal behavior that we have discussed throughout the book (e.g., peers, employment/education, and family), we know that many of those with SPMIs live complicated lives and often struggle with a lack of community resources, unemployment, homelessness, and addictions

---

[1]The SPMI category most often refers to schizophrenia, bipolar, and major depressive disorders.

BOX 6.1   SPOTLIGHT: MENTAL HEALTH COURTS

The problem solving court model became popular in the late 1980s with the creation of the first drug court. Mental health courts first developed in the late 1990s. While much of the research on drug courts is supportive of its ability to reduce drug use and recidivism among participants, fewer studies have been conducted on mental health courts.

The Mental Health Court model is modeled after the drug court model. This model is considered a wraparound service-based approach designed to provide dedicated court-based treatment to those with serious mental illnesses. In 2007, the Council of State Governments issued a report outlining the 10 key components of mental health courts:

1. Planning and administration

   A broad array of stakeholders guides the planning and administration of the court.
2. Target population

   The client's mental illness should be interfering with his or her life circumstances and related to the current offense.
3. Timely identification and linkage to services

   The client should be screened and placed in services as soon as possible.
4. Detailed terms of participation

   The least restrictive supervision and length of services should not exceed what the client would have experienced had he or she been placed on probation or institutionalized.
5. Informed consent is key

   It is imperative that it is determined that the client is competent to grant consent to participate.
6. Individualized treatment and support

   Targeted case management is recommended to increase the client's ability to be self-sufficient. The need for treatment for co-occurring disorders should be assessed.
7. Maintained confidentiality

   Privacy of the client's diagnoses and treatment information should be kept completely confidential.
8. Specialized and ongoing training

   Depending on the team members, specialized training should take place to ensure all members are well versed in the treatment and support of those with serious mental illnesses.
9. Continual monitoring and support

   Status review hearings with the judge and team are necessary to track progress through the system.

(Continued)

> **BOX 6.1 SPOTLIGHT: MENTAL HEALTH COURTS—Continued**
>
> **10.** Evaluation to encourage sustainability
>
> > Monitoring fidelity to the model and evaluating the impact of the court is imperative to understanding which features work best with clients. This should be an ongoing process.
>
> ---
>
> *Source:* Thompson, M., Osher, F., & Tomasini-Joshi, D. (2007). *Improving responses to people with mental illnesses: The essential elements of a mental health court.* New York: Council of State Governments.

(James & Glaze, 2006). For example, clients who are homeless and reside in a shelter are often at risk for criminal behavior in the community that surrounds the shelter and are difficult to engage in treatment due to their chaotic living situation. Mental health may also coexist with cognitive functioning issues, as discussed in the previous section.

Mental health stabilization may become a key responsivity issue that must be addressed before a counselor can begin addressing core criminogenic needs. Ignoring mental health issues would be akin to ignoring motivation and just hoping that the client figures it out along the way. The key issue here, however, is that once the client is stabilized in the area of mental health (note that we are not using the word "cured"), the full course of services around core criminogenic needs begins.

Related is the concept of the dually diagnosed offender. Clients with a dual diagnosis in mental health and substance abuse disorders can be more challenging to treat. We know that the relationship between substance abuse and mental illness is strong. For example, a study by Ogloff et al. (2004) found that two-thirds of the mentally disordered offenders they studied also had a substance abuse problem. In addition, those with co-occurring disorders are more likely to engage in criminal behavior than those with just a mental health diagnosis (Bonta et al., 1998; Rice & Harris, 1995). We discuss this issue in greater detail in the chapter regarding substance abuse, but it is imperative to note here that the research suggests that substance abuse disorders are often not "cured" by simply attending to the mental illness. In the case of the dually diagnosed offender, program staff should proceed in similar ways as discussed previously.

Personality

As discussed at the beginning of this chapter, personality can exist as both a risk/need factor and a responsivity factor. From the risk/need perspective, studies suggest that certain personality characteristics, such as extraversion, psychoticism, neuroticism/ negative affectivity, and low constraint/self-control, are related to criminal behavior (Caspi et al., 1994; Eysenck, 1996; Listwan, Van Voorhis, & Ritchey, 2007; Pratt & Cullen, 2000). Personality traits can influence the situations people place themselves into and the relationships they have with others (Eysenck & Eysenck, 1985). For example, studies show that individuals higher in trait anxiety are consistently more prone to perceive greater danger in their relationships and respond with greater elevations of stress (Speilberger, 1985). They also tend to be distressed and have a very negative view of themselves, often worry, and tend to dwell on frustrations and disappointments. Although some individuals may experience these feelings as a state of mind during times of stress, those high in negative affectivity manifest these feelings even in the absence of stress (Watson & Clark, 1984).

From a risk/need standpoint, individuals with antisocial attitudes that are high on neuroticism need intensive treatment toward increasing their self-regulation. Cognitive and behavioral approaches may be well suited for this task. From a responsivity perspective, however, neuroticism can impede treatment in several ways. For example, individuals with this tendency toward hostility need to be paired with staff members who are willing to continually challenge their antisocial attitudes. In addition, not all neurotics are hostile and negative in an aggressive manner as described previously. Neuroticism may also manifest as general anxiety. Highly anxious clients may not perform well in certain settings (e.g., therapeutic communities) that utilize highly confrontational techniques.

Psychopathy or antisocial personality disorder is another particularly challenging personality type. Psychopaths tend to be highly manipulative yet intelligent and often exhibit callousness and little concern for others (Hare, 1999). Much like the neurotics mentioned previously, these individuals can often benefit from intensive therapy centered on increasing their self-regulation skills. However, from a responsivity standpoint, staff should be cautious when placing psychopaths in therapeutic groups. A study by Seto and Barbaree (1999) found that subjects characterized as psychopaths did well in treatment but were more likely to reoffend than non-psychopaths. This paradox has been discussed extensively by Robert Hare (1999), the developer of the Psychopathy Checklist Revised, a well-known assessment tool used to diagnose psychopathy. The typical features of a psychopath are listed in Figure 6.2. He writes that aggressive psychopaths tend to seek out treatment primarily when it will benefit them, such as when attempting to obtain release or privileges. He and others surmise that group therapy may provide these clients with insight into others' thinking that they may use to manipulate others. These offenders can co-opt groups by manipulating others, creating infighting, or simply parroting what the counselor wants to hear. This may imply that certain psychopaths are

- Superficial
- Grandiose
- Deceitful
- Lacks remorse
- Lacks empathy
- Does not accept responsibility

- Impulsive
- Poor behavioral controls
- Lacks goals
- Irresponsible
- Antisocial behavior

FIGURE 6.2 Psychopathic traits: Psychopathy Checklist Revised.

more likely to appear to make progress in treatment but in reality do not internalize the appropriate skills.

However, as we have indicated with other types of offenders, it is not to suggest that treatment strategies cannot work with psychopaths. In fact, Robert Hare and colleagues have developed a handbook referred to as *Guidelines for a Psychopathy Treatment Program* that outlines the importance of skill-building and relapse prevention strategies with these types of offenders (Wong & Hare, 2005). In addition, studies have found that behavioral therapy (i.e., contingency management) is an effective approach with clients exhibiting antisocial personality disorder (Messina, Farabee, & Rawson, 2003).

Trauma

An area that has received much attention lately is the role of trauma in predicting criminal behavior. Trauma can be defined as an event or multiple events that are emotionally disturbing. The impact and types of traumatic events are widely discussed in the psychological literature. Unfortunately, the focus around trauma is often limited to women. Although it may be true that women are at greater risk for certain types of abuses, research suggests that the vast majority of individuals (60% of men and 40% of women) have experienced a traumatic event in their lifetime (*Harvard Mental Health Letter*, 2007).

The debate surrounding trauma is similar to that of mental illness. Although we know that many people experience trauma during their lifetime, its role in predicting criminal behavior is less clear. The majority of the literature regarding the impact of trauma focuses on the psychological implications. For example, there is a clear relationship between trauma exposure and the occurrence of post-traumatic stress syndrome (PTSD). However, exposure to trauma does not create PTSD symptoms in all people (Benotsch et al., 2000). As we would expect, the differences in vulnerability or susceptibility and trauma vary quite a bit based on both individual and situational circumstances. For example, Steve Hobfoll and colleagues (1991) found that intensity is important in that stressful situations that are high in magnitude and frequency will have a greater impact on psychological health. Also, we see that brief traumas may have only limited effects on the individual, whereas repeated trauma may lead to significant mental health and behavior problems (Davies & Flannery, 1998; Terr, 1991). One such tool to measure trauma is the Trauma Symptom Checklist. Noted in Table 6.2, the checklist asks clients to report symptoms they may be experiencing in a variety of domains. The scoring allows the staff member to obtain an overall score for the client (1–40) as well as subdomain scores in the areas of anxiety, dissociation, anxiety, depression, sexual problems, and sleep disturbances (Briere & Runtz, 1989).

One particular type of traumatic event that may be more likely among offenders is exposure to violence. Exposure to violence can occur in many forms. For example, individuals may be exposed to violence in their communities, in prison, or within intimate relationships. Women are more likely to experience domestic violence and sexual abuse in their lifetimes. Similar to the previous discussion, victimization research indicates that

Table 6.2   Trauma Symptom Checklist Items

TSC-40

How often have you experienced each of the following in the last two months?

0 = Never to 3 = Often

1. Headaches	0 1 2 3
2. Insomnia (trouble getting to sleep)	0 1 2 3
3. Weight loss (without dieting)	0 1 2 3
4. Stomach problems	0 1 2 3
5. Sexual problems	0 1 2 3
6. Feeling isolated from others	0 1 2 3
7. "Flashbacks" (sudden, vivid, distracting memories)	0 1 2 3
8. Restless sleep	0 1 2 3
9. Low sex drive	0 1 2 3
10. Anxiety attacks	0 1 2 3
11. Sexual overactivity	0 1 2 3
12. Loneliness	0 1 2 3
13. Nightmares	0 1 2 3
14. "Spacing out" (going away in your mind)	0 1 2 3
15. Sadness	0 1 2 3
16. Dizziness	0 1 2 3
17. Not feeling satisfied with your sex life	0 1 2 3
18. Trouble controlling your temper	0 1 2 3
19. Waking up early in the morning and can't get back to sleep	0 1 2 3
20. Uncontrollable crying	0 1 2 3
21. Fear of men	0 1 2 3
22. Not feeling rested in the morning	0 1 2 3
23. Having sex that you didn't enjoy	0 1 2 3
24. Trouble getting along with others	0 1 2 3
25. Memory problems	0 1 2 3
26. Desire to physically hurt yourself	0 1 2 3
27. Fear of women	0 1 2 3
28. Waking up in the middle of the night	0 1 2 3
29. Bad thoughts or feelings during sex	0 1 2 3
30. Passing out	0 1 2 3
31. Feeling that things are "unreal"	0 1 2 3
32. Unnecessary or overfrequent washing	0 1 2 3
33. Feelings of inferiority	0 1 2 3
34. Feeling tense all the time	0 1 2 3
35. Being confused about your sexual feelings	0 1 2 3
36. Desire to physically hurt others	0 1 2 3
37. Feelings of guilt	0 1 2 3
38. Feelings that you are not always in your body	0 1 2 3
39. Having trouble breathing	0 1 2 3
40. Sexual feelings when you shouldn't have them	0 1 2 3

Source: Briere, J., & Runtz, M. (1989). The Trauma Symptom Checklist (TSC-33): Early data on a new scale. *Journal of Interpersonal Violence, 4,* 151–163.

victims of violence often suffer from increased levels of stress, anxiety, emotional discomfort, and a variety of health-related concerns (Briere & Jordan, 2004; Nicolaidis, Curry, McFarland, & Gerrity, 2004; Sommers & Buschur, 2004). However, as discussed in the previous section, mental health is not a strong predictor of criminal behavior. If recent trauma is currently impacting mental health, then logically staff should attend to that issue as a responsivity consideration. Or it may be that some who have experienced domestic abuse may not do as well with male staff members who are highly confrontational in their approach or male-led groups that are highly confrontational in nature (e.g., some techniques commonly used in therapeutic communities).

It is worth noting that the Substance Abuse Mental Health Administration (SAMSHA) has emphasized the importance of taking trauma into consideration when designing treatment strategies. This is often referred to as trauma-informed care. The agency argues that a "definition of **trauma-informed approach** incorporates three key elements: (1) *realizing* the prevalence of trauma; (2) *recognizing* how trauma affects all individuals involved with the program, organization, or system, including its own workforce; and (3) *responding* by putting this knowledge into practice" (SAMSHA, 2013). Strategies noted by SAMHSA include building trusting relationships and creating mutual respect between staff and clients. It is important to note, however, that that trauma-informed care should not be misconstrued as a treatment modality (e.g., cognitive, behavioral). Rather, the perspective is most congruent with the argument that trauma should be taken into consideration as a responsivity factor. This makes sense if we can consider that trauma and mental health (depression and anxiety) can influence core criminogenic needs such as relationships with families, performance at work, or addiction to alcohol or other drugs.

Demographic and Cultural Characteristics

A number of other individual-level factors should be taken into consideration when designing treatment programs. For example, demographic characteristics such as age, gender, race, and ethnicity can play a role in how people respond to treatment or to staff.

With regard to age, it is well-known that young people tend to fail at higher rates in treatment programs (Olver et al., 2011). The staff must be very mindful of being responsive to this age group. For example, younger clients tend to be more impulsive and may be resistant to change. Younger clients may be less eager to change their behavior and feel more inclined to drop out of programs, particularly ones that are encouraging them to change their peer networks and abstain from alcohol use. Motivational interviewing strategies have been found to be particularly useful in changing the client's perspective about his or her life circumstance(s) and can help younger offenders as well.

With regard to gender, the idea of gender-responsive treatment has been the source of considerable debate in the field of corrections. Chapter 9 covers this issue in more detail; however, there are some issues that are important responsivity considerations for some women. For example, Holtfreter and Morash (2003) found that women with the highest risk of recidivism tended to be drug-addicted and were more likely to have mental health issues, employment difficulties, and educational deficits. Consistent with these findings, others have found that women are also more likely to be primary caretakers of dependent children (Gregoire & Snively, 2001; Grella & Greenwell, 2006). Program staff would need to attend to mental health issues in the ways discussed in the previous section and consider child care options for those who exhibit a need in this area.

Finally, with regard to race and ethnicity, one important issue confronting treatment agencies is maintaining **multicultural sensitivity**. Multicultural sensitivity is an awareness and action that embraces diversity (Wing Sue & Sue, 2012). It actually fits well with the core logic of considering responsivity conditions in treatment. To be culturally competent is to understand that different people respond differently to treatment based on a myriad of factors. To respect diversity, however, does not suggest that we should stereotype clients based on their race, culture, or ethnicity. For example, to suggest that certain cultures need different treatment modalities would be incorrect. Rather, it is more appropriate to respect that people differ based on their individual characteristics and design their treatment plans accordingly.

Although the word "diversity" has varied meanings, the notion that someone's background or cultural experiences can impact or impede the treatment process is understandable. Again, this is not to suggest that treatment modality should be tailored to individuals of different backgrounds but, rather, that the counselors should be aware of any barriers that might exist with clients. One obvious barrier would be language difficulties. Staff members need to plan for how to conduct groups with non-English-speaking clients or how they will complete materials that are written in English.

Also in the area of multicultural communication, this can mean needing to talk audibly, distinctly, limit slag or jargon, and take extra time for those struggling to understand the context of certain assignments. Counselors should also be aware of their potential tendency to judge people with certain accents or language fluency or whether they become frustrated when trying to communicate with those who do not speak English.

Agencies should be mindful of whether these factors (race, ethnicity, and cultural background) may be impacting outcomes. For example, studies find that African-American and Hispanic clients are less likely to complete treatment compared to Caucasian clients (Saloner & LeCook, 2013). Some studies suggest, for example, that African-American clients are more weary and distrustful of counseling services than are Caucasian clients and believe that the system is biased against minority group members (Sussman, Robins, & Earls, 2007; Senturia, Sullivan, Cixke, & Shiu-Thorton, 2000). In this example, it is important to consider two issues. First, depending on the client's level of motivation and mistrust of the system, the staff members must work to reduce the resistance and build trust with the client. Reducing resistance could occur via motivational interviewing strategies discussed previously in this chapter. Second, it should also be a consideration when matching clients to treatment staff. For example, agencies should seek out a diverse workforce when hiring qualified staff to work in the program. Although it should not be assumed that clients can only benefit from counselors who are from their own race or heritage, matching along demographic lines may be beneficial for some clients. The same logic should be used when matching staff to clients on the basis of gender and age.

As discussed throughout this chapter, there are a variety of internal responsivity characteristics that can have an impact on treatment effectiveness. Similarly, there are remaining barriers or factors that may exist in a client's life that can have an impact.

Other Barriers

In this section, we outline several other factors that may impede the process, including homelessness, lack of transportation, and general instability among certain offenders.

Housing is another example of an issue that can be both a risk/need factor and a responsivity factor. Studies show that at any given time, between 20 and 50% of parolees are homeless (Rodriquez & Brown, 2005). Inadequate housing and program attrition are highly correlated. Clients who are homeless have more difficulty securing employment, maintaining conditions of parole, and are at greater risk of arrest and reincarceration (Metraux & Culhane, 2004; Roman & Travis, 2004).

From a responsivity standpoint, housing is important as well. Individuals who live in shelters or in unstable living conditions (e.g., living in transitional housing) are faced with constant uncertainty and disruption. For example, lack of housing makes it more difficult for the client to attend treatment, complete homework assignments, and attend to parole or probation requirements (e.g., drug testing and paying court fees). In addition, studies find that women in shelters are at increased risk of violence and assault (Bassuk et al., 1996).

Jewell and Wormith (2010) refer to this constellation of factors as an issue of lifestyle instability among offenders. They note that staff should attend to these lifestyle issues in treatment. In particular, agencies should make treatment services flexible for those at greater risk of dropping out of the program. They also note the importance of providing ancillary services around these issues and making efforts to contact participants who fail to attend treatment to encourage them to stick with the program.

In conclusion, the responsivity principle outlines the importance of providing the most appropriate type and level of treatment matched to the characteristic of the client. We began this chapter by noting that the responsivity is often referred to as the neglected principle in the RNR model. Many agencies may find that they devote considerable resources and time attending to risk and need without giving full consideration to these "other" issues. The importance of attending to these issues, however, cannot be understated. As programs develop risk and need assessment tools to guide placement and dosage levels for treatment, they should also assess clients for other issues that can impede the process.

Summary

- Treatment effectiveness can be enhanced if the program staff take into consideration the characteristics of the clients.

- The general responsivity principle suggests that cognitive behavioral approaches are the most effective way to teach people new behaviors.
- The specific responsivity principle suggests that treatment should be tailored to individual characteristics that may impact its success.
- Staff characteristics and therapeutic skills should be taken into consideration when matching to groups and clients.
- Individual responsivity factors include motivation, cognitive functioning, mental illness, and demographic characteristics.
- External responsivity factors include transportation, child care, and homelessness.
- The assessment process should include an assessment of these domains to plan for how these barriers will be alleviated during the treatment process.

References

American Psychiatric Association. (2000). *Diagnostic and statistical manual of mental disorders* (4th ed., text rev.). Washington, DC: Author.

Andrews, D. A., & Bonta, J. (2010a). *The psychology of criminal conduct* (5th ed.). New Providence, NJ: LexisNexis Matthew Bender.

Andrews, D. A., & Bonta, J. (2010b). Rehabilitating criminal justice policy and practice. *Psychology, Public Policy and Law, 16,* 39–55.

Andrews, D. A., & Kiessling, J. J. (1980). Program structure and effective correctional practices: A summary of the CaVIC research. In R. R. Ross, & P. Gendreau (Eds.), *Effective correctional treatment* (pp. 441–463). Toronto: Butterworths.

Bassuk, E. L., Weinreb, L. F., Buckner, J. C., Browne, A., Salomon, A., & Bassuk, S. (1996). The characteristics and needs of sheltered homeless and low-income housed mothers. *Journal of the American Medical Association, 276,* 640–646.

Benotsch, E. G., Brailey, K., Vasterling, J. J., Uddo, M., Constans, J. I., & Sutker, P. B. (2000). War zone stress, personal and environmental resources, and PTSD symptoms in Gulf War veterans: A longitudinal perspective. *Journal of Abnormal Psychology, 109,* 205–213.

Bonta, J. (1995). The responsivity principle and offender rehabilitation. *Forum on Corrections Research, 7,* 34–37.

Bonta, J., & Andrews, D. A. (2007). *Risk–need–responsivity model for offender assessment and treatment (User Report No. 2007-06).* Ottawa, Ontario: Canada. Public Safety Canada.

Bonta, J., Law, M., & Hanson, R. K. (1998). The prediction of criminal and violent recidivism among mentally disordered offenders: A meta-analysis. *Psychological Bulletin, 123,* 123–142.

Briere, J., & Jordan, C. E. (2004). Violence against women: Outcome complexity and implications for assessment and treatment. *Journal of Interpersonal Violence, 19,* 1252–1276.

Briere, J., & Runtz, M. (1989). The Trauma Symptom Checklist (TSC-33): Early data on a new scale. *Journal of Interpersonal Violence, 4,* 151–163.

Caspi, A., Moffitt, T. E., Silva, P. A., Stouthamer-Loeber, M., Krueger, R. F., & Schmutte, P. S. (1994). Are some people crime prone? Replications of the personality–crime relationship across countries, genders, races, and methods. *Criminology, 32,* 163–195.

Cullen, F. T., Gendreau, P., Jarjoura, G. R., & Wright, J. P. (1997). Crime and the bell curve: Lessons from intelligent criminology. *Crime & Delinquency, 43,* 387–411.

Davies, H., & Flannery, D. (1998). Post-traumatic stress disorder in children and adolescents exposed to violence. *Pediatric Clinics of North America, 45*, 341–353.

Eysenck, H. J. (1996). Personality and crime: Where do we stand. *Psychology, Crime & Law, 2*, 143–152.

Eysenck, H. J., & Eysenck, M. W. (1985). *Personality and individual differences: A natural science approach.* New York: Plenum.

Gregoire, T., & Snively, C. (2001). The relationship of social support and economic self-sufficiency to substance abuse outcomes in a long-term recovery program for women. *Journal of Drug Education, 31*, 221–237.

Grella, C. E., & Greenwell, L. (2006). Parental status and attitudes toward parenting among substance-abusing female offenders. *Prison Journal, 86*, 89–113.

Hare, R. D. (1999). Psychopathy as a risk factor for violence. *Psychiatric Quarterly, 70*, 181–197.

Harvard Mental Health Letter. (2007, February). *The risk for PTSD: New findings.* Retrieved July 2009 from https://www.health.harvard.edu/newsletters/Harvard_Mental_Health_Letter/2007/February.

Herrnstein, R. J., & Murray, C. (1996). *Bell curve: Intelligence and class structure in American life.* New York: Free Press.

Hobfoll, S. E., Spielberger, C. D., Breznitz, S., Figley, C., Folkman, S., Lepper-Green, B., & van der Kolk, B. (1991). War-related stress. *American Psychologist, 46*, 848–855.

Holtfreter, K., & Morash, M. (2003). The needs of women offenders: Implications for correctional programming. *Women & Criminal Justice, 14*, 137–160.

James, D. J., & Glaze, L. E. (2006). *Mental health problems of prison and jail inmates.* Washington, DC: U.S. Department of Justice, Office of Justice Programs.

Jewell, L. M., & Wormith, J. S. (2010). Variables associated with attrition from domestic violence treatment programs targeting male batterers: A meta-analysis. *Criminal Justice and Behavior, 37*, 1086–1113.

Joe, G. W., Simpson, D. D., Dansereau, D. F., & Rowan-Szal, G. A. (2001). Relationships between counseling rapport and drug abuse treatment outcomes. *Psychiatric Services, 52*, 1223–1229.

Listwan, S. J., Van Voorhis, P., & Ritchey, N. P. (2007). Personality, criminal behavior, and risk assessment: Implications for theory and practice. *Criminal Justice and Behavior, 34*, 37–59.

Marshall, W. L. (2005). Therapist style in sexual offender treatment: Influences on indices of change. *Sexual Abuse: A Journal of Research and Treatment, 17*, 109–116.

McConnaughy, E. N., Prochaska, J. O., & Velicer, W. F. (1983). Stages of change in psychotherapy: Measurement and sample profiles. *Psychotherapy: Theory, Research and Practice, 20*, 368–375.

Messina, N., Farabee, D., & Rawson, R. (2003). Treatment responsivity of cocaine-dependent patients with antisocial personality disorder in cognitive behavioral and contingency management interventions. *Journal of Consulting and Clinical Psychology, 71*, 320–329.

Metraux, S., & Culhane, D. P. (2004). Recent incarceration history among a sheltered homeless population. *Crime and Delinquency, 52*, 504–517.

Miller, W. R., & Rollnick, S. (2012). *Motivational interviewing* (3rd ed.). New York: Guilford.

Morgan, R. D., Fisher, W. H., Duan, N., Mandracchia, J. T., & Murray, D. (2010). Prevalence of criminal thinking among state prison inmates with serious mental illness. *Law & Human Behavior, 34*, 324–336.

Nicolaidis, C., Curry, M., McFarland, B., & Gerrity, M. (2004). Violence, mental health, and physical symptoms in an academic internal medicine practice. *Journal of General Internal Medicine, 19*, 819–827.

Ogloff, J. R., Lemphers, A., & Dwyer, C. (2004). Dual diagnosis in an Australian forensic psychiatric hospital: Prevalence and implications for services. *Behavioral Sciences and the Law, 22,* 543–562.

Olver, M. E., Stockdale, K. C., & Wormith, S. J. (2011). A meta-analysis of predictors of offender treatment attrition and its relationship to recidivism. *Journal of Consulting and Clinical Psychology, 79,* 6–21.

Patterson, G. R., & Yoerger, K. (1993). Developmental models for delinquent behavior. In S. Hodgins (Ed.), *Mental disorder and crime.* Newbury Park, CA: Sage.

Pratt, T. C., & Cullen, F. T. (2000). The empirical status of Gottfredson and Hirschi's general theory of crime: A meta-analysis. *Criminology, 38,* 931–964.

Prochaska, J. O., & DiClemente, C. C. (1983). Stages and processes of self-change of smoking: Toward an integrative model of change. *Journal of Consulting and Clinical Psychology, 51,* 390–395.

Rice, M. E., & Harris, G. T. (1995). Psychopathy, schizophrenia, alcohol abuse, and violent recidivism. *International Journal of Law and Psychiatry, 18,* 333–342.

Rodriguez, N., & Brown, B. (2003). *Preventing homelessness among people leaving prison.* New York: Vera Institute of Justice.

Roman, C. G., & Travis, J. (2004). *Taking stock: Housing, homelessness, and prisoner reentry.* Washington, DC: Urban Institute Justice Policy Center.

Saloner, B., & LeCook, B. (2013). Black and Hispanics are less likely than whites to complete addiction treatment, largely due to socioeconomic factors. *Health Affairs, 32,* 135–145.

Senturia, K., Sullivan, M., Cixke, S., & Shiu-Thorton, S. (2000). *Cultural issues affecting domestic violence service utilization in ethnic and hard to reach populations.* Rockville, MD: National Criminal Justice Reference Service.

Seto, M. C., & Barbaree, H. E. (1999). Psychopathy, treatment behavior, and sex offender recidivism. *Journal of Interpersonal Violence, 14,* 1235–1248.

Simpson, D. D., Joe, G. W., Greener, J. M., & Rowan-Szal, G. A. (2000). Modeling year 1 outcomes with treatment process and post-treatment social influences. *Substance Use & Misuse, 35,* 1911–1930.

Skeem, J., Manchak, S., & Peterson, J. (2011). Correctional policy for offenders with mental illness: Creating a new paradigm for recidivism reduction. *Law and Human Behavior, 35,* 110–126.

Sommers, M. S., & Buschur, C. (2004). Injury in women who are raped. *Dimensions of Critical Care Nursing, 23,* 62–68.

Spielberger, C. D. (1985). Anxiety, cognition, and affect: A state-trait perspective. In A. H. T. J. Maser (Ed.), *Anxiety and the anxiety disorders* (pp. 171–182). Hillsdale, NJ: Erlbaum.

Steadman, H. J., Osher, F. C., Robbins, P. C., Case, B., & Samuels, S. (2009). Prevalence of serious mental illness among jail inmates. *Psychiatric Services, 60,* 761–765.

Substance Abuse Mental Health Administration. (2013). *Trauma definition.* Available at http://www.samhsa.gov/traumajustice/traumadefinition/approach.aspx.

Sussman, L. K., Robins, L. N., & Earls, F. (2007). Treatment seeking for depression by African American and white Americans. *Social Science and Medicine, 24,* 187–196.

Taylor, J., Lindsay, W., & Willner, P. (2008). CBT for people with intellectual disabilities: Emerging evidence, cognitive ability and IQ effects. *Behavioural and Cognitive Psychotherapy, 36,* 723–733.

Terr, L. C. (1991). Childhood traumas: An outline and overview. *American Journal of Psychiatry, 48,* 10–20.

Ward, D. A., & Tittle, C. R. (1994). IQ and delinquency: A test of two competing explanations. *Journal of Quantitative Criminology, 10,* 189–212.

Watson, D., & Clark, L. (1984). Negative affectivity: The disposition to experience aversive emotional states. *Psychological Bulletin, 96*, 465–490.

Wing Sue, D., & Sue, D. (2012). *Counseling the culturally diverse: Theory and practice*. Indianapolis, IN: Wiley.

Wolf, N., Frueh, B. C., Shi, J., & Schumann, B. E. (2012). Effectiveness of cognitive behavioral trauma treatment for incarcerated women with mental illnesses and substance abuse disorders. *Journal of Anxiety Disorders, 26*, 703–710.

Wong, S., & Hare, R. (2005). *Guidelines for a psychopathy treatment program*. Toronto: Multihealth Systems.

7

What Works with Drug Courts

Introduction

As discussed in previous chapters, substance abuse is considered a dynamic risk factor for recidivism. This is not surprising when we consider the relationship between substance abuse and crime. Although the number of drug offenders sent to prison is decreasing, they still account for 17% of all state prisoners and almost half of federal inmates (Carson & Sabol, 2012). Among those on probation in 2011, 25% had a drug offense as their most serious charge, and nearly one-third of parolees had a drug offense as their most serious charge (Maruschak & Parks, 2012). Beyond those sentenced for drug offenses, it is important to recognize that many more may have been under the influence of alcohol or other drugs at the time of their arrest, and others engaged in crime in an effort to fund their illegal drug habit. A study conducted by the researchers at the Bureau of Justice Statistics revealed that more than one-half of state inmates and 45% of federal inmates met the criteria for drug dependence or abuse. However, less than half of those in need of treatment received it (Mumola & Karberg, 2006). Although statistics regarding probationers are slightly more promising, it appears that more opportunities for treatment are still needed (Mumola, 1998).

Drug courts have emerged as one method for providing community-based treatment and supervision to drug offenders. With the goal of reducing substance abuse and subsequent crime, drug courts have proven to be widely popular. The federal government regularly funds the implementation and expansion of drug courts. Between 1995 and 2008, Congress authorized more than $500 million to fund drug courts (Franco, 2010), and it is estimated that another $52 million will be appropriated in fiscal year 2013 to support problem-solving courts (Office of National Drug Control Policy, 2012). The success and support of drug courts have led to the development of a number of other "problem-solving courts," including juvenile drug courts, family courts, mental health courts, reentry courts, and veterans' courts. Whereas relatively little is known about the effectiveness of the variety of problem-solving courts, a great deal of research has been conducted on adult drug courts. Using this as our basis, this chapter explores the development of the drug court model, its effectiveness, and the characteristics associated with the most effective drug courts.

What Is a Drug Court?

Judge Herbert Klein presided over the first drug court in Miami in 1989. Miami was hit particularly hard by the war on drugs. As the war on drugs escalated, the system became clogged with drug-abusing offenders. They were often sent to prison for short periods of time, where they did not receive treatment, and they often reoffended upon release. Judge Klein grew tired of this revolving door of offenders and, in collaboration with other stakeholders including then-State Attorney Janet Reno, proposed a new approach for managing drug offenders. Rather than simply locking them up, they suggested that drug offenders be allowed to stay in the community as long as they were subjected to supervision and participated in treatment. In contrast to traditional probation, they also proposed that offenders remain under the supervision of the court through regular status hearings. It was believed that by merging treatment with close judicial supervision, drug courts would alleviate court dockets while reducing substance use and criminal activity.

The first drug court was deemed a great success, and other jurisdictions soon began to replicate the model. Anecdotal success, along with preliminary empirical support, led to a rapid growth in drug courts. Within the first 10 years of their existence, there were nearly 500 drug courts in place or in the process of being implemented, and it was estimated that more than 100,000 offenders had been served (Drug Courts Program Office, 1998). This growth has continued. Drug courts exist in every state, with more than 2600 in operation in the United States (Figure 7.1; National Drug Court Institute, 2012). Beyond the United States, drug courts now exist in a number of other countries, including Australia, New Zealand, Norway, and Jamaica.

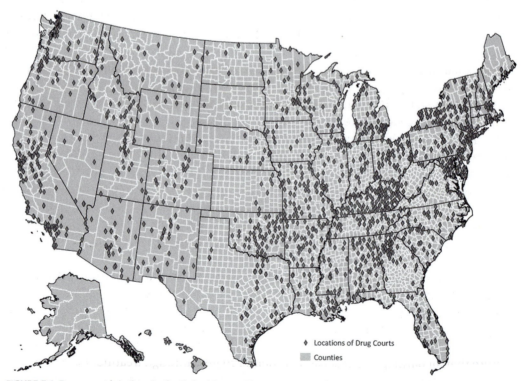

FIGURE 7.1 **Drug court locations in the United States.** There were 2644 drug courts as of December 31, 2011. *Source: National Drug Court Institute (2012). Drug court locations in the United States, 2011. Washington, DC: Author.*

Table 7.1   Comparing the Drug Court Model to Traditional Court

	Traditional court	Drug court
Work group	Judge, prosecutor, defense	Judge, prosecutor, defense, probation, treatment
Relationship	Adversarial	Nonadversarial
Goal	Process case, apply law	Restore offender as productive member of society
Judicial supervision	Limited	Central
Treatment requirements	Discretion of judge at sentencing	Formalized, structured activities; ongoing
Relapse	Jail	Graduated sanctions

As seen in Table 7.1, the drug court model is very different from the traditional court setting. In a traditional criminal court setting, the goal is simply to process cases and apply the law judiciously. However, drug courts are designed with the specific goal of restoring the offender as a productive member of society. The difference in this overarching goal is evident when we compare a typical court to a drug court. One main difference relates to the courtroom work group. In a traditional criminal court, the work group largely consists of the judge, prosecutor, and defense. Each player has a clearly defined role and rarely deviates from it. Given the competing goals of the attorneys, the relationship is often characterized as adversarial, with prosecutors advocating on behalf of the state and defense attorneys seeking to protect the rights of their clients. In contrast, the work group under the drug court model is expanded to include the probation department, treatment provider, and, often, a member of law enforcement. The team works collaboratively with the unified goals of effectively supervising and treating participants while keeping the community safe.

Perhaps the major difference between a traditional court setting and a drug court is the involvement of the judge. In our typical system, the judge provides a sentence, which may or may not include treatment recommendations, and has rather limited contact with an offender. Rarely does the offender return to court, other than for new cases or as the result of technical violations. In contrast, the judge plays a critical role in the drug court setting. The role of the judge is central to all proceedings, and the drug court judge is actively involved in making decisions regarding treatment and monitoring move through the program. Monitoring often occurs through status review hearings, which often occur on a weekly or biweekly basis. In this way, drug court participants interact with the judge regularly, not just upon getting into trouble again.

Because the goal of the drug court is to rehabilitate participants, treatment is a formalized part of the drug court program. Again, this is in contrast to a typical court case. Depending on the jurisdiction, treatment may or may not be required of offenders who struggle with addiction or dependence. In some states, this decision rests with the judge, whereas it rests with the supervising agency in other jurisdictions. Drug courts, however, require that all participants receive treatment. Progress through treatment is discussed at regular team meetings, and participants are provided feedback on their progress during their status hearings with the judge. Given the relatively small percentage of offenders who receive treatment services in a traditional setting, this focus on treatment is an important element of the drug court program.

A final difference between the traditional court setting and the drug court model involves the response to relapse. In a traditional court setting, relapse is likely to be responded to punitively and may result in jail time or even a probation revocation. Although this can also happen in a drug court, the perception of relapse often differs. Rather than viewed as an indication of noncompliance, relapse is often viewed as part of the recovery process and as an indication that the level of care may need to be adjusted. Graduated sanctions are often used in response to relapse, and any jail time is generally brief; sometimes as little as a few hours. Collectively, these differences result in a unique approach to the treatment of substance abusing offenders.

You may be wondering what a drug court looks like in practice. In a typical drug court, an offender is screened for admission into the program by a drug court coordinator. This is often done before a conviction is entered so that the case is transferred to the drug court docket. Once admitted into the drug court, participants move through a phase system and are subjected to a number of requirements. During the first phase of the program, the participant usually appears before the judge at least once every other week. During these status review hearings, the judge inquires about progress in treatment and any challenges the participant may be facing. The judge often praises participants who are doing well, but he or she may also use this time to admonish a participant or provide a sanction. In addition to status review hearings, participants often submit to regular drug testing, meet with their probation officer regularly, and attend substance abuse treatment.

This same process is continued through subsequent phases of the program. However, the intensity of the status review hearings, drug testing, and probation visits often decreases over time. As those requirements decrease, many drug courts increase requirements relating to work or school and often require participation in peer support groups such as Alcoholics Anonymous (AA) or Narcotics Anonymous (NA). Movement through the phases is often marked with some type of acknowledgment of progress, and completion of the program is often celebrated with a graduation ceremony. Although drug court participants are quite active in programming, the drug court team is also very involved. Team members often attend meetings prior to status review hearings where they discuss new intakes, review progress, identify violators, and discuss phase movement and graduation.

Although drug courts tend to follow the model as described, there is much inconsistency across the programs. In part, this is probably because the early drug courts developed quickly and with only limited guidance. Several years after Judge Klein held the first drug court hearing, a group of practitioners, researchers, and stakeholders met in Washington, DC, to identify the key components of a drug court. These are listed in Table 7.2. As you can see, the 10 key components provide an overview of the *elements* associated with drug courts but fail to provide much detail in terms of *how* a drug court should operate. The National Association of Drug Court Professionals (NADCP) convened

Table 7.2   Ten Key Components of Drug Courts

1. Integrate alcohol and other drug treatment with justice system case process.
2. Using a nonadversarial approach, prosecution and defense counsel promote public safety while protecting participants' due process rights.
3. Eligible participants are identified clearly and promptly placed in the drug court program.
4. Drug courts provide access to a continuum of alcohol, drug, and other related treatment and rehabilitation services.
5. Abstinence is monitored by frequent alcohol and other drug testing.
6. A coordinated strategy governs drug court response to participants' compliance.
7. Ongoing judicial interaction with each drug court participant is essential.
8. Monitoring and evaluation measure the achievement of program goals and gauge effectiveness.
9. Continuing interdisciplinary education promotes effective drug court planning, implementation, and operations.
10. Forging partnerships among drug courts, public agencies, and community-based organizations generates local support and enhances drug court program effectiveness.

Source: National Association of Drug Court Professionals. (1997). *Defining drug courts: The key components.* Washington, DC: U.S. Department of Justice.

a work group in 2011 to develop a revised set of standards. The standards will be based on the results of various research studies, including both meta-analyses and multisite studies, and are expected to be released in 2013 and 2014.

Do Drug Courts Work?

Although early outcome studies on drug courts were somewhat mixed, the research has consistently found that drug courts can reduce recidivism. A number of meta-analyses have been conducted examining their effectiveness, and they generally conclude that drug courts can reduce recidivism between 8 and 13%. The most recent meta-analysis was completed O. J. Mitchell and colleagues (2012). This study updated an earlier meta-analysis by the same group of researchers (Wilson, Mitchell, & MacKenzie, 2006) and included evaluations of 92 adult drug courts. Among these, nearly all (88%) had been found to be effective, and the meta-analysis found that the drug courts reduced recidivism in general along with drug offenses and drug use. Figure 7.2 illustrates the impact on recidivism. Assuming members of the comparison group recidivated at a 50% rate, Mitchell et al.'s findings suggest drug court participants recidivate at a 38% rate.

In addition to meta-analyses, a number of multisite evaluations have taken place, including one conducted by researchers at the Urban Institute, RTI International, and the Center for Court Innovation. The Multi-Site Adult Drug Court Evaluation (MADCE) is the largest study of its kind and included 23 drug courts across eight states (Rossman et al., 2011). The researchers compared the experiences of 1,157 drug court participants to 627 comparison group members, most of whom were on probation. Offenders were interviewed when the study began, 6 months later, and again 18 months after the initial interview. During the interviews, participants were asked about both their drug use and their criminal behavior in the preceding 6 months. In addition to interviews, arrest records were collected 24 months after the initial interview.

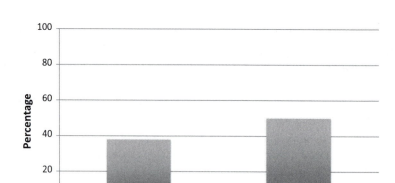

FIGURE 7.2 Recidivism rates of drug court participants and comparison group members. *Source: Wilson, D. B., Mitchell, O., & MacKenzie, D. L. (2006). A systematic review of drug court effects on recidivism.* Journal of Experimental Criminology, 2, *459–487.*

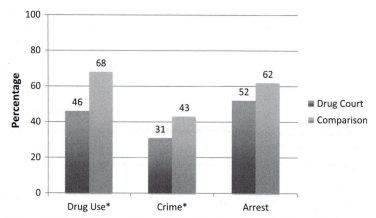

FIGURE 7.3 Results from the Multi-Site Adult Drug Court Evaluation. *p < .05. Source: Rossman, S. B., Rempel, M., Roman, J. K., Zweig, J. M., Lindquist, C. H., Green, M., & Farole D. J., Jr. (2011).* The Multi-Site Adult Drug Court Evaluation: The impact of drug courts *(Vol. 4). Washington, DC: National Institute of Justice.*

As indicated in Figure 7.3, the self-report data suggest the drug courts had an impact. Drug court participants reported significantly less drug use and criminal behavior 18 months after entering the program. However, whereas participation had an impact on self-reported behaviors, it did not have a significant impact on arrest. After 24 months, 52% of the drug court participants had been arrested compared to 62% of the comparison group. This difference was not statistically significant.

How do we reconcile the findings between the meta-analyses, which indicated drug courts reduce recidivism, and the MADCE study? First, it is important to remember that this is one study. The research has consistently found that most, but not all, drug courts work to reduce recidivism. Quite simply, some are better than others. Differences across the drug courts in the MADCE study can help to explain the findings. Related to this point, it is important to remember that drug courts, on average, reduce recidivism only approximately 10%. Although significant, it also suggests that a number of drug courts have relatively weak effects. Remember, as noted in Chapter 2, programs that adhere to the principles of risk, need, and responsivity can reduce recidivism up to 30% (Andrews et al., 1990; Dowden & Andrews, 1999, 2000, 2004). It seems that drug courts should be able to do much better.

In recent years, a number of researchers have begun to explore what works with drug courts. Although it can be assumed that the general literature of effective interventions applies to drug courts, the reality is that the model is much broader than just treatment. In other words, we need to consider not only risk, need, and responsivity but also the structure of the drug court itself. One of the challenges in determining "what works" with drug courts is the need for a large sample of drug courts and having details about who they serve, what they do, and how they do it.

There have been several efforts to explore what works with drug courts, including a 2011 meta-analysis (Shaffer, 2011). By interviewing drug court coordinators about their processes (e.g., assessment, treatment, and intensity) and structure (e.g., target population, leverage, and staff), details about drug court activities were able to be linked to their effects on recidivism. Other efforts to explore the impact of various drug court components include the MADCE study and research efforts by Michael Finegan, Shannon Carey, and their colleagues at NPC Research in Portland, Oregon. Between 2000 and 2010, they conducted evaluations of more than 125 adult drug courts. As part of their research, they collected information about drug court practices including issues related to each of the 10 key components discussed previously. Because they used similar methodologies for several of the studies, they were able to explore the impact of these practices on both recidivism and cost-effectiveness using a sample of 69 drug courts (Carey, Mackin, & Finigan, 2012).

Given the complexity of the drug court model, it is not yet known how the various elements work together to create an effective model. However, the studies described above, along with other studies testing the impact of drug courts for different types of offenders, provide important information about drug courts. Collectively, the research studies and multisite outcome evaluations can help us identify when and how drug courts work best. It is important to note that when we talk about "what works" regarding drug courts, we are specifically talking about what works with *adult* drug courts. As previously noted, relatively little is known about the various extensions of the model, and we should be careful about assuming too much about how they work. Finally, although risk, need, and responsivity all relate to the practices of effective drug courts, consideration must also be given to the broader structure of the drug court, its processes, and those working within it.

The Drug Court Team

The drug court team and role of the judge are perhaps two of the more novel elements of the drug court model. The people working in drug courts should understand the nature of addiction, work well together, and be committed to being active participants in the drug court process.

Drug Court Judge

The role of the drug court judge is perhaps one of the most studied components of drug courts. John Goldkamp and colleagues confirmed the importance of judges' participation in drug courts through interviews with 150 participants in drug courts throughout the country, including those in New York, Las Vegas, and Philadelphia. When asked, participants consistently reported that they developed a close relationship with the judge while in the program and that this relationship was an important part of their willingness to stay in the program (Goldkamp, White, & Robinson, 1998). Although it is difficult to isolate the impact of this relationship, it seems clear that feeling supported by the judge is an important element of the model's success.

Because of the importance of the drug court judge, a number of researchers have explored the characteristics of effective drug court judges. It appears that the most effective drug courts are those that have a regular judge who has a minimum of a 2-year appointment. The research by Shannon Carey and colleagues (2012) found that a minimum of a 2-year appointment helps to ensure continuity in programming and gives the judge ample time to become a knowledgeable member of the team. Courts with more frequent turnover among the judges tend to be less effective (Carey et al., 2012).

In addition to examining length of time on the drug court bench, others have examined the nature of interactions between the judge and participants. It has been suggested that judges should spend at least 3 minutes with each participant before the bench (Figure 7.4; Carey et al., 2012). This allows time for the judge to inquire about progress, give meaningful feedback, and address any concerns that may arise. It also increases the

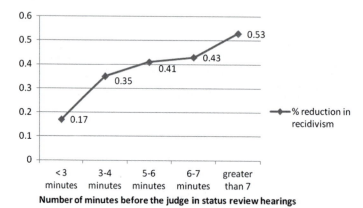

FIGURE 7.4 **Impact of judicial interaction on recidivism.** *Source: Carey, S. M., Mackin, J. R., & Finigan, M. W. (2012). What works? The ten key components of drug court: Research-based best practices. Drug Court Review, 8, 6–42.*

likelihood that judges are perceived as fair, which has been found to be related to improved outcomes (Farole & Cissner, 2007).

It is important that the new drug court judges receive training on the drug court itself, as well as substance abuse and addiction. Therapeutic jurisprudence is a legal theory that has been used to explain the success of drug courts (Hora, 2002). One of the basic tenets of the theory is that judicial interactions with clients have the ability to reinforce and shape behaviors (Wexler, 2000). Although relatively few drug court judges are identified as being primarily therapeutic in their role (Shaffer, 2011), the type of feedback provided to participants seems to matter. A study by Scott Senjo and Leslie Leip (2001) found that participants who received more positive (as opposed to negative) feedback from the judge were more likely to graduate from the program. Training can help to ensure judges are acting within a therapeutic jurisprudence approach.

Finally, training is important when we consider that the judge is generally responsible for making the final decision regarding participants, despite the collaborative nature of the team. Understanding the characteristics of effective treatment, the importance of assessment, and how to use behavioral techniques can help to make the judge even more efficient and fair when making decisions.

Drug Court Team

As previously noted, the drug court team should include the judge, drug court coordinator, prosecutor, defense attorney, treatment provider, probation officer, and a representative from law enforcement (Figure 7.5). Drug courts often face challenges with

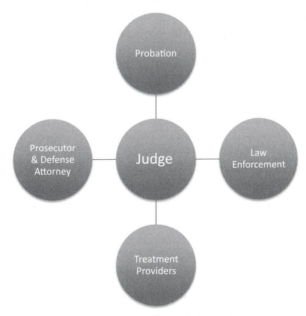

FIGURE 7.5 The drug court team.

regard to finding law enforcement representatives. However, having a member of law enforcement on the team is important because they often have a better sense of what is happening in the communities in which participants reside. In this way, law enforcement officers can provide context for understanding some of the challenges that participants face. Drug courts that enjoy this type of collaboration reduce recidivism 88% more than those that do not include law enforcement (Carey et al., 2012).

Another challenge related to the drug court team involves the role of the treatment provider. Many drug courts utilize multiple treatment providers or provide treatment within the context of the drug court itself. The meta-analyses consistently find that this approach is more effective than using a single provider (Mitchell et al., 2012; Shaffer, 2011). It is likely that the reason for this difference is related to participation on the drug court team. For example, Carey et al. (2012) found that having two providers is just as effective as having a single provider, but that the quality of participation matters. Drug courts are more effective when treatment providers attend both team meetings and status review hearings. Often, treatment providers are not represented on the team, which undermines the ability to provide input regarding the progress of participants in treatment. Drug courts should make sure that (1) providers are active members of the team and (2) when multiple providers are utilized, all providers are involved in the drug court process.

It is also important that team meetings are held regularly. Although the research on the frequency of meetings is less clear, there is some indication that weekly meetings are warranted (Shaffer, 2011). Beyond including treatment providers and law enforcement officers on the team, it is important that all members of the team are active and knowledgeable participants in the process. Unfortunately, this rarely seems to happen, with almost half of the drug courts in Shaffer's study reporting less than perfect attendance. Carey et al. (2012) found that having active participation at the team meetings was associated with better outcomes. The research is less clear on the importance of attendance at status review hearings, although the trend suggests this also likely has an impact (Carey et al., 2012).

As with the judge, it is important that all members of the drug court are trained and knowledgeable about the drug court program, the nature of addiction, and the methods for addressing it. The National Drug Court Institute provides training and technical support to drug courts throughout the country. Training is offered to jurisdictions that are in the process of designing a drug court as well as those that are already in existence. For existing drug courts, NADCP provides discipline-specific trainings aimed at enhancing the roles of each individual team member. "Older" drug courts are also eligible for advanced training, which focuses on topics such as evaluation, incentives and rewards, and improving programming.

New drug courts are generally required to participate in an initial training as part of the federal funding requirements. The goals of training were to educate new drug court team members about the drug court model and the roles of each member on the team. As with treatment programs in general, the research indicates that ongoing training is important. Training can occur in a number of ways, including attendance at NADCP's annual conference. During these conferences, team members have a chance to learn about the latest research, learn new strategies, and receive reminders about the most effective practices. Drug courts do better when their teams regularly attend these conferences (Shaffer, 2011).

How Should Drug Courts Be Structured?

The structure of drug courts is particularly important because it often provides the foundation for the entire program. Drug courts should be designed to accept offenders either before a guilty plea or before sentencing. They should be designed to last between 12 and 24 months and should cap their capacity at 125 participants. A phase system should be utilized to move participants through the program and should guide the frequency of status review hearings and drug testing. Finally, drug courts should identify completion criteria that require both stable housing and demonstrated sobriety.

Point of Entry

One of the important elements of the early drug courts was the focus on early intervention. An arrest was often perceived as a motivating event, and it was believed that offenders would be more responsive to treatment if the intervention began immediately following arrest. Because of this, many of the early drug courts were pre-plea drug courts. Participants often agreed to enter the drug court, with their charges held pending completion of the program. Upon successful completion of the court, charges were typically reduced or dismissed and participants were free from further supervision. Variations on this approach included a pre-adjudication model in which participants entered a guilty plea but their sentence was held in abeyance pending completion of the program. Over time, the model has largely shifted to a post-adjudication model. As with a post-plea model, participants plead guilty. However, they are then sentenced to drug court. The motivation for pleading guilty is often reduced charges (e.g., felony to misdemeanor) or the promise of staying in the community.

Over time, the differences between the two models began to be thought of as leverage (Longshore et al., 2001). That is, the amount of leverage a drug court holds over participants differs depending on the consequence of failure. With what were historically called pre-plea courts, the "stick" was being convicted of charges. In contrast, the stick associated with post-plea models is often a prison sentence. The meta-analyses on drug courts have found that both approaches are effective. That is, one is not considered to be more effective than the other. However, some drug courts combine the approaches, allowing participants to enter the drug court under a number of legal statuses. Whereas the earlier meta-analyses found a mixed model to be less effective (Lowenkamp, Holsinger, & Latessa, 2005; Shaffer, 2011; Wilson et al., 2006), a recent meta-analysis found a mixed model to be equally effective at reducing recidivism (Mitchell et al., 2012).

It is not entirely clear why the mixed model sometimes fails, but it is likely that the failure is more a function of mixing offenders rather than differences in legal statuses alone. That is, it may be that the drug court receives lower-risk participants through one track and higher-risk participants through the other. Mixed models, for example, may include people coming in on new charges (pre-adjudication) and those coming in on technical violations (post-adjudication). In this case, there may be systematic differences between offender types dependent on their entry point into the program.

As a general rule, it is still recommended that drug courts select a "pure" rather than hybrid model. However, the reality is that many drug courts wish to serve both populations. In that case, it is important that the drug court clearly identify any systemic differences between the entry points and tailor services appropriately. In this way, the drug court may be able to serve a wider range of offenders while still maintaining program integrity.

Drug Court Phases and Length of Programming

As discussed in other chapters, the most effective treatment programs should be designed to last between 3 and 9 months (Gendreau, 1996). Given the combination of treatment and supervision, the most effective drug courts should be designed to last longer—ideally at least 12 months (Carey et al., 2012). This does not mean participants should be in primary treatment for the entire time. Rather, the last phase of the program should be viewed as a stepped-down phase with minimal supervision.

The majority of drug courts utilize a three- or four-phase system in which participants are rewarded for their progress with decreasing program requirements over time. For example, during the first phase of a drug court, participants may be required to appear before the judge weekly, submit to twice-weekly urinalysis, meet with their probation officer weekly, and be subjected to other requirements as dictated by the court. However, over time, continued compliance and the use of prosocial behaviors are rewarded with phase advancement and fewer requirements. That is, rather than weekly status review hearings, participants may be required to come in only once or twice a month. Similarly, the frequency of urinalysis and meetings with probation officers may also decrease.

There are several important considerations when developing phase requirements. First, the requirements for phase advancement must be both formalized and realistic. This allows participants to predict when advancement will occur and helps to ensure that timely progress is made. Informal guidelines may lead participants to be less compliant with the rules because they may not see a need for adherence. Moreover, unrealistic requirements may make it nearly impossible for participants to move up through the program despite making significant progress. For example, imagine that a drug court requires participants to obtain employment prior to moving out of the first phase. This may not always be realistic in times of high unemployment rates or for participants with limited job skills. As a result, participants may remain in a phase for much longer than expected because of an inability to meet unrealistic expectations. This could translate to noncompliance, and participants begin to feel hopeless about the possibility of making progress through the program.

Second, decreases in drug testing should not occur at the same time as decreases in other phase requirements. In other words, the frequency of drug testing should decrease only after participants have demonstrated continued compliance with the program following a decrease in the frequency of status review hearings and other monitoring activities. This increases the likelihood that participants will continue to be successful following their movement to a less intensive phase.

Finally, treatment phases and drug court phases should be viewed as two separate concepts. Treatment progress should not be used to impede a participant from moving through the drug court phases, nor should movement through the drug court phases dictate the level of service in treatment. Decisions regarding the level of care and intensity of services should be decided clinically and not tied to compliance with the drug court rules. For example, a drug court participant with a severe drug problem may need intensive outpatient treatment services. It may be decided to advance the participant to the next drug court phase as a result of progress in the program and completion of phase requirements. However, the level of care should be decided independently of this change.

Status Review Hearings

Progress through the drug court is generally monitored through status review hearings. Depending on their phase in the program, participants may appear before the judge as frequently as once a week or as little as once every month or so. Both the drug court team and program participants are in the court for status hearings. During a typical session, new participants will be welcomed, rewards will be issued for those doing well in the program, and sanctions will be meted out for those that have violated the rules of the program.

The structure of court sessions tends to vary by drug court and drug court judge. In some cases, the sessions are conducted in a very formal manner with the judge dressed in robes and sitting on the bench. In other instances, sessions are much more informal and may have all team members seated around a table. To date, there is no research to indicate which method is preferred. It is likely that the content of the session matters much more than the structure of the session.

The drug court team should meet prior to the court hearings to review cases, discuss new intakes, identify any violations that must be addressed, and recommend participants for phase advancement. The nature of these meetings should be collaborative, and disagreements between team members should be resolved prior to the status review hearings.

Graduation

As we would expect, participants who successfully graduate from drug court fare much better than those who are unsuccessfully terminated. However, drug courts should use care in determining when someone is ready to graduate. Just like other types of programs, drug courts should have clear completion criteria in place. The completion criteria should be centered on behavioral change and not just participating in the drug court for a set amount of time. One important criterion relates to abstinence. The NPC research found

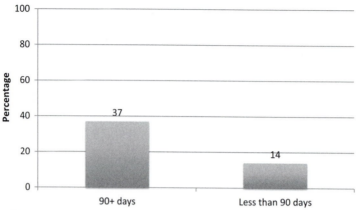

FIGURE 7.6 Effect of abstinence on recidivism. *Source: Carey, S. M., Mackin, J. R., & Finigan, M. W. (2012). What works? The ten key components of drug court: Research-based best practices.* Drug Court Review, 8, 6–42.

that drug courts that required participants to have at least 90 days abstinent were more effective (Carey et al., 2012). Figure 7.6 shows the difference in effect sizes between drug courts that require 90 days or more of negative drug tests and those that do not. Clearly, a period of demonstrated abstinence makes a difference. In addition to abstinence, it is also important that participants have stable housing and an aftercare plan in place (Carey et al., 2012).

It should not be expected that every participant successfully completes the drug court. Using objective, behaviorally based criteria should help to distinguish between those who are appropriate for graduation and those who are not. Mitchell et al.'s (2012) meta-analysis examined the impact of graduate rates on effectiveness. Drug courts that had graduation rates ranging between 51 and 75% were most effective compared to drug courts with lower graduation rates.

Capacity

Finally, when considering the structure of effective drug courts, it is important to think about capacity. By definition, drug courts are thought to be intensive programs and, as we have discussed, judicial interaction and supervision are critical components of the drug court. This begs the question of how big, or small, should a drug court be? The researchers at NPC examined this issue in their study of 69 drug courts (Carey et al., 2012). They found that the effectiveness of a drug court diminishes when it becomes larger than 125 participants (Figure 7.7). Specifically, they found that drug courts with fewer than 125 participants reduced rearrest by 40%, whereas those with more than 125 participants reduced recidivism by only 6%.

Obviously, some jurisdictions may need larger drug courts, and a number of drug courts far exceed 125 participants (Shaffer, 2011). The drug courts in New York City, for example, serve hundreds of offenders each year. Large programs can still be effective. In a study of New York's drug courts, Mike Rempel and colleagues (2003) found that the drug

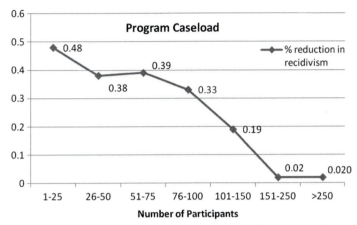

FIGURE 7.7 Relationship between program capacity and reductions in recidivism. Note that the difference is significant at *p* < .05. *Source: Carey, S. M., Mackin, J. R., & Finigan, M. W. (2012). What works? The ten key components of drug court: Research-based best practices.* Drug Court Review, 8, 6–42.

court participants in New York City had rearrest rates between 11 and 25% lower than probationers. For large drug courts to be successful, however, they must have policies and procedures in place to ensure the integrity of the model is upheld.

Who Should Be in a Drug Court?

The existing research makes it clear that drug courts can serve a wide range of offenders. Researchers have examined the impact of drug courts across gender, drug of choice, and risk level. In general, drug courts should target high-risk offenders, regardless of gender or drug of choice.

The Role of Gender

In general, the "what works" literature suggests treatment programs need to be responsive to gender differences. Men and women should not be treated in the same groups, and there is debate regarding whether different factors predict risk for men and women. It has also been found that men and women use drugs and other illicit substances for different reasons. Women are more likely to use drugs as a form of self-medication, whereas men tend to use drugs for recreational or social purposes (Newcomb, Chou, Bentler, & Huba, 1988; Novacek, Raskin, & Hogan, 1991; Toray, Coughlin, Vuchinich, & Patricelli, 1991). In addition to differences in why people use drugs, it is also important to consider the role of mental health. Gray and Saum (2005) found that female participants are more likely to report depression, present with anxiety, and use prescription medications compared to male participants. Despite these differences, the existing research suggests drug courts work equally well for both groups. Whereas some of the outcome studies find that men are more likely to be rearrested compared to women (Spohn, Pipier, Martin, & Frenzel, 2001;

Wolfe, Guydish, & Termondt, 2002), others find that women are more likely to be rearrested and specifically for drug-related offenses (Listwan, Sundt, Holsinger, & Latessa, 2003; Peters & Murrin, 2000).

The key to really understanding whether drug courts work for women is to compare female drug court participants to female probationers. In this area, the research is still mixed. Adele Harrell and colleagues (2001) were the first to examine this issue. When comparing female probationers and female drug court participants, they found both groups were rearrested at relatively equal rates. However, a recent study found the opposite to be true. Shaffer, Hartman, and Listwan (2009) found that only 25% of drug court participants had new charges filed on them compared to 63% of the comparison group. One explanation for the contradictory findings may be that the drug courts operated differently from one another. More research is needed to more fully understand the drug court processes as they relate to female offenders. However, it seems clear that drug courts can serve both men and women.

Drug of Choice

Another important consideration when discussing whom drug courts work best with is drug of choice. Despite differences in the addiction process, it is generally believed that no one should be excluded from participation simply because of their drug of choice. This does not mean all drug offenders are equally successful in drug courts. Depending on the court under study, research has found that crack/cocaine addicts are less likely to graduate from drug court (Hartley & Phillips, 2001; Miller & Shutt, 2001; Schiff & Terry, 1997), marijuana users are less likely to graduate than alcohol users (Shaffer, Hartman, Listwan, Howell, & Latessa, 2011), and heroin users are more likely to self-report rearrest than other types of drug users (Harrell et al., 2001). However, this does not mean that drug courts do not work for these folks. Instead, as with gender, it is important that drug courts are responsive to the nature of the drug addiction and needs of the participants.

Concerns regarding the treatment of methamphetamine users can help to illustrate this point (Listwan, Shaffer, & Hartman, 2009). Just as there was panic over crack use in the 1980s, methamphetamine use was viewed to be of epidemic proportions in the 2000s and though to be highly addictive and untreatable. As a result, many drug courts questioned whether they should accept methamphetamine users. Researchers found that there were differences between methamphetamine users and non-users. For example, Stoops, Tindall, Mateyoke-Scrivner, and Leukefeld (2005) found that drug participants who had tried methamphetamine generally had more severe drug use histories but less severe criminal histories. Despite these differences, Listwan et al. (2009) found that drug court participants who identified methamphetamine as their drug of choice performed just as well as those participants who identified other drugs as their primary drug of choice. Collectively, the findings appear to suggest that drug of choice likely matters less than the methods for targeting it.

Risk Level

A final characteristic to consider when identifying appropriate offenders for drug court participation is risk of recidivism. Despite the fact that drug courts are intended to divert offenders from prison, many focus on low-risk offenders instead (Lowenkamp, Latessa, & Smith, 2006; Shaffer, 2006). In part, this may be because drug courts screen for substance abuse but not risk of recidivism. It is also likely that drug courts fear accepting high-risk offenders because of the potential for higher recidivism rates. However, given the intensive nature of drug courts, they should be targeting higher-risk offenders to be more effective (Lowenkamp et al., 2006).

Doug Marlowe and colleagues at the Treatment Research Institutes conducted one of the few studies to explicitly test this issue. They received a federal grant to examine the impact of status review hearings on outcomes and were interested in knowing how risk interacted with frequency. Because they did not have a measure of risk level, they defined high-risk participants as those who met the *Diagnostic and Statistical Manual of Mental Disorders*, fourth edition (American Psychiatric Association, 1994) criteria for antisocial personality disorder or had a history of drug abuse treatment. They found that high-risk participants who had more frequent judicial status hearings were able to abstain from drugs and alcohol for longer periods of time compared to those who had fewer status hearings (Festinger et al., 2002; Marlowe, Festinger, Dugosh, Lee, & Benasutti, 2006).

In a recent study examining the importance of risk, Deborah Koetzle and her colleagues (2012) compared recidivism rates for high-risk participants to those of high-risk probationers in Ada County, Idaho. Using the Level of Service Inventory–Revised (LSI-R) as a measure of risk, they defined high-risk participants as those scoring 34 or higher on the assessment. They found that drug court participants recidivate significantly less than probationers. As illustrated in Figure 7.8, 44% of the drug court participants had

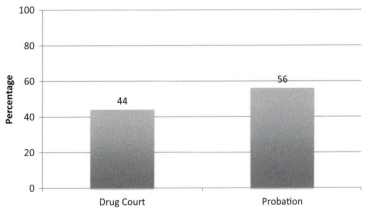

FIGURE 7.8 Recidivism levels for high-risk offenders. *Source: Koetzle, D., Listwan, S. J., Guastaferro, W. P., & Kobus, K. (2012).* Treating high risk offenders in the community: The potential of drug courts. *Manuscript submitted for publication.*

new charges filed compared to 56% of the probationers. When controlling for differences in the group, they found that probationers were almost two times more likely to be rearrested compared to drug court participants. This provides more evidence that drug courts should purposefully target high-risk offenders rather than systematically exclude them.

What Services Should Be Provided?

A meta-analysis on drug courts by Leticia Gutierre and Guy Bourgon in Canada focused on the role of risk, need, and responsivity (RNR) as they relate to effectiveness. As part of the study, they assessed whether each drug court adhered to these principles. As we would expect, they found that drug courts that adhered to a greater number of principles did better. Figure 7.9 shows the differences in effect sizes by the number of RNR principles followed. Note that none of the drug courts in their study followed all three principles. However, those that followed at least two principles reduced recidivism 31%. Obviously, this result is much better than that of those which failed to follow any of the principles and reduced recidivism only 5%. Clearly, then, drug courts should adhere to RNR when considered the types of services provided. The following section details what this looks like in a drug court setting.

Assessment

As noted in Chapter 2, assessment is a critical part of any effective program. Like other treatment programs, drug courts should assess participants for risk, need, and responsivity using standardized, actuarial assessments. Although many drug courts assess substance abuse, they often fail to assess for risk and other criminogenic needs. Moreover, like many programs, they fail to assess for responsivity as well (Shaffer, 2011).

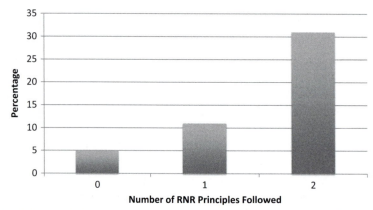

FIGURE 7.9 **RNR and drug court effectiveness.** *Source: Gutierrez, L., & Bourgon, G. (2012). Drug treatment courts: A quantitative review of study and treatment quality.* Justice Research and Policy, 14, 47–77.

However, assessment is just as important for drug courts as it is for other types of correctional treatment programs.

Although drug courts do a fairly good job of screening for substance abuse, it is not clear whether most programs assess participants for substance abuse. Many use screening tools such as the SASSI or the TCU drug screen. However, as noted by Roger Peters and Elizabeth Peyton (1998), screening tools are not the same as assessment instruments. Whereas screening can help to determine if an individual is appropriate for placement, assessment provides a clinical diagnosis and can be used for treatment planning. One example of an assessment instrument is the Addiction Severity Index (ASI), which provides an indication of the severity of substance abuse and its relationship to several life areas, including medical status, family/social status, and psychiatric status.

In addition to using tools such as the ASI, drug courts may consider using the *American Society of Addiction Medicine Patient Placement Criteria* (ASAM PPC-2R) for determining the level of care as it relates to substance abuse treatment. Drug courts should refrain from automatically placing all participants into the same level of service (e.g., intensive outpatient) and should instead use the PPC to drive such decisions. The PPC-2R has been widely adopted throughout the country and has been found to accurately predict level of care (Magura et al., 2003).

In addition to assessing for substance abuse, drug courts must also assess for risk and other criminogenic needs. As noted previously, drug courts are most effective when they treat higher-risk offenders. Using a standardized risk assessment is critical for ensuring the drug court is receiving higher-risk participants. Simply addressing substance abuse without addressing other needs is likely to undermine a drug court's effectiveness. As a refresher, other criminogenic needs include antisocial attitudes, poor problem solving, criminal friends, and poor family communication. A discussion of tools used to assess risk and need (e.g., LSI-R, Ohio Risk Assessment System, and COMPAS) can be found in Chapter 2.

Substance Abuse Treatment

One challenge in providing effective drug treatment to offenders is the "disconnect" between the substance abuse treatment literature and the criminal justice treatment literature (Gendreau, 1995). This often results in programs failing to use empirically supported principles and techniques (Maynard, 2010). Programs are often designed with a general population in mind, which can result in "correctional quackery" as discussed in Chapter 5.

Efforts by agencies such as the Substance Abuse and Mental Health Services Administration (SAMHSA), the National Institute of Corrections, and the National Institute of Drug Abuse (NIDA) are aimed at helping to bridge the gap and improve services for offenders by identifying effective programs and by publishing standards related to effective strategies. NIDA's *Principles of Drug Abuse Treatment for Criminal Justice Populations* (2012) is one such example. Developed by a panel of experts and based on empirical evidence regarding drug treatment of offenders, the principles are intended to serve as a guide for those working with drug-abusing offenders. Just as SAMHSA makes the distinction between the general population and criminal justice-involved participants, so should treatment providers working with drug courts.

Although not specific to drug courts, there is ample evidence that programs should use a cognitive behavioral approach and manualized curricula to target substance abuse. Many drug courts continue to rely on eclectic treatment models, yet this approach has been found to be less effective (Wilson, Bouffard, & Mackenzie, 2005). Using a cognitive behavioral approach can help to address thinking errors and provide participants the opportunity to practice and adopt new skills relating to problem solving, interpersonal relationships, and emotional regulation, including coping skills and tolerance for distress (McHugh, Hearon, & Otto, 2010). Examples of curricula include *Criminal Conduct and Substance Abuse Treatment: Strategies for Self-Improvement, Moral Reconation Therapy, New Directions,* and *Cognitive Behavioral Interventions for Substance Abuse Treatment.*

Beyond more traditional cognitive behavioral treatment approaches, there is a growing discussion regarding the use of medically assisted treatment (MAT). In 2011, the NADCP passed a resolution that drug courts should not have "blanket prohibitions" against the use of MAT. Although MAT should not be relied on as a primary treatment strategy, there is evidence that it increases treatment retention and delays time to recidivism (Gordon, Kinlock, Schwarz, & O'Grady, 2008). In one of the few experimental studies on this issue, James Cornish and colleagues (1997) found that opiate-addicted parolees receiving MAT were less likely to relapse and be incarcerated compared to opiate-addicted parolees who received just standard parole supervision. Although the results are encouraging, the follow-up period was brief and caution is warranted before fully adopting this approach. Much more research is needed to fully understand when and how MAT should be used within a drug court setting.

Other Criminogenic Needs

As noted with assessment, drug court participants are likely to have a number of needs beyond substance abuse. Drug courts that address substance abuse without targeting these other criminogenic needs are less likely to be effective. As a reminder, criminogenic needs include those factors that are predictive of recidivism but can be changed. For participants in drug courts, this may translate into the need to target peer associations, attitudes surrounding criminal behavior, problem-solving skills, and relapse prevention. Many participants may have alienated family members as a result of their substance use and may need help in repairing those relationships. Despite the need for treatment in these areas, Shaffer (2011) found that many drug courts fail to provide these types of services, unless they are specifically tied to traditional substance abuse approaches (e.g., relapse prevention). Finally, many drug courts require participants to be employed or seeking work (Shaffer, 2011). However, drug courts should recognize that whereas some participants are likely able to maintain employment once abstinent, others may need vocational training or treatment targeting their attitudes about work.

Reinforcers and Sanctions

The use of a contingency management system or rewards and punishers is a key component of the drug court model. However, relatively few drug courts have formalized procedures in place, and the use of rewards and sanctions varies widely (Burdon, Roll, Prendergast, & Rawson, 2001; Shaffer, 2011). Table 7.3 illustrates reinforcers and sanctions recommended by NADCP. Although the recommendations include many appropriate examples, they tend to focus on those applicable within the context of drug court hearings. However, a wider range of reinforcers can be identified. For example, all members of the team, including the treatment provider, should provide verbal praise. Reinforcers can also be expanded to include other symbolic and tangible rewards, including certificates of completion for drug court phases and treatment phases, gift certificates, treats, and bus tokens. As with praise, all members of the drug court team should be encouraged to provide verbal redirection when warranted, and other punishers may include extra work outside community service or a loss of privileges as they relate to the treatment facility.

Despite the recognized need for rewards and sanctions, not all contingency management systems have worked well within the drug court setting. For example, one study evaluated the use of gift certificates as an enhancement to the normal reinforcement system used by a drug court in Philadelphia (Marlowe, Festinger, Dugosh, Arabia, & Kirby, 2008). The researchers compared the outcomes across three groups of drug court participants: those that did not receive the enhanced reinforcers, those that received enhanced reinforcers of relatively equal value but less frequent over time, and those that received enhanced reinforcers in a way that allowed for the gift certificate amount to continually

Table 7.3 Examples of Rewards and Sanctions

Rewards	Sanctions
Praise and encouragement from the judge	Warnings or admonishment from the judge
Ceremonies marking advancement to the next phase	Moving back a phase
Tokens indicating progress	Increased drug testing
Reduced supervision	Increased court appearances
Less frequent court appearances	Isolation in the courtroom
Reduced fees or fines	Increased monitoring
Dismissal of charges/reduction in sentence	Increased treatment intensity
Graduation	Fines
	Community services
	Jail
	Termination from the program

Source: National Association of Drug Court Professionals. (1997). *Defining drug courts: The key components.* Washington, DC: U.S. Department of Justice.

increase over time. Marlowe and colleagues failed to find that the use of gift certificates had an effect on performance in the drug court. However, this may be the result of the difficulties in incorporating a meaningful contingency management system into the drug court setting because gift certificates were only awarded once every 4–6 weeks.

Faye Taxman and colleagues have created a contingency management system known as JSTEPS, which is designed for criminal justice populations. At a presentation at the NADCP conference, Maxine Spitzer (2011) noted that one of the challenges in implementing a contingency management system into drug courts is simply not knowing where it should be used in the system. Many drug courts rely on the judge to hand out sanctions or rewards. However, status review hearings are often a minimum of 2 weeks apart, and the intervals can sometimes be as much as 4–6 weeks, as in the Philadelphia drug court. Given that rewards and sanctions should be offered immediately, it may be that relying on the judge undermines the ability of a contingency management system to be effective. Spitzer recommended that drug courts place contingency management systems within the context of probation instead because responses can be more immediate. Although research on the use of JSTEPS with drug courts is ongoing, it seems obvious that integrating a system of rewards and punishers *throughout* the drug court is important as drug courts continue to improve.

Alcoholics Anonymous/Narcotics Anonymous

Perhaps one of the more controversial elements of treatment within a drug court setting surrounds the use of AA/NA. More than half of the drug courts included in Shaffer's (2011) meta-analysis required participants to attend AA/NA. However, research has failed to find that this approach is effective with an offender treatment program (Shaffer, 2011; Wells-Parker & Bangert-Drowns, 1995). There is also growing concern about the legal and ethical issues of mandating participants to services with a religious or spiritual element to them.

However, some type of peer support group is warranted for drug court participants because there is evidence that peer support groups can help participants be successful (McClellan et al., 1998). Connecting participants with peers can help to provide emotional support and provide opportunities for participation in prosocial activities such as sports and other recreational activities (SAMHSA, 2009). Although drug courts should not mandate participants to attend AA/NA, they should recommend and encourage participation in some type of peer support group. Drug courts may want to create alumni groups in an effort to address the need for peer support.

Aftercare

Finally, aftercare is a critical part of any effective treatment program, including drug courts. In a typical treatment program, aftercare is a stepped-down service occurring after the primary treatment is completed. Given the structure and length of drug courts, some courts build aftercare into the final phase of the drug court program. That is, rather than have participants enter aftercare following graduation, they move through an aftercare phase prior to graduation. During this phase, participants may still have supervision and treatment requirements. However, they are much less intensive than during previous phases.

Relatively little research has explored the role of aftercare within a drug court setting. In part, this may be the result of the complexity of the model in general. However, there is a great deal of evidence to suggest aftercare is an important part of drug treatment programs. For example, Steven Martin and colleagues at the University of Delaware found that drug offenders returning from prison had improved outcomes when they participated in aftercare services in addition to treatment (Martin, Butzin, Saum, & Inciardi, 1999). Moreover, Chris Lowenkamp and researchers at the University of Cincinnati examined the relationship between program quality and reductions in recidivism (Lowenkamp et al., 2006). Providing aftercare was one indicator of quality. As expected, they found that higher-quality programs had greater reductions in recidivism.

A Note on Juvenile Drug Courts

Finally, it is important to consider the effectiveness of juvenile drug courts. Given the initial success of drug courts, jurisdictions sought to replicate the model with juvenile participants as early as 1995. Today, there are more than 450 juvenile drug courts in operation. However, the research on the juvenile model has been less than promising. Meta-analyses have largely failed to find a treatment effect for juvenile drug courts, and a recent multisite study found that juvenile drug courts did not have an effect, with drug court participants often doing worse than members of the comparison group (Latessa, Sullivan, Blair, Sullivan, & Smith, 2012; Shaffer, 2006; Wilson et al., 2006). However, a recent meta-analysis found that juvenile drug courts did reduce general recidivism (Mitchell et al., 2012). One criticism of juvenile drug courts has been that they target experimental drug users rather than those with serious addiction and dependence issues. It may be that the most recent findings by Mitchell reflect a trend toward improving juvenile drug courts to be more effective.

A number of efforts have sought to improve juvenile drug court outcomes. Recognizing differences between juveniles and adults, an interdisciplinary group of researchers and practitioners identified *16 Strategies in Practice* to guide juvenile drug courts (Table 7.4; National Council of Juvenile and Family Court Judges, 2003). Much like the adult model, research suggests that programs adhering to these principles have improved outcomes (van Wormer & Lutze, 2011).

Although limited research on juvenile drug courts precludes us from being able to prescribe specific practices regarding the structure of the program, it is likely that many of the general principles of effective interventions hold true. Drug courts should use sound assessment processes to identify appropriate participants and should use cognitive behavioral approaches in working with them. As with adult drug courts, it is likely that the most effective juvenile drug courts will be those targeting higher-risk youths with a demonstrated need for services.

Table 7.4   Strategies in Practice

1. Engage all stakeholders in creating an interdisciplinary, coordinated, and systemic approach to working with youth and their families.
2. Develop and maintain an interdisciplinary, nonadversarial team.
3. Define a target population and eligibility criteria that are aligned with the program's goals and objectives.
4. Schedule frequent judicial reviews and be sensitive to the effect court proceedings can have on youth and their families.
5. Establish a system for program monitoring and evaluation.
6. Build partnerships with community organizations to expand the range of opportunities available to youth and their families.
7. Tailor interventions to the complex and varied needs of youth and their families.
8. Tailor treatment to the developmental needs of adolescents.
9. Design treatment to address the unique needs of each gender.
10. Create policies and procedures that are responsive to cultural differences and train personnel to be culturally competent.
11. Maintain a focus on the strengths of youth and their families.
12. Recognize and engage the family as a valued partner in all components of the program.
13. Coordinate with the school system to ensure that each participant enrolls.
14. Design drug testing to be frequent, random, and observed.
15. Respond to compliance and noncompliance with incentives and sanctions designed to reinforce or modify the behavior of youth and their families.
16. Establish a confidentiality policy and procedure that guard the privacy of the youth.

Source: National Council of Juvenile and Family Court Judges (2003). *Juvenile drug courts: Strategies in practice.* Washington, DC: Bureau of Justice Assistance.

Summary

- Drug courts offer an effective solution for communities wishing to keep drug offenders out of prison and in the community.
- By providing a coordinated effort of judicial supervision, community monitoring, and treatment, drug courts are able to reduce criminal behavior and drug use.
- Reserving drug courts for higher-risk offenders results in greater reductions in recidivism than when placing low-risk offenders into the program.
- Like other programs, drug courts should utilize cognitive behavioral interventions and use risk and need assessments to guide decision making.
- Drug court judges play in integral role in the success of the program, and having involved, dedicated drug court team members helps to increase the effectiveness of drug courts.

References

American Psychiatric Association. (1994). *Diagnostic and statistical manual of mental disorders* (4th ed.). Washington, DC: Author.

Andrews, D. A., Zinger, I., Hodge, R. D., Bonta, J., Gendreau, P., & Cullen, F. T. (1990). Does correctional treatment work? A clinically relevant and physiologically informed meta-analysis. *Criminology, 28,* 369–404.

Burdon, W. M., Roll, J. M., Prendergast, M. L., & Rawson, R. A. (2001). Drug courts and contingency management. *Journal of Drug Issues, 37*(1), 73–90.

Carey, S. M., Mackin, J. R., & Finigan, M. W. (2012). What works? The ten key components of drug court: Research-based best practices. *Drug Court Review, 8,* 6–42.

Carson, E. A., & Sabol, W. J. (2012). Prisoners in 2011 *NCJ 23908.* Washington, DC: Bureau of Justice Statistics.

Cornish, J. W., Metzger, D., Woody, G. E., Wilson, D., McLellan, A. T., Vangergrift, B., & O'Brien, C. P. (1997). Naltrexone pharmacotherapy for opioid dependent federal probationers. *Journal of Substance Abuse Treatment, 14,* 529–534.

Dowden, C., & Andrews, D. A. (1999). What works for female offenders: A meta-analytic review. *Crime and Delinquency, 45,* 438–452.

Dowden, C., & Andrews, D. A. (2000). Effective correctional treatment and violent reoffending. *Canadian Journal of Criminology, 42,* 449–467.

Dowden, C., & Andrews, D. A. (2004). The importance of staff practice in delivering effective correctional treatment: A meta-analytic review of core correctional practice. *International Journal of Offender Therapy and Comparative Criminology, 48,* 203–214.

Drug Courts Program Office. (1998). *Looking at a decade of drug courts.* Washington, DC: Author.

Farole, D. J., & Cissner, A. B. (2007). Seeing eye to eye: Participant and staff perspectives on drug courts. In G. Berman, M. Rempel, & R. V. Wolf (Eds.), *Documenting results: Research on problem-solving justice* (pp. 51–73). New York: Center for Court Innovation.

Festinger, D. S., Marlowe, D. B., Lee, P. A., Kirby, K. C., Bovasso, G., & McLellan, A. T. (2002). Status hearings in drug court: When more is less and less is more. *Drug and Alcohol Dependence, 68,* 151–157.

Franco, C. (2010). *Drug courts: Background, effectiveness, and policy issues for Congress.* Washington, DC: Congressional Research Service.

Gendreau, P. (1995). Technology transfer in the criminal justice field: Implications for substance use. In T. E. Backer, S. L. David, & G. Saucy (Eds.), *Reviewing the behavioral science knowledge base on technology transfer..* Rockville, MD: U.S. Department of Health and Human Services.

Gendreau, P. (1996). The principles of effective intervention with offenders. In A. Harland (Ed.), *What works in community corrections.* Thousand Oaks, CA: Sage.

Goldkamp, J. S., White, M. D., & Robinson, J. (1998). *An honest chance: Perspectives of drug court participants—Findings from focus groups in Brooklyn, Miami, Seattle, Las Vegas, and San Bernadino.* Philadelphia: Crime and Justice Research Institute.

Goldkamp, J. S., White, M. D., & Robinson, J. B. (2002). An honest chance: Perspectives on drug courts. *Federal Sentencing Reporter, 6,* 369–372.

Gordon, M. S., Kinlock, T. W., Schwartz, R. P., & O'Grady, K. E. (2008). A randomized clinical trial of methadone maintenance for prisoners: Findings at 6 months post-release. *Addiction, 103,* 1333–1342.

Gray, A. R., & Saum, C. A. (2005). Mental health, gender, and drug court completion. *American Journal of Criminal Justice, 30,* 55–69.

Gutierrez, L., & Bourgon, G. (2012). Drug treatment courts: A quantitative review of study and treatment quality. *Justice Research and Policy, 14,* 47–77.

Harrell, A., Roman, J., & Sack, E. (2001). *Drug court services for female offenders, 1996–1999: Evaluation of the Brooklyn Treatment Court.* Washington, DC: Urban Institute. Justice Policy Center. Retrieved February 2004 from http://www.urban.org/url.cfm?ID=410356.

Hartley, R. E., & Phillips, R. C. (2001). Who graduates from drug courts? Correlates of client success. *American Journal of Criminal Justice, 26,* 107–119.

Hora, P. F. (2002). A dozen years of drug treatment courts: Uncovering our theoretical foundation and the construction of a mainstream paradigm. *Substance Use & Misuse, 37,* 1469–1488.

Koetzle, D., Listwan, S. J., Guastaferro, W. P., & Kobus, K. (2012). *Treating high risk offenders in the community: The potential of drug courts.* Unpublished manuscript.

Latessa, E. J., Sullivan, C., Blair, L., Sullivan, C. J., & Smith, P. (2012). *Outcome and process evaluation of juvenile drug courts, draft report.* Cincinnati, OH: University of Cincinnati, Center for Criminal Justice Research.

Listwan, S. J., Shaffer, D. K., & Hartman, J. L. (2009). Combating methamphetamine use in the community. *Crime & Delinquency, 55,* 627–644.

Listwan, S. J., Sundt, J., Holsinger, A. M., & Latessa, E. J. (2003). The effect of drug court programming on recidivism: The Cincinnati experience. *Crime & Delinquency, 49,* 389–411.

Longshore, D., Turner, S., Wenzel, S., Morral, A., Harrell, A., McBride, D., Deschenes, E., & Iguchi, M. (2001). Drug courts: A conceptual framework. *Journal of Drug Issues, 31,* 7–26.

Lowenkamp, C. T., Holsinger, A. M., & Latessa, E. J. (2005, Fall). Are drug courts effective? A meta-analytic review. *Journal of Community Corrections,* 5–10, 28.

Lowenkamp, C. T., Latessa, E. J., & Smith, P. (2006). Does correctional program quality really matter? The impact of adhering to the principles of effective intervention. *Criminology & Public Policy, 5,* 575–594.

Magura, S., Staines, G., Kosanke, N., Rosenblum, A., Foote, J., DeLuca, A., & Bali, P. (2003). Predictive validity of the ASAM patient placement criteria for naturalistically matched vs. mismatched alcoholism patients. *American Journal on Addictions, 12*(5), 386–397.

Marlowe, D. B., Festinger, D. S., Dugosh, K. L., Arabia, P. L., & Kirby, K. C. (2008). An effectiveness trial of contingency management in a felony pre-adjudication drug court. *Journal of Applied Behavior Analysis, 41,* 565–577.

Marlowe, D. B., Festinger, D. S., Dugosh, K. L., Lee, P. A., & Benasutti, K. M. (2006). Adapting judicial supervision to the risk level of drug offenders: Discharge and 6-month outcomes from a prospective matching study. *Drug and Alcohol Dependence, 88,* 4–13.

Martin, S. S., Butzin, C. A., Saum, C. A., & Inciardi, J. A. (1999). Three-year outcomes of therapeutic community treatment for drug-involved offenders in Delaware: From prison to work release to aftercare. *Prison Journal, 79,* 294–320.

Maruschak, L. M., & Parks, E. (2012). *Probation and parole in the United States, 2011* (NCJ 239686). Washington, DC: Bureau of Justice Statistics.

Maynard, B. R. (2010). Social service organizations in the era of evidence-based practice: The learning organization as a guiding framework for bridging science to service. *Journal of Social Work, 10,* 301–316.

McHugh, R. K., Hearon, B. A., & Otto, M. W. (2010). Cognitive behavioral therapy for substance abuse disorders. *Psychiatric Clinics of North America, 33,* 511–525.

McClellan, A. T., Hagan, T. A., Levine, M., Gould, F., Meyers, K., Bencivengo, M., et al. (1998). Research report: Supplemental social services improve outcomes in public addiction treatment. *Addiction, 93*(10), 1489–1499.

Miller, J. M., & Shutt, J. E. (2001). Considering the need for empirically grounded drug court screening mechanisms. *Journal of Drug Issues, 31,* 91–106.

Mitchell, O., Wilson, D. B., Eggers, A., & MacKenzie, D. L. (2012). Assessing the effectiveness of drug courts on recidivism: A met-analytic review of traditional and non-traditional drug courts. *Journal of Criminal Justice, 40,* 60–71.

Mumola, C. J. (1998). (with Bonczar, T. P) (NCJ 166611) *Substance abuse and treatment of adults on probation, 1995.* Washington, DC: Bureau of Justice Statistics.

Mumola, C. J., & Karberg, J. C. (2006). *Drug use and dependence, state and federal prisoners, 2004* (NCJ 213530). Washington, DC: Bureau of Justice Statistics.

National Association of Drug Court Professionals. (1997). *Defining drug courts: The key components.* Washington, DC: U.S. Department of Justice.

National Council of Juvenile and Family Court Judges. (20030). Juvenile drug courts: Strategies in practice. Washington, DC: Bureau of Justice Assistance

National Drug Court Institute. (2012). *Drug court locations in the United States, 2011.* Washington, DC: Author.

National Institute of Drug Abuse. (2012). *Principles of drug abuse treatment for criminal justice populations: A research-based guide.* Rockville, MD: National Institutes of Health.

Newcomb, M. D., Chou, C., Bentler, P. M., & Huba, G. J. (1988). Cognitive motivations for drug use among adolescents: Longitudinal tests of gender differences and predictors of change in drug use. *Journal of Counseling Psychology, 35,* 426–438.

Novacek, J., Raskin, R., & Hogan, R. (1991). Why do adolescents use drugs? Age, sex and user differences. *Journal of Youth and Adolescence, 20,* 475–492.

Office of National Drug Control Policy. (2012). *National drug control budget.* Washington, DC: Author.

Peters, R. H., & Murrin, M. R. (2000). Effectiveness of treatment-based drug courts in reducing criminal recidivism. *Criminal Justice and Behavior, 27,* 72–96.

Peters, R. H., & Peyton, E. (1998). *Guidelines for drug courts on screening and assessment.* Washington, DC: Drug Courts Program Office.

Rempel, M., Fox-Kralstein, D., Cissner, A., Cohen, R., Labriola, M., Farole, D., Bader, A., & Magnani, M. (2003). *The New York State Adult Drug Court Evaluation: Policies, participants and impacts* (Tech. Rep.). New York: Center for Court Innovation.

Rossman, S. B., Rempel, M., Roman, J. K., Zweig, J. M., Lindquist, C. H., Green, M., & Farole, D. J., Jr. (2011). *The Multi-Site Adult Drug Court Evaluation: The impact of drug courts,* Vol. 4. Washington, DC: National Institute of Justice.

Schiff, M., & Terry, W. C., III. (1997). Predicting graduation from Broward County's dedicated drug treatment county. *Justice Systems Journal, 19,* 291–310.

Senjo, S. R., & Leip, L. A. (2001). Testing and developing theory in drug court: A four-part logit model to predict program completion. *Criminal Justice Policy Review, 12*(1), 66–87.

Shaffer, D. K. (2006). Reconsidering drug court effectiveness: A meta-analytic review [Doctoral dissertation, University of Cincinnati, 2006]. *Dissertation Abstracts International, 67,* 09A (AAT No. 3231113).

Shaffer, D. K. (2011). Looking inside the black box of drug courts: A meta-analytic review. *Justice Quarterly, 28,* 493–521.

Shaffer, D. K., Hartman, J. L., & Listwan, S. J. (2009). Drug abusing women in the community: The impact of drug court involvement on recidivism. *Journal of Drug Issues, 39,* 803–827.

Shaffer, D. K., Hartman, J. L., Listwan, S. L., Howell, T., & Latessa, E. J. (2011). Outcomes among drug court participants: Does drug of choice matter? *International Journal of Offender Therapy and Comparative Criminology, 55,* 155–174.

Spitzer, M. (2011). *Contingency management in drug courts: Research and resources.* Paper presented at the annual meeting of the National Association of Drug Court Professionals. Retrieved February 2012 from http://www.gmuace.org/documents/presentations/2011/NADCP%202011%20Stitzer.pdf.

Spohn, C., Piper, R. K., Martin, T., & Frenzel, E. D. (2001). Drug courts and recidivism: The results of an evaluation using two comparison groups and multiple indicators of recidivism. *Journal of Drug Issues, 31,* 149–176.

Stoops, W. W., Tindall, M. S., Mateyoke-Scrivner, A., & Leukefeld, C. (2005). Methamphetamine use in non-urban and urban drug court clients. *International Journal of Offender Therapy and Comparative Criminology, 49*, 260–276.

Substance Abuse and Mental Health Services Administration. (2009). *What are peer recovery support services?* (HHS Publication No. (SMA) 09–4454). Rockville, MD: Author.

Toray, T., Coughlin, C., Vuchinich, S., & Patricelli, P. (1991). Gender differences associated with adolescent substance abuse: Comparisons and implications for treatment. *Family Relations, 40*, 338–344.

Wells-Parker, E., & Bangert-Drowns, R. (1995). Final results from a meta-analysis of remedial interventions with drink/drive offenders. *Addiction, 90*, 907–927.

Wexler, D. (2000). Therapeutic jurisprudence: An overview. *Thomas M. Cooley Law Review, 17*, 125–134.

Wilson, D. B., Bouffard, L. A., & Mackenzie, D. L. (2005). A quantitative review of structured group-oriented, cognitive-behavioral programs for offenders. *Criminal Justice and Behavior, 32*, 172–204.

Wilson, D. B., Mitchell, O., & MacKenzie, D. L. (2006). A systematic review of drug court effects on recidivism. *Journal of Experimental Criminology, 2*, 459–487.

Wolfe, E., Guydish, J., & Termondt, J. (2002). A drug court outcome evaluation comparing arrests in a two year follow-up period. *Journal of Drug Issues, 32*, 1155–1172.

8

What Works with Sex Offenders

Paula Smith, Myrinda Schweitzer, Ronen Ziv

UNIVERSITY OF CINCINNATI, CINCINNATI, OHIO

Introduction

The current empirical literature provides clear direction with respect to "what works" in reducing recidivism with offender populations (Andrews & Bonta, 2010). Specifically, this research suggests that corrections professionals can influence change in offenders and reduce post-release recidivism when they design and deliver services consistent with certain core principles of effective intervention (Andrews et al., 1990). Although it is clear that such services must be structured, planned, and require a considerable amount of effort to implement well, there is good reason to be optimistic about rehabilitative efforts with offenders, including sex offender populations in particular. At the center of this framework are the risk, need, and responsivity (RNR) principles. In short, the risk principle refers to *who* should be targeted for correctional treatment, the need principle refers to *what* should be targeted for change, and the responsivity principle refers to *how* these factors should be targeted. This chapter discusses each of these principles in detail, and it describes the application to sex offenders in particular. Additional emphasis is also given to the *fidelity principle*, which underscores the importance of ensuring adherence to the RNR principles through intentional efforts to measure and improve the quality of such services.

Rationale for the Treatment of Sex Offenders

In comparison with the overall population of offenders, individuals convicted of sexual offenses constitute a relatively small proportion (Brown, 2005). Furthermore, many authors have raised pertinent concerns about the level of resources required to produce a meaningful impact on sexual recidivism (for a more detailed review, see Brown, 2005). For these reasons, it is reasonable to critically examine the rationale for the treatment of sex offenders within the criminal justice system. It is worth noting, however, that the vast majority of sex offenders either remain in the community under some form of supervision or return to the community after serving a custodial sentence (Brown, 2005). From the perspective of reducing victimization alone, therefore, it makes sense to generate research and cumulate knowledge about "what works" to reduce recidivism in this important population of offenders.

Although support for the application of the principles of effective intervention has been consistently found with general offenders, researchers have also found support for these concepts with sex offender populations. There are now more than 40 published meta-analyses of the correctional treatment literature alone, and the importance of the RNR principles has been replicated with remarkable consistency (Smith, Gendreau, & Swartz, 2009). In a review of 374 treatment effect sizes, Andrews and Bonta (2010) estimated that programs not in adherence with any of the principles were associated with slight increases in recidivism ($r = -.02$), whereas interventions in adherence with one of the principles (i.e., risk, need, or responsivity) produced a slight decrease ($r = .02$). Furthermore, interventions in adherence with two principles produced a larger decrease ($r = .18$), and those in adherence with all three principles produced the most dramatic reductions ($r = .26$) in offender recidivism. Similarly, in a meta-analysis examining the effectiveness of treatment for sex offenders, Hanson, Bourgon, Helmus, and Hodgson (2009) found that programs in adherence with the principles of effective intervention showed the largest reductions in both general and sexual recidivism.

The Risk Principle

The risk principle states that the level and intensity of services should be matched to the offender's risk level (Andrews et al., 1990). As such, intensive services of a greater duration should be reserved for higher-risk offenders, and less intense services of a shorter duration should be reserved for lower-risk offenders (Andrews & Bonta, 2010; Lowenkamp & Latessa, 2004; Lowenkamp, Latessa, & Holsinger, 2006). Andrews and Bonta also strongly encourage the separation of services by risk level to ensure that higher-risk offenders do not expose lower-risk offenders to antisocial attitudes and behaviors.

At the most basic level, the risk principle also maintains that criminal behavior is predictable using actuarial assessments of static and dynamic risk factors. Static factors are those factors that cannot be targeted for change (e.g., criminal history), whereas dynamic risk factors are those that are amenable to change (Andrews & Bonta, 2010). Within this context, dynamic risk factors can increase or decrease, whereas static risk factors can only increase.

Risk factors for general recidivism include criminal history (a static risk factor) and dynamic characteristics such as antisocial attitudes, antisocial peers, antisocial temperament/personality factors, family dynamics, education/employment, substance abuse, as well as leisure and recreation (Andrews & Bonta, 2010). In contrast, the risk factors emphasized for the prediction of sexual recidivism have historically been more static in nature. Examples include age, previous offense history, onset of sexually deviant interests, marital status, and specific offense characteristics such as stranger victim, male victim, and contact/noncontact offense (Harris, 2006; Hanson & Bussière, 1998). Recently, however, researchers have also identified dynamic risk factors for sexual recidivism. In addition, these dynamic risk factors have been further divided into stable and acute risk factors (Hanson & Harris, 2000). This further division separates dynamic risk factors into relatively enduring problems and offender characteristics (i.e., stable risk factors) from those that can rapidly change and signal the timing of reoffending (i.e., acute risk factors). Stable dynamic risk factors (Hanson & Harris, 2000; Hanson & Morton-Bourgon, 2004) include the following:

- Social influences
- Sexual entitlement
- Attitudes
- Sexual self-regulation
- General self-regulation

The following are examples of acute dynamic factors (Hanson & Harris, 2000):

- Access to victims
- Noncooperation with supervision
- Anger

Mann, Hanson, and Thornton (2010) have suggested an alternative—and perhaps more sophisticated—perspective to understand risk factors by considering those factors that are *psychologically meaningful.* These authors use the term to refer to psychologically meaningful risk factors as propensities or characteristics of individuals that interact with their specific environments to place them at risk for reoffending (Mann et al., 2010). Although they do not necessarily classify propensities as static or dynamic, they agree that some propensities can change, whereas others cannot change and might instead be managed through specific strengths or external supports (Mann et al., 2010). For example, Seto (2008) suggested that current research has yet to demonstrate that some deviant sexual preferences are mutable. Specifically, Seto highlighted that pedophilia may be immutable and best managed with the purposeful removal of triggering stimuli and other community risk management techniques. Within this context, Mann et al. examined the psychological factors that demonstrated the strongest empirical evidence as risk factors for sexual recidivism. Empirically supported risk factors (Mann et al., 2010) include the following:

- Sexual preoccupation
- Deviant sexual interest
- Offense-supportive attitudes
- Emotional congruence with children
- Lack of emotionally intimate relationships with adults
- Lifestyle impulsivity
- General self-regulation problems
- Poor cognitive problem solving
- Resistance

Promising risk factors in their study included the following:

- Hostility toward women
- Machiavellianism
- Callousness
- Dysfunctional coping

The results of their study are similar to the dynamic factors suggested by others, such as Hanson and Harris (2000). However, what is clear about the previous studies related to the dynamic risk factors for sex offenders is that research is still in the early phases of development (Harris & Hanson, 2001; Mann et al., 2010). It is anticipated that further research will continue to clarify those factors that are most likely to predict future offending.

Recall that the risk principle states that criminal behavior is predictable using actuarial assessments of both static and dynamic risk factors. Static risk assessment tools include items that have been demonstrated, through longitudinal research, to be related to reoffending (Andrews & Bonta 2010; Bonta, 1996). An example of a static risk assessment tool for general recidivism is the Salient Factor Score (SFS) (Hoffman, 1994). In contrast, the most commonly used static risk assessment tools for sexual recidivism include the Static-99 (Hanson & Thornton, 2000), Risk Matrix 2000 (Thornton et al., 2003), and the Sex Offender Risk Appraisal Guide (Quincy, Harris, Rice, & Cormier, 1998).

The utility of static risk assessment tools is their ability to predict risk for future recidivism and to support correctional programs in the classification of offenders. However, these tools are composed of only static risk factors and therefore cannot assist in the identification of targets for correctional intervention or the measurement of change (Andrews & Bonta 2010; Bonta, 1996). Improving on static assessments of risk, tools that assess both static and dynamic risk factors (risk/need assessments) have been developed for both general and sexual recidivism in order to more accurately measure changes in key life areas, fluctuations in risk level, and the impact of treatment on the risk of recidivism. These tools provide an overall composite risk score while also providing information about specific dynamic risk areas. Examples of risk/need assessments for general recidivism include the Level of Service Inventory–Revised (Andrews & Bonta, 2004), the Wisconsin Risk Needs Assessment (Baird, Heinz, & Bemus, 1979), and the Correctional Offender Management Profiling for Alternative Sanctions (COMPAS) (http://www.northpointeinc.com). Recently, the Violence Risk Scale–Sex Offender version (VRS-SO) (Olver, Wong, Nicholaichuk, & Gordon, 2007) and the Structured Assessment of Risk and Need (Webster et al., 2006) have been developed to capture both static and dynamic risk factors for sexual recidivism.

When considering risk assessment tools for sex offenders, it is important to consider both sexual and general recidivism. Hanson and Morton-Bourgon (2004) found that risk assessments designed to assess risk for general recidivism were able to accurately predict general recidivism in sex offenders. The interesting finding, however, is that many sex offenders tend to score low-risk for general recidivism on these tools but continue to be high risk for sexual recidivism. This underscores the importance of also using a sex offense-specific risk assessment tool in conjunction with a measure of general recidivism (McGrath, Lasher, & Cumming, 2011). Failure to use a sex offense-specific tool could result in the misclassification of sex offenders and poor outcomes.

The accurate assessment of risk for sexual offenders supports adherence to the risk principle; those offenders identified as high-risk for recidivism should receive more intensive services than those identified as low-risk for recidivism. In the literature, the evidence supporting the application of the risk principle to sex offenders is beginning to emerge. For example, Hanson et al. (2009) found stronger treatment effects for higher-risk offenders compared to lower-risk offenders, although the effect did not reach statistical significance. Similarly, Lovins, Lowenkamp, and Latessa (2009) found that higher-risk sex offenders had lower rates of general recidivism when they received more intensive services, such as residential placement, compared to less intensive services. Finally, in a review of research on the risk principle with sex offenders, Wakeling, Mann, and Carter (2012) concluded that lower-risk sex offenders would benefit most from no more than 100 hours of treatment. In addition, they suggest that lower-risk offenders should be kept separate from higher-risk offenders, and treatment services should not interfere with other activities that encourage a prosocial lifestyle.

Need Principle

The need principle highlights the importance of targeting dynamic risk factors, otherwise known as *criminogenic needs,* in order to reduce an offender's likelihood of future criminal behavior (Andrews et al., 1990). In terms of sex offenders, the need principle suggests that corrections professionals should measure the dynamic risk factors of sex offenders and focus intervention efforts on those factors identified as predictive of sexual reoffending. Recall that dynamic risk factors are those risk factors that are amenable to change. Many of the major risk factors introduced previously are relevant criminogenic targets for change that should be the focus of interventions. As a review, sex offender research suggests that a deviant sexual interest, offense-supportive attitudes, lack of emotionally intimate relationships with adults, lifestyle impulsivity, general self-regulation problems, resistance to rules and supervision, grievance/hostility, and negative social influences are important criminogenic needs (Hanson & Harris, 2000; Harris, 2006; Mann et al., 2010;). In addition, the evidence suggests the importance of targeting emotional congruence with children and targeting poor cognitive problem solving (Mann et al., 2010).

As noted previously, the field has developed assessment tools to specifically assess both static and dynamic risk factors for sexually offending. Some of these tools have been developed to measure strictly static factors (e.g., Static-99), whereas other instruments have been developed to measure the combination of static and dynamic factors (e.g., Structured Assessment of Risk and Need). However, tools are also available to measure only the dynamic risk factors—or criminogenic needs—of sex offenders. Examples of tools designed to specifically assess stable and acute factors include the Stable-2007 and the Acute-2007 (Hanson, Harris, Scott, & Helmus, 2007) and the Sex Offender Treatment Needs and Progress Scale (McGrath & Cumming, 2003). As previously mentioned, these tools have the added benefit of identifying specific targets for change while also allowing for the measurement of change related to these target areas.

When the assessment of dynamic risk factors is coupled with a static measure of risk (e.g., Static-99), studies have demonstrated that the addition of dynamic risk factors adds incremental predictive validity beyond static measures of risk, such as the Static-99 (Beech, Friendship, Erikson, & Hanson, 2002; Knight & Thornton, 2007; Olver et al., 2007; Thornton, 2002). Thus, the assessment of overall risk is improved while also providing clear targets for change to reduce the likelihood of sexual recidivism. In addition, studies examining the use of both static and dynamic assessments have found an association between positive treatment progress and reductions in recidivism (Beggs & Grace, 2011; Olver & Wong, 2011). In a meta-analysis by Hanson and colleagues (2009), programs that targeted the criminogenic needs of sex offenders were more effective at reducing the likelihood of sexual recidivism of sex offenders than programs that failed to target criminogenic needs. In fact, the results suggested that adherence to the need principle in particular demonstrated the most powerful effect on recidivism. These studies support the assessment of dynamic risk factors for sex offenders and stress the importance of targeting those areas for change in order to reduce recidivism.

Responsivity Principle

The responsivity principle refers to the fact that the most effective modes of treatment are those based on behavioral, cognitive, and social learning theories (Andrews, 1995). This is referred to as *general responsivity*, suggesting that offenders respond best to techniques grounded in cognitive, behavioral, and social learning theories. In addition to the concept of general responsivity, the term *specific responsivity* is used to emphasize that correctional interventions should be tailored to the learning style, motivation level, mental abilities, and strengths of individual offenders (Andrews & Bonta, 2010). Allowing for the assessment of responsivity factors supports the offender's success with correctional programming by minimizing potential barriers.

In examining the concept of general responsivity in more detail, three clear theories are evident: cognitive, behavioral, and social learning. Cognitive theories recognize the importance of cognitions and how thinking can influence behavior. Behavioral theories state that human behavior can be shaped through the regular and consistent use of purposeful reinforcement and punishment (Speigler & Guevrement, 2010). Social learning theory states that learning occurs through a process of observational learning, with role models playing a crucial role (Bandura, 1977). In particular, the direct teaching of the new skill, with repetitive modeling of the new behavior in alternative situations, occurs along with plenty of opportunities to practice. These opportunities are followed by the purposeful reinforcement of the new behavior attempts (Bandura, 1977).

These theories have been extended into cognitive behavioral interventions and social skills training. Cognitive behavioral interventions focus on restructuring antisocial thoughts with prosocial thoughts and teaching skills such as cognitive problem solving. *Cognitive restructuring* involves teaching offenders how to recognize and identify antisocial thinking, how to stop or challenge the thinking, and ultimately how to replace the risky thinking with more prosocial thoughts. *Cognitive behavioral coping skills* involve the structured teaching of specific skills designed to teach offenders how to maintain and adapt cognitive and behavioral responses to difficult situations. For sex offenders specifically, this entails targeting the offenders' denial, minimization, rationalizations, or other cognitive distortions that have served to maintain their sexual offending and related behaviors over time.

On the other hand, *social skills training* attempts to teach new skills to offenders in a structured manner that relies on observational learning, behavioral rehearsal, and the use of reinforcement. Social skills training has important relevance within the context of sex offender treatment. First, it can be used to teach skills that can be used to support decreasing sexual arousal while simultaneously increasing appropriate arousal (Brown, 2005). These strategies can also be used to impart the specific skills necessary to enhance social functioning, which includes skills to initiate and maintain appropriate intimate relationships (Hanson et al., 2009). Finally, social skills training can be applied to life management more generally, including developing appropriate leisure activities and improving employment skills (Brown, 2005).

The extant literature is clear that cognitive behavioral and social learning approaches are effective techniques in reducing the risk of general recidivism. From the earliest reviews, there is support for the importance of targeting criminogenic needs with such an approach (Lipsey & Cullen, 2007). Researchers were careful to examine whether these approaches worked for females, juveniles, and violent offenders (Dowden & Andrews 1999a, 1999b, 2000). In three separate meta-analyses, Dowden and Andrews confirmed that programs in which the criminogenic needs of higher-risk offenders are targeted using a cognitive behavioral approach do in fact reduce the recidivism of females, juvenile offenders, and even violent offenders. Smith et al. (2009) made a similar observation when they noted that more than 40 meta-analyses have been conducted on effective correctional treatment and across all studies the treatment of choice for offenders is cognitive behavioral.

Considering the studies that carefully assess the use of cognitive behavioral interventions with sex offenders, the research demonstrates similar findings. For example, one of the earliest meta-analyses found both cognitive behavioral and behavioral treatments to be effective at reducing sexual recidivism (Gallagher, Wilson, Hirschfield, Coggeshall, & MacKenzie, 1999). In a meta-analysis conducted with 32 European studies, cognitive behavioral and behavioral models proved to be the most beneficial (Illescas, Sanchez-Meca, & Genoves, 2001). Hanson et al. (2002) conducted a quantitative review of 43 studies and found that cognitive behavioral treatments along with systemic treatments produced the largest effects on both sexual and general recidivism. In 2005, Walker and colleagues conducted a meta-analysis and review of 10 treatment studies for adolescent sexual recidivism (Walker, McGovern, Poey, & Otis, 2005). They found that treatment was beneficial for juvenile sex offenders and, more important, that cognitive behavioral treatments were the most effective. Finally, in a systematic review of 69 controlled outcome evaluations, Schmucker and Lösel (2008) found that both cognitive behavioral and behavioral approaches demonstrated significant positive treatment effects.

The Good Lives Model

Although there is evidence for the importance of cognitive behavioral and behavioral approaches to the treatment of sex offenders, an alternative approach many practitioners have recently considered is the Good Lives Model. The Good Lives Model is a strength-based approach that aims to provide a comprehensive rehabilitation theory to the treatment of sex offenders (GLM-C) (Ward, Mann, & Gannon, 2006). The model takes a positive psychology approach to the treatment of offenders while holding practical reasoning as its core idea (Ward, 2010). The GLM suggests that offenders who desist from crime are healthier, happier individuals with fewer negative emotions and problems in life (Porporino, 2010). There are three components to the GLM-C approach to the treatment of sex offenders: (1) a set of general principles and assumptions that specify the values that underlie rehabilitation practice and the kind of overall aims that clinicians should be striving for; (2) the implications of these general assumptions for explaining and understanding sexual offending and its functions; and (3) the treatment implications of a focus on goals, self-regulation strategies, and ecological variables (Ward et al., 2006).

As laid out by Ward and colleagues (2006), the first assumption of GLM-C is that sex offenders, like all human beings, seek out primary goods such as states of affairs and of the mind, personal characteristics, activities, or experiences that will increase psychological well-being. The second assumption states that rehabilitation involves a variety of different values reflecting the individual offender, the interests of the community, and the practices and methods supported in the treatment field. As Maruna (2001) clearly explained, according to the GLM, it is imperative not only to teach offenders new skills to manage their risk factors but also to help them foster a meaningful personal identity. The fourth and fifth assumptions suggest that the treatment plan should include all areas related to a good life (the primary goods identified previously) along with considerations related to the necessary coping skills for the environment in which the offender will return. Finally, the treatment plan should be developed in collaboration between the corrections professional and the offender and emphasize the formation of a therapeutic alliance and motivating offenders to engage in the change process.

The implications of these general assumptions for explaining and understanding sexual offending and its functions are such that offenders are either directly seeking basic goods through the act of offending or else commit an offense as a result of an unanticipated conflict between goods (Ward et al., 2006). Furthermore, according to the GLM-C, risk factors represent problem areas in the internal and external conditions required to implement a good lives plan. Naturally, GLM-C recommends that treatment should directly address the problem areas within the individual (i.e., skills, values, and beliefs) and the external problem areas (resources, social supports, and opportunities) to reduce each individual's level of risk. Therefore, the GLM-C approach involves a focus on goals, self-regulation strategies, and ecological variables to equip the offender with the skills, values, attitudes, and resources necessary to lead a healthy life that is filled with meaning (Ward et al., 2006).

In order to meet the GLM-C proposed purpose of correctional rehabilitation, that rehabilitation should help offenders develop competencies necessary to lead a healthy lifestyle while also effectively coordinating and managing their goals to meet their current external contingencies. Ward (2010) reviews five phases of the GLM rehabilitation framework. The first phase involves careful identification of the social, psychological, and material factors related to the offender's criminal behavior. Here, there is a strong developmental focus with an emphasis on the past. Standardized risk/need assessment tools should be used, but GLM also supports the use of clinical interviews, phallometric tests, and other unstandardized assessment tools (Yates et al., 2010). The second phase involves identifying what the offender hopes to achieve through offending (goods), whereas the third phase develops a plan to achieve these goods prosocially. The fourth phase involves recognizing the required environments and resources needed to achieve the desired goods. The fifth phase brings together the previous phases in a detailed intervention plan (good lives plan). Within the plan, the necessary offender competencies are identified and can be targeted. Although cognitive and behavioral techniques can be utilized to target and develop competencies, the model does not clearly state the specific approach that the treatment provider should take (Ward, 2010). There appears to be significant discretion awarded to the treatment provider throughout the treatment process (Yates et al., 2010) and no mechanisms to ensure known effective methods are being used. Despite these concerns, GLM aims to reduce offender risk through living a more fulfilling life by taking a strength-based approach to addressing both internal and external problems of offenders (Ward et al., 2006). Despite the newfound popularity of the GLM, critics note that there is little empirical evidence to support this approach (Andrews, Bonta, & Wormith, 2011; Cullen, 2012). It will be important for proponents of this approach to develop both the technology to translate theory into practice moving forward and specific measures of treatment fidelity.

Program Integrity and Treatment Fidelity

As a final note, the importance of program integrity and treatment fidelity cannot be understated. As previously noted, it requires considerable time and effort to design and implement services that align with the RNR framework, and this is particularly true in the case of sex offenders. Previous research has underscored the importance of program integrity with general offenders (Lowenkamp, Latessa, & Smith, 2006), and recent reviews of the state of practice with sex offenders (e.g., Brown, 2005) have suggested that there is considerable variation in the content of services. This is attributable, at least in part, to the resistance to the relevance of treatment efforts with sex offenders and the fact that there is less research with this special population. As Hanson et al. (2009) have noted, careful empirical evaluations of high-fidelity cognitive behavioral treatment programs in the future will provide important contributions to the research literature.

Summary

The mere mention of sex offenders often invokes fear and strong emotions, yet we know that sex offenders are a very diverse group. Research indicates that the most effective interventions for sex offenders follow the principles of effective intervention and are based on risk, needs, responsivity, and fidelity. The following are some of the key points in the chapter:

- Sex offenders represent a relatively small percentage of the offender population.
- Meta-analysis supports that treatment of sex offenders can be effective when it adheres to the principles of effective intervention.
- Risk factors for sex offenders include both static and dynamic factors, including psychologically meaningful risk factors.
- There are a number of risk assessment tools specifically designed to be used with sex offenders.
- Research has demonstrated that the risk principle is applicable to sex offenders— stronger treatment effects were found with higher-risk sex offenders.
- Research supports the use of cognitive behavioral treatment for sex offenders.
- The Good Lives Model has been offered as an alternative to traditional cognitive behavioral approaches; however, there is little empirical evidence to support this approach.

References

Andrews, D. A. (1995). The psychology of criminal conduct and effective treatment. In J. McGuire (Ed.), *What works: Reducing reoffending-guidelines from research and practice.* New York: Wiley.

Andrews, D. A., & Bonta, J. (2004). *The Level of Service Inventory–Revised.* Toronto: Multi-Health Systems.

Andrews, D. A., & Bonta, J. (2010). *The psychology of criminal conduct* (5th ed.). Newark, NJ: LexisNexis.

Andrews, D. A., Bonta, J., & Wormith, S. (2011). The risk–need–responsivity (RNR) model: Does adding the Good Lives Model contribute to effective crime prevention? *Criminal Justice and Behavior, 38,* 735–755.

Andrews, D. A., Zinger, I., Hoge, R. D., Bonta, J., Gendreau, P., & Cullen, F. T. (1990). Does correctional treatment work? A clinically-relevant and psychologically-informed meta-analysis. *Criminology, 28,* 369–404.

Baird, C., Heinz, R., & Bemus, B. (1979). *The Wisconsin Case Classification/Staff Deployment Project: Two-year follow-up report.* Madison, WI: Wisconsin Division of Corrections.

Bandura, A. (1977). *Social learning theory.* Englewood Cliffs, NJ: Prentice Hall.

Beech, A. R., Friendship, C., Erikson, M., & Hanson, R. K. (2002). The relationship between static and dynamic risk factors and reconviction in a sample of UK child abusers. *Sexual Abuse: A Journal of Research and Treatment, 14,* 155–167.

Beggs, S. M., & Grace, R. C. (2011). Treatment gain for sexual offenders against children predicts reduced recidivism: A comparative validity study. *Journal of Consulting and Clinical Psychology, 79*(2), 182–192.

Bonta, J. (1996). Risk–needs assessment and treatment. In A. T. Hartland (Ed.), *Choosing correctional interventions that work: Defining the demand and evaluating the supply* (pp. 18–32). Newbury Park, CA: Sage.

Brown, S. (2005). *Treating sex offenders: An introduction to sex offender treatment programs.* Devon, UK: Willan.

Cullen, F. T. (2012). Taking rehabilitation seriously: Creativity, science, and the challenge of offender change. *Punishment and Society, 14,* 94–114.

Dowden, C., & Andrews, D. A. (1999a). What works for female offenders: A meta-analytic review. *Crime and Delinquency, 45*(4), 438–452.

Dowden, C., & Andrews, D. A. (1999b). What works in young offender treatment: A meta-analysis. *Forum on Corrections Research, 11,* 21–24.

Dowden, C., & Andrews, D. A. (2000, October). Effective correctional treatment and violent offending: A meta-analysis. *Canadian Journal of Criminology,* 449–467.

Gallagher, C. A., Wilson, D. B., Hirschfield, P., Coggeshall, M. B., & MacKenzie, D. L. (1999). A quantitative review of the effects of sex offender treatment on sexual reoffending. *Corrections Management Quarterly, 3,* 19–29.

Hanson, R. K., Bourgon, G., Helmus, L., & Hodgson, L. (2009). The principles of effective correctional treatment also apply to sexual offenders: A meta-analysis. *Criminal Justice and Behavior, 36,* 865–891.

Hanson, R. K., & Bussière, M. T. (1998). Predicting relapse: A meta-analysis of sexual offender recidivism studies. *Journal of Consulting and Clinical Psychology, 66,* 348–362.

Hanson, R. K., Gordon, A., Harris, A. J. R., Marques, J. K., Murphy, W., Quinsey, V. L., & Seto, M. C. (2002). First report of the Collaborative Outcome Data Project on the effectiveness of psychological treatment of sex offenders. *Sexual Abuse: A Journal of Research and Treatment, 14,* 169–194.

Hanson, R. K., & Harris, A. J. (2000). Where should we intervene? Dynamic predictors of sexual offender recidivism. *Criminal Justice and Behavior, 27*(1), 6–35.

Hanson, R. K., Harris, A. J. R., Scott, T., & Helmus, L. (2007). *Assessing the risk of sex offenders on community supervision* (User Report No. 2007-05). Ottawa, Ontario, Canada: Public Safety and Emergency Preparedness Canada.

Hanson, R. K., & Morton-Bourgon, K. (2004). *Predictors of sexual recidivism: An updated meta-analysis* (Corrections Research User Report No. 2004-02). Ottawa, Ontario, Canada: Public Safety Canada.

Hanson, R. K., & Thornton, D. (2000). Improving risk assessment for sex offenders: A comparison of three actuarial scales. *Law and Human Behavior, 24*(1), 119–136.

Harris, A. J. (2006). Risk assessment and sex offender community supervision: A context-specific framework. *Federal Probation, 70*(2), 36–43.

Harris, A. J., & Hanson, R. K. (2001). A structured approach to evaluating change among sexual offenders. *Sexual Abuse: A Journal of Research and Treatment, 13*(2), 105–122.

Hoffman, P. (1994). Twenty years of operational use of a risk prediction instrument: The United States Parole Commission's Salient Factor Score. *Journal of Criminal Justice, 22,* 477–494.

Illescas, S. R., Sanchez-Meca, J., & Genoves, V. G. (2001). Treatment of offenders and recidivism: Assessment of the effectiveness of programs applied in Europe. *Psychology in Spain, 5,* 47–62.

Knight, R. A., & Thornton, D. (2007). *Evaluating and improving risk assessment schemes for sexual recidivism: A long-term follow-up of convicted sexual offenders* (Document No. 217618). Washington, DC: U.S. Department of Justice.

Lipsey, M. W., & Cullen, F. T. (2007). The effectiveness of correctional rehabilitation: A review of systemic reviews. *Annual Review of Law and Social Science, 3,* 297–320.

Lovins, B., Lowenkamp, C. T., & Latessa, E. J. (2009). Applying the risk principle to sex offenders: Can treatment make some sex offenders worse? *Prison Journal, 89,* 344–357.

Lowenkamp, C., & Latessa, E. (2004). Increasing the effectiveness of correctional programming through the risk principle: Identifying offenders for residential placement. *Criminology and Public Policy, 4,* 501–528.

Lowenkamp, C. T., Latessa, E., & Holsinger, A. (2006). The risk principle in action: What have we learned from 13,676 offenders and 97 correctional programs? *Crime & Delinquency, 51,* 1–17.

Lowenkamp, C. T., Latessa, E. J., & Smith, P. (2006). Does correctional program quality really matter? The impact of adhering to the principles of effective intervention. *Criminology and Public Policy, 5*(3), 575–594.

Mann, R., Hanson, K., & Thornton, D. (2010). Assessing risk for sexual recidivism: Some proposals on the nature of psychologically meaningful risk factors. *Sexual Abuse: A Journal of Research and Treatment, 22,* 172–190.

Maruna, S. (2001). *Making good: How ex-convicts reform and rebuild their lives.* Washington, DC: American Psychological Association.

McGrath, R. J., & Cumming, G. F. (2003). *Sex offender treatment needs and progress scale manual.* Silver Spring, MD: Center for Sex Offender Management, U.S. Department of Justice. Retrieved from http://www.csom.org/pubs/SexOffTreatScale.pdf.

McGrath, R. J., Lasher, M. P., & Cumming, G. F. (2011). *A model of static and dynamic sex offender risk assessment.* Washington, D.C: U.S. Department of Justice, National Institute of Corrections.

Olver, M. E., & Wong, S. C. P. (2011). A comparison of static and dynamic assessment of sexual offender risk and need in a treatment context. *Criminal Justice and Behavior, 38,* 113–126.

Olver, M. E., Wong, S. C. P., Nicholaichuk, T., & Gordon, A. (2007). The validity and reliability of the Violence Risk Scale–Sexual Offender version: Assessing sex offender risk and evaluating therapeutic change. *Psychological Assessment, 19*(3), 318–329.

Porporino, F. J. (2010). Bringing sense and sensitivity to corrections: from programmes to "fix" offenders to services to support desistence. In *What else works? Creative work with offenders* (pp. 61–85). Devon, UK: Willan.

Quincy, V. L., Harris, G. T., Rice, M. E., & Cormier, C. A. (1998). *Violent offenders: Appraising and managing risk.* Washington, DC: American Psychological Association.

Schmucker, M., & Lösel, F. (2008). Does sexual offender treatment work? A systematic review of outcome evaluations. *Psicothema, 2,* 10–19.

Seto, M. C. (2008). Pedophilia: Psychopathology and theory. In D. R. Laws, & W. T. O'Donohue (Eds.), *Sexual deviance: Theory, assessment, and treatment* (pp. 164–182). New York: Guilford.

Smith, P., Gendreau, P., & Swartz, K. (2009). Validating the principles of effective intervention: A systematic review of the contributions of meta-analysis in the field of corrections. *Victims and Offenders, 4,* 148–169.

Spiegler, M., & Guevremont, D. (2010). *Contemporary behavior therapy* (5th ed.). Pacific Grove, CA: Brooks/Cole.

Thornton, D. (2002). Constructing and testing a framework for dynamic risk assessment. *Sexual Abuse: A Journal of Research and Treatment, 14,* 137–151.

Thornton, D., Mann, R. E., Webster, S., Blud, L., Travers, R., Friendship, C., & Erikson, M. (2003). Distinguishing and combining risks for sexual and violent recidivism. *Annals of the New York Academy of Science, 989,* 225–235.

Wakeling, H., Mann, R., & Carter, A. J. (2012). Do low-risk sexual offenders need treatment? *Howard Journal, 51*(3), 286–299.

Walker, D. F., McGovern, S. K., Poey, E. L., & Otis, K. E. (2005). Treatment effectiveness for male adolescent sexual offenders: A meta-analysis and review. *Journal of Child Sexual Abuse, 13*(3-4), 281–293.

Ward, T. (2010). The good lives model of offender rehabilitation: Basic assumptions, aetiological commitments, and practice implications. In F. McNeill, P. Raynor, & C. Trotter (Eds.), *Offender supervision: New directions in theory, research and practice* (pp. 41–64). New York: Willan.

Ward, T., Mann, R. E., & Gannon, T. A. (2006). The Good Lives Model of offender rehabilitation: Clinical impressions. *Aggression and Violent Behavior, 12,* 87–107.

Webster, S. D., Mann, R. E., Carter, A. J., Long, J., Milner, R. J., O'Brien, M. D., & Ray, N. (2006). Inter-rater reliability of dynamic risk assessment with sexual offenders. *Psychology, Crime & Law, 12,* 439–452.

Yates, P. M., Prescott, D. S., & Ward, T. (2010). *Applying the Good Lives and Self-Regulation models to sex offender treatment: A practical guide for clinicians.* Brandon, VT: Safer Society Press.

9

What Works with Women

Introduction

Although the majority of people under correctional supervision are men, the number of women in prison and on community supervision is still substantial. Specifically, women account for 25% of probationers, 11% of parolees, and nearly 7% of state and federal prisoners (Carson & Sabol, 2012; Maruschak & Parks, 2012). Given that women make up a relatively small proportion of offenders overall, many of the programs and services provided to them were initially designed for men. This chapter reviews the gender-specific literature as it relates to assessment and treatment, and it offers recommendations for providing services that are responsive to women while keeping the general principles of effective intervention in mind.

Women, Girls, and Crime

When we compare female and male offenders, it is easy to see there are differences in their entry into offending behavior and the nature of their offending. Women are less prone to violent crime and less likely to be arrested compared to men. In 2011, nearly 2.5 million women were arrested, accounting for 26% of the total number arrested that same year. Although substantial, the number of women arrested has decreased during the past 5 years. When examining offense type, women account for 20% of all violent arrests and 37% of all property offenses (Figure 9.1). Compared to male offenders, they are less likely to be arrested for all *Uniform Crime Reports* (UCR) offenses with the exception of prostitution and vice and embezzlement. Despite the gendered differences in arrest rates, men and women are similar in terms of their most common offense types. Table 9.1 lists the top five offense types for men and women. For both, the most common offenses are larceny–theft, other (nonaggravated) assaults, drug abuse violations, driving under the influence, and "all other offenses (except traffic)" (Federal Bureau of Investigation, 2012).

Like women, the number of girls coming to the attention of the court has increased since the 1980s. In 2009, girls accounted for 28% of all delinquent cases, up from 19% in 1985 (Knoll & Sickmund, 2012). As illustrated in Figure 9.2, girls accounted for 19% of violent offenses, 34% of property offenses, 18% of drug law violations, and 28% of public order offenses that were brought to court in 2010 (Puzzanchera & Kang, 2013). In that same year, there were nearly 10,000 girls in residential placement, accounting for 13% of all juveniles in placement (Sickmund, Sladky, Kang, & Puzzanchera, 2011). As can be seen in Figure 9.3, the majority of these girls were removed from the home for personal offenses. However, a sizable number were also placed in residential services for status offenses and technical offenses.

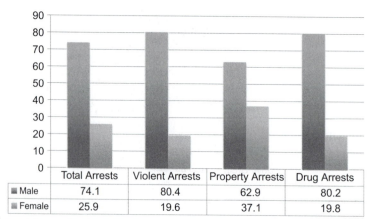

	Total Arrests	Violent Arrests	Property Arrests	Drug Arrests
▪ Male	74.1	80.4	62.9	80.2
▪ Female	25.9	19.6	37.1	19.8

FIGURE 9.1 2011 arrests by gender. *Source: Federal Bureau of Investigation. (2012).* Crime in the United States, 2011. *Available at http://www.fbi.gov/about-us/cjis/ucr/crime-in-the-u.s/2011/crime-in-the-u.s.-2011/tables/table-42.*

Table 9.1   Most Common Offenses by Gender

Male arrests	Female arrests
"Other offenses" (28.9%)	"Other offenses" (26.9%)
Drug abuse violations (13.3%)	Larceny–theft (17.2%)
Driving under the influence (9.9%)	Other assaults (10.6%)
Other assaults (9.8%)	Drug abuse violations (9.4%)
Larceny–theft (7.9%)	Driving under the influence (9.3%)

Source: Federal Bureau of Investigation. (2012). *Crime in the United States, 2011.* Available at http://www.fbi.gov/about-us/cjis/ucr/crime-in-the-u.s/2011/crime-in-the-u.s.-2011/tables/table-42.

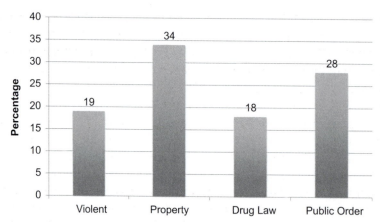

FIGURE 9.2 Female juvenile court cases. *Source: Puzzanchera, C., & Kang, W. (2013).* Easy access to juvenile court statistics: 1985–2010. *Available at http://www.ojjdp.gov/ojstatbb/ezajcs.*

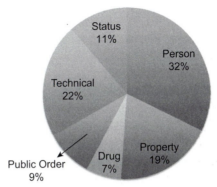

FIGURE 9.3 Most serious offense for girls in residential placement. *Source: Sickmund, M., Sladky, T. J., Kang, W., & Puzzanchera, C. (2011). Easy access to the census of juveniles in residential placement. Available at http://www.ojjdp. gov/ojstatbb/ezacjrp.*

Table 9.2   National Profile of Women Offenders

Disproportionately African American or Hispanic
Early to mid-thirties
Convicted of a drug or drug-related offense
Has a family member in the criminal justice system
History of physical and/or sexual abuse
Drug and alcohol problems
Physical and mental health difficulties
Single parents
High school graduate (or GED)
Limited vocational training and work histories

Source: Bloom, B., Owen, B., & Covington, S. (2003). *Gender-responsive strategies: Research, practice, and guiding principles for women offenders.* Washington, DC: National Institute of Corrections.

In addition to considering the prevalence and incidence of females involved in the criminal justice system, it is also important to think about their characteristics. In their review of gender-responsive strategies, Barbara Bloom, Barbara Owen, and Stephanie Covington (2003) offer a profile of women offenders. Table 9.2 illustrates the national profile of women offenders. Compared to men, women are more likely to have custody of minor children, have higher incidences of mental health problems, have more physical health difficulties, and are more likely to have histories of mental health. Although both men and women struggle with substance abuse, national surveys of offenders suggest that women in prison have higher rates of drug use than men (Harlow, 1999).

When considering the profiles of girls, Meda Chesney-Lind, Merry Morash, and Tia Stevens (2008) note that girls' early delinquent behavior is often less serious and less chronic than that of boys. Like women, delinquent girls have extensive histories of abuse, often have challenging familial relationships, and struggle with alcohol and other drug use. Many girls have age-inappropriate boyfriends, struggle academically, and, like their adult counterparts, have a number of physical and mental health problems.

Extent of Services for Women and Girls

Given the increased number of women and girls in the criminal justice system, relative to the 1990s, programs are increasingly developing services designed for women and girls. In a review of substance abuse treatment programs, Christine Grella (2008) noted that 41% of substance abuse programs report providing services geared specifically toward women. This suggests that the number of services designed for girls and women is increasing. In their review of gender-responsive programming, Chesney-Lin et al. (2008) found that most surveys of programs reported that less than 25% of services were designed for delinquent girls through the 1980s and 1990s.

Although the number of services aimed at women and girls in increasing, the quality of these programs is questionable. The reality is that relatively few programs for women and girls have been evaluated, and the existing evaluations often rely on small samples and fail to use experimental design. Moreover, services for women are often replicas of those for men. For example, in a survey of state prison systems, Patricia Van Voorhis and Lois Presser (2001) found that 36 states had classification systems in place that had not been tested for women. The assumption was made, however, that the systems worked equally well for women as they did for men.

A number of initiatives have been undertaken in an effort to improve the quality of knowledge and services. The National Institute of Corrections has been particularly influential in this regard and has funded a number of publications and tools aimed at improving practices. These include reports such as *Gender-Responsive Strategies: Research, Practice, and Guiding Principles for Women Offenders* and the development of a risk/needs assessment and a case management model designed specifically for women (Van Voorhis, 2012).

Despite these initiatives, there remains a great deal of debate in the existing literature concerning what approaches are most effective for women. Whereas many argue that the same strategies that work for women work for men, others argue for the need for gender-specific or gender-responsive strategies. In the next sections, we examine the emergence of gender-specific services, the differences between male and female offenders, and review the attempt to reconcile this perspective with the more general literature on what works.

Development of Gender-Specific and Gender-Responsive Strategies

Grella's (2008) review of the paradigm shift regarding the treatment of women is useful for understanding the development of gender-specific and gender-responsive services. As she notes, gender was not recognized as an important factor until the 1970s. Prior to that time, treatment programs were male centered, and it was readily assumed the same programs worked for both men and women. Partially a response to the women's movement, a shift occurred during the 1970s whereby gender differences were given greater regard. However, during this time, the focus tended to be on biological and psychological differences. Also during this time, greater attention began to be paid to the unique treatment needs of women, although the focus was often related to factors such as parenting and pregnancy. Over time, the growing emphasis on gender differences led to the emergence of gender-specific services in the 1980s. At this point, programs began to recognize the need for separate facilities and groups. Still, an emphasis remained on parenting, pregnancy, and child care. Finally, the 1990s saw the emergence of gender-responsive strategies. Advocated by researchers such as Stephanie Covington and Barbara Bloom, gender-responsive strategies are often conceptualized as including trauma-informed services utilizing a strengths-based approach and based on relational theory.

The terms *gender-specific* and *gender-responsive* are often used interchangeably. For our purposes, we refer to gender-specific services (GSS) throughout the chapter. It should be clear that a consideration of GSS is important given that much of the general treatment literature has been criticized for its failure to account for differences between men and women. Because researchers often treat men and women as identical, many of the assessments and programs identified with the "what works" or risk–need–responsivity (RNR) literature were designed for and tested on male offenders. Although many of these services have been found to be effective for women, gender-specific advocates would suggest that programs designed specifically for women and tested on women may be more effective than the RNR programs (Van Voorhis, 2012). In other words, GSS advocates might agree that RNR programs work for women, but they would argue that GSS programs work better.

The main debate between GSS and RNR researchers centers on whether the differences between male and female offenders necessitate the need for gender-specific services. RNR advocates contend that gender differences are a responsivity consideration, whereas GSS advocates contend that the differences result in distinct risk and need factors for females. For example, both camps agree that many female offenders have experienced trauma. However, whereas GSS advocates see trauma as a risk factor, RNR advocates see it as a responsivity consideration. In part, these differences are the result of contrasting theoretical perspectives on why women engage in criminal behavior.

Theoretical Perspectives

A number of theoretical perspectives explain why and how crime occurs. Depending on the perspective, the emphasis may be on biological factors, environmental factors, societal factors, or individual factors. The "what works" literature has been guided by individual-level theories of crime. As described by Jill Rettinger and Don Andrews (2010), a general personality and cognitive social learning (GPCSL) perspective offers a gender-neutral explanation of criminality. This perspective contends that criminal behavior is learned through interaction with others and that it is repeated, or not, depending on the reward or punishment associated with the behavior. Within this perspective, broader social conditions are thought to influence behavior indirectly. In other words, issues of race, age, gender, and social class have a relatively minimal effect on behavior compared to factors such as peers, attitudes, and personality.

In contrast, feminist theories of crime often highlight the role of gender in explaining criminal behavior among women (Rettinger & Andrews, 2010). This perspective often emphasizes the mental health problems and histories of trauma and abuse as explanations of criminal involvement. Kathleen Daly's (1992) work on female pathways to crime has helped to guide this perspective. She reviewed the presentence investigation reports of 40 women whose cases were being heard in felony court. Her review found that women often experienced physical or sexual abuse as children and had mothers who were distant or uncaring. The majority of women lacked both a high school education and the skills and training necessary for stable employment. Most of the women had at least one child, but few were raising their children at the time of the arrest. Finally, many of the women had substance abuse problems.

Based on her review, Daly (1992) identified five pathways to criminal behavior: street women, harmed and harming women, battered women, drug-connected women, and other, which some have argued could be viewed as economically motivated (Reisig, Holtfreter, & Morash, 2006). As described by Daly, street women generally have serious criminal histories and became criminal after fleeing abusive homes and becoming drug addicts. For these women, crime offers a means of survival. Harmed and harming women are those who experienced abuse/neglect as children and were often identified as "problem children." These women may be violent, especially when drinking, may be drug-addicted, and may have psychological problems. They are often unable to cope with problems. Whereas harmed and harming women experienced abuse as children, battered women experienced abuse in their romantic relationships. Although violence in relationships was a common theme for many of the women in Daly's study, battered women were unique in that their criminal involvement was a direct by-product of their violent relationship. Drug-connected women are those who use or sell drugs as a result of relationships with boyfriends or family members. In contrast to some of the other categories, these women were not drug addicts and did not have extensive criminal histories. The final group of women ("other") did not have substance abuse problems or abusive backgrounds. Instead, their crimes were largely economically motivated.

Emily Salisbury and Patricia Van Voorhis (2009) tested three distinct pathways: childhood victimization, relational model, and a social capital model. The childhood victimization model was somewhat similar to Daly's (1992) harmed and harming model, with the assumption that child abuse and mental illness precede substance abuse. The relational model emphasizes the role of dysfunctional intimate relationships, which lead to reduced levels of self-efficacy and increased likelihood of victimization. They hypothesized that this leads to depression and anxiety and substance abuse. The social and human capital model focused on the role of social relationships in producing human capital, which provides alternative opportunities to criminal behavior. Human capital includes factors such as education, self-efficacy, employment, and fewer financial difficulties. In their analysis, they found support for the notion that unhealthy relation-ships, mental illness, trauma, and substance abuse lead to recidivism. For example, although childhood abuse was not directly relatedly to recidivism, they found that it was related to depression, anxiety, and substance abuse, which were related to recidivism. Finally, they found that human capital was also important. As with men, financial and employment struggles, along with educational deficits, all contributed to recidivism. However, unlike men, they found that these needs were made worse coupled with a lack of social support through family and intimate relationships.

Across these different pathways, we can see patterns of abuse, trauma, drug addiction, and poor relationships in explaining criminal patterns of behavior. Feminist scholars have argued that these factors represent treatment needs of criminally involved women that the criminal justice system has largely failed to address (Belknap, 2007; Chesney-Lind, 2000). Moreover, it has been argued that treatment programs are often male centered and, when available to women, are often exact replicas of services offered to men or sexist in nature (e.g., those that increase domestic capabilities or increase femi-ninity) (Belknap, 2007). The challenge for treatment programs, then, is determining what works for women. Doing this requires that we seek to reconcile these two conflicting perspectives.

Reconciling GSS and RNR

Dana Hubbard and Betsy Matthews (2008) have attempted to reconcile the GSS literature and RNR literature as it relates to girls and juvenile delinquency. In terms of girls, they note six substantive differences between the two camps:

1. Theoretical foundation
2. Program goals
3. Consideration of risk
4. Assessment techniques
5. Criminogenic needs
6. Therapeutic approach

As we have seen, the GSS camp views delinquency and criminality among girls and women as a response to sexual abuse and societal factors that marginalize them. In contrast, the RNR camp views delinquency and crime as a response to individual-level factors drawing from social learning, control, and strain theories. Because of the theo-retical differences in why crime occurs, the goals of programming are also viewed differently across the two camps. Whereas the RNR camp firmly contends the purpose of services should be to reduce recidivism, the GSS camp views the empowerment of girls and women and an improved quality of life as the primary goals.

Ultimately, these differences in goals can help to explain the difference in approaches between the two camps. As noted by Hubbard and Mathews (2008), the GSS camp argues that high-risk girls are more of a risk to themselves rather than others and that their risk level should not be used to justify incarceration. In contrast, the RNR camp argues that risk level should be used to drive placement decisions. Moreover, the RNR camp, as has been discussed throughout this book, advocates for the use of objective, standardized assessments to determine risk and need. The GSS camp, in contrast, advocates for a qualitative review of social history to understand the female pathway into criminal behavior. Once assessed, the GSS camp advocates treatment for all needs, not just criminogenic needs, and suggests that the needs for girls and women differ from those of boys and men. In contrast, the RNR camp argues that the needs are similar across groups and that the emphasis should be placed on criminogenic needs rather than on non-criminogenic needs. Finally, the theoretical differences between the two camps translate to differences in the therapeutic approach. As we have seen, the RNR camp emphasizes the use of cognitive behavioral interventions. This perspective argues for action-based groups that are structured in nature. In contrast, the GSS camp argues for process-oriented groups that are based on relational and empowerment models.

As can be seen, many of the recommendations made by the GSS camp are inconsistent with the research we have reviewed in this book. We should not, however, simply discount the recommendations of the GSS scholars. Instead, it is important that we understand the limitations and criticisms of the competing literature. The GSS research is often criticized for using small samples; qualitative methods, which lack generalizability; and outcome measures other than recidivism (Dowden & Andrews, 1999). At the same time, the RNR literature is often criticized for relying on male-centered samples and assuming that the findings hold true for women and girls. For example, much of the RNR principles derive from meta-analyses, which are largely based on studies that often use male-only or male-dominated samples. Moreover, many of the programs tested within the RNR camp were originally designed for male offenders.

Although both camps suffer limitations, there is evidence that many of the recommendations made by the RNR camp are empirically supported. For example, Dowden and Andrews (1999) conducted a meta-analysis to test the RNR principles for women. As evidence of the limited research on women, they were only able to find 26 studies that used women-only or predominately female samples with a comparison group and an outcome measure related to recidivism. Consistent with the more general meta-analysis on effective interventions (Andrews et al., 1990), Andrews and Dowden found support for the risk, need, and responsivity principles. Figure 9.4 illustrates their findings for the female-only samples. As can be seen, as with the more general meta-analysis, the same principles hold true. That is, programs for women are more effective when they provide human service, target high-risk women for more intensive services, target criminogenic needs, and utilize cognitive behavioral or social learning approaches.

Although the RNR principles appear to be supported for women, it is imperative that we consider them within the context of the GSS literature and gender differences. Doing so should help to make programs even more effective in working with women. In the next section, we more closely consider the role of RNR as it relates to female offenders.

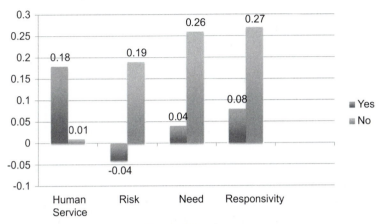

FIGURE 9.4 RNR and women.

What Works for Women?

Risk Assessment

As we see from Dowden and Andrews (1999), the role of risk matters for women. The question becomes, How do we best measure risk? There is ample evidence that the basic risk factors discussed elsewhere throughout this text hold true for women. As with men, antisocial attitudes, antisocial peers, poor family relationships, substance abuse, and criminal history are important for women (Dowden & Andrews, 1999). Moreover, commonly used risk assessments such as the Level of Service Inventory–Revised (LSI-R) have been found to predict female recidivism (Smith, Cullen, & Latessa, 2009). However, there is some criticism that these male-based instruments may overclassify women and ignore risk factors relevant to women (Van Voorhis, Wright, Salisbury, & Bauman, 2010).

Matthews and Hubbard (2008) recommend using a traditional risk/needs assessment and supplementing it with assessments of other factors known to be important for girls and women. In other words, rather than focus on one area or the other, use both gender-neutral and gender-responsive instruments. A collaboration between the National Institute of Corrections and researchers at the University of Cincinnati sought to develop and test the usefulness of a gender-based supplement to gender-neutral risk assessments. Using a sample of women probationers, prisoners, and those in pre-release units, Van Voorhis and colleagues (2010) examined whether supplementing the LSI-R with gender-responsive items improves predictions of recidivism. Gender-responsive measures included parental stress, self-efficacy, relationship dysfunction, adult physical abuse, unsafe housing, anxiety/depression, current psychosis, anger/hostility, family support, and educational assets. Consistent with prior research, they found that the LSI-R, composed of gender-neutral factors, predicted recidivism. However, they found that adding gender-responsive factors to the model helped to improve its predictive validity.

One limitation to the study by Van Voorhis et al. (2010) is that the nature and importance of gender-responsive factors varied depending on the sample used (prison, probation, and pre-release) and site (Maui, Minnesota, and Missouri). This limitation does not mean the findings should be ignored; rather, more research is needed to fully understand the types of gender-responsive factors that should be included in supplements to gender-neutral risk assessments.

Targeting Criminogenic Needs

In addition to identifying appropriate risk factors, it is important to consider the role of criminogenic needs in terms of treatment planning. As we have seen throughout this book, common treatment targets should include changing criminal thinking, improving problem solving, reducing antisocial peers, reducing substance abuse, improving family communication, and providing vocational training. All of these factors remain true for women. However, as noted by Van Voorhis and colleagues (2010), criminal thinking may be less important for women compared to factors such as substance abuse and relationships. Specifically, they concluded that substance abuse, economic factors, educational deficits, parenting, and mental health needs are among the most important treatment needs for women in the community. For women in prison, trauma, dysfunctional relationships, and mental health concerns are critical needs.

Ultimately, the criminogenic needs identified by Van Voorhis et al. (2010) can be largely viewed as consistent with both the RNR literature and the GSS literature. For example, although parenting is rarely identified as a criminogenic need in the RNR literature, the reality is that many of the skills included in a parenting class are often emphasized in other groups. Specifically, skills related to decision making, problem solving, understanding the feelings of others, and listening are commonly addressed in groups such as Thinking for a Change and can also be used in parenting classes.

The larger debate involves factors such as trauma and mental health needs. RNR scholars generally view these factors within the context of responsivity. As a reminder, responsivity refers to the general notion that we need to match the characteristics of the offender to the characteristics of the facilitator and treatment. Doing so helps to increase the likelihood of successful program completion and, therefore, remaining crime-free. When we consider the pathways literature, issues such as trauma and mental health are a consistent theme in explaining why women and girls become criminal. The question, then, is whether we address these factors as criminogenic needs or responsivity considerations.

The research by Van Voorhis et al. (2010) provides evidence that we should address these as criminogenic needs, at least for some women. The issue then becomes the method for addressing them. Rather than using client-centered groups to process past traumas, we argue that trauma and mental health should be targeted by providing groups related to coping skills and the identification of triggers for when these factors are likely to lead to substance abuse or other criminal behaviors. Learning to manage these factors becomes a target that should be amenable to both groups.

Responsivity

As noted in Chapter 6, responsivity involves the approach with how we provide treatment. As you saw, responsivity involves both specific and general responsivity, both of which are aimed at removing barriers to success in treatment. Here, we review a few basic responsivity considerations important for the treatment of girls and women.

Cognitive Behavioral Interventions

There appears to be agreement between both camps that cognitive behavioral interventions are effective for women and girls (Covington & Bloom, 2006; Dowden & Andrews, 1999; Matthews & Hubbard, 2008). However, as noted by Matthews and Hubbard, the structure of the groups may need some modification. A typical cognitive behavioral therapy group should be very structured, with an emphasis on reviewing the previous group lesson, introducing a new topic, and rehearsing the new skill or behavior. Given the relational orientation of women and girls, Matthews and Hubbard suggest that some flexibility be built into the group protocol to allow for conversation between participants aimed at supporting one another's efforts. This does not mean that groups should allow for free-for-all conversation but, rather, time for reinforcement and mutual understanding of the challenges and benefits in applying the new skills, behaviors, and attitudes. This also means that facilitators need to be skilled at moving groups along to ensure the curricula are followed while allowing for peer support between participants.

Therapeutic Alliance

As with any treatment group, the development of a therapeutic alliance is also important for girls and women. A therapeutic alliance is generally defined as one in which there is agreement and collaboration between the facilitator and the client, along with the presence of a trusting and respectful relationship (Matthews & Hubbard, 2008). Given the challenges many women and girls have with relationships, having a therapeutic alliance can be critical for helping them to be successful within the group setting and beyond. This approach is supported within both the GSS literature and the RNR literature; however, relatively little training is given to correctional staff on how to develop these helping relationships (Taxman, 2002). Programs should work to hire staff with characteristics supportive of developing a therapeutic alliance, including being empathetic, genuine, and accepting (Miller & Rollnick, 1991).

Mental Health

Although mental health issues such as depression and anxiety can be criminogenic needs for some women, they can be responsivity considerations for others. When working with women, it is important to assess the impact of mental health on recidivism. Whether there is a direct impact or not, however, it is also important to consider how mental health may make it more difficult to achieve treatment goals for all women. The high rates of trauma and abuse can often contribute to a number of mental health challenges; post-traumatic stress disorder and depression are two examples of factors that may pose a challenge to success. Program staff should be trained to recognize the signs of these factors and provide treatment aimed at reducing the symptoms (Matthews & Hubbard, 2008).

Single-Sex Groups

A review of the research on substance abuse treatment by Grella (2008) makes it clear that women have better outcomes when they are placed in single-sex groups. Compared to women in co-ed groups, women in single-sex programs tend to utilize more treatment services and treatment has a greater impact on drug use and legal outcomes. An-Pyng Sun (2006) also found that women in single-sex groups are more likely to complete treatment compared to those in mixed groups.

Why are single-sex groups important? According to Covington and Bloom (2006), single-sex groups make it easier for women to share their experiences, thoughts, and feelings; help women to become empowered; and allow a safe place for women who have experienced sexual abuse. Andrews and Bonta (2006) are equally supportive of this position in their book *The Psychology of Criminal Conduct*. On this point, then, both groups readily agree on the need for single-sex services.

Summary

- The number of women and girls under supervision has increased since the 1980s but has begun to decline in recent years.
- The identification of effective treatment strategies for girls and women has been subject to a great deal of debate.
- Feminist scholars often point to the role of trauma and abuse in explaining female criminality, whereas gender-neutral scholars often point to individual factors, including peer associations, antisocial attitudes, and antisocial personality characteristics, in explaining criminality.
- Research suggests the need for both gender-neutral risk factors (e.g., attitudes, associations, family, and substance abuse) and gender-responsive factors (e.g., trauma, mental health, and relationships) in predicting recidivism.
- Programs should target criminogenic needs, including substance abuse, employment, education, and relationships.
- There should be recognition that factors such as trauma and mental health may be criminogenic for some women. Efforts should be made to teach women prosocial techniques to manage and cope with the challenges presented by these factors.

- Programs should provide separate groups for women and girls. As with male groups, female groups should rely on cognitive behavioral interventions, with some allowance for peer support within the group setting.

References

Andrews, D. A., & Bonta, J. (2006). *The psychology of criminal conduct.* Cincinnati, OH: Anderson.

Andrews, D. A., Zinger, L., Hoge, R. D., Bonta, J., Gendreau, P., & Cullen, F. T. (1990). Does correctional treatment work? A clinically relevant and psychologically informed meta-analysis. *Criminology, 28,* 369–404.

Belknap, J. (2007). *The invisible woman: Gender, crime and justice* (3rd ed.). Stamford, CT: Wadsworth.

Bloom, B., Owen, B., & Covington, S. (2003). *Gender-responsive strategies: Research, practice, and guiding principles for women offenders.* Washington, DC: National Institute of Corrections.

Carson, E. A., & Sabol, W. J. (2012). *Prisoners in 2011* (NCJ 239808). Washington, DC: Bureau of Justice Statistics.

Chesney-Lind, M. (2000). Women and the criminal justice system: Gender matters. In *Topics in community corrections: Responding to women offenders in the community* (pp. 7–10). Washington, DC: National Institute of Corrections.

Chesney-Lind, M., Morash, M., & Stevens, T. (2008). Girls troubles, girls' delinquency, and gender responsive programming: A review. *Australian & New Zealand Journal of Criminology, 41,* 162–189.

Covington, S. S., & Bloom, B. E. (2006). Gender-responsive treatment and services in correctional settings. *Women and Therapy, 29(3/4),* 9–33.

Daly, K. (1992). Women's pathways to felony court: Feminist theories of lawbreaking and problems of representation. *Southern California Review of Law and Women's Studies, 2,* 11–52.

Dowden, C., & Andrews, D. A. (1999). What works for female offenders: A meta-analytic review. *Crime & Delinquency, 45,* 438–452.

Federal Bureau of Investigation. (2012). Crime in the United States, 2011. Retrieved April 2013 from http://www.fbi.gov/about-us/cjis/ucr/crime-in-the-u.s/2011/crime-in-the-u.s.-2011/tables/table-42.

Grella, C. E. (2008). From generic to gender-responsive treatment: Changes in social policies, treatment services, and outcomes of women in substance abuse treatment. *Journal of Psychoactive Drugs, 40,* 327–343.

Harlow, C. W. (1999). *Prior abuse reported by inmates and probationers* (NCJ 172879). Washington, DC: Bureau of Justice Statistics.

Hubbard, D. J., & Matthews, B. (2008). Reconciling the difference between the "gender-responsive" and the "what works" literatures to improve services for girls. *Crime & Delinquency, 54,* 225–258.

Knoll, C., & Sickmund, M. (2012). *Delinquency cases in juvenile court, 2009.* Washington, DC: Office of Juvenile Justice and Delinquency Prevention.

Maruschak, L. M., & Parks, E. (2012). *Probation and parole in the United States, 2011* (NCJ 239686). Washington, DC: Bureau of Justice Statistics.

Matthews, B., & Hubbard, D. J. (2008). Moving ahead: Five essential elements for working effectively with girls. *Journal of Criminal Justice, 36,* 494–502.

Miller, W. R., & Rollnick, S. (1991). Motivational interviewing: Preparing people to change addictive behavior. New York: Guilford.

Puzzanchera, C., & Kang, W. (2013). Easy access to juvenile court statistics: 1985–2010. Available at http://www.ojjdp.gov/ojstatbb/ezajcs.

Reisig, M. D., Holtfreter, K., & Morash, M. (2006). Assessing recidivism risk across female pathways to crime. *Justice Quarterly, 23,* 384–405.

Rettinger, L. J., & Andrews, D. A. (2010). General risk and need, gender specificity, and the recidivism of female offenders. *Criminal Justice and Behavior, 37,* 29–46.

Salisbury, E. J., & Van Voorhis, P. (2009). Gendered pathways: A quantitative investigation of women probationers' paths to incarceration. *Criminal Justice and Behavior, 36,* 541–566.

Sickmund, M., Sladky, T. J., Kang, W., & Puzzanchera, C. (2011). Easy access to the census of juveniles in residential placement. Available at http://www.ojjdp.gov/ojstatbb/ezacjrp.

Smith, P., Cullen, F. T., & Latessa, E. J. (2009). Can 17,737 women be wrong? A meta-analysis of the LSI-R and recidivism for female offenders. *Criminology & Public Policy, 8,* 183–207.

Sun, A. (2006). Program factors related to women's substance abuse treatment retention and other outcomes: A review and critique. *Journal of Substance Abuse Treatment, 30,* 1–20.

Taxman, F. (2002). Supervision: Exploring the dimensions of effectiveness. *Federal Probation, 66,* 14–27.

Van Voorhis, P. (2012). On behalf of women offenders: Women's place in the science of evidence-based practice. *Criminology & Public Policy, 11,* 111–145.

Van Voorhis, P., & Presser, L. (2001). *Classification of women offenders: A national assessment of current practices.* Washington, DC: National Institute of Corrections, U.S. Department of Justice.

Van Voorhis, P., Wright, E. M., Salisbury, E., & Bauman, A. (2010). Women's risk factors and their contributions to existing risk/needs assessment: The current status of a gender-responsive supplement. *Criminal Justice and Behavior, 37,* 261–288.

10

What Works in Prison

Introduction

Nearly 1.6 million people older than the age of 18 years were housed in state and federal prisons in the United States in 2011 (Carson & Sabol, 2012). In addition, nearly 90,000 juveniles were incarcerated in 2007 (Sickmund, 2010). Although the number of incarcerated persons in the United States is declining, the simple fact remains that the United States continues to have one of the highest rates of incarceration, with 492 of every 100,000 residents incarcerated. Among individuals convicted of felony offenses, 40% are sent to prison and 30% are sent to jail (Durose & Langan, 2007). The majority of these individuals return home at some point; on average, felony offenders sent to prison receive a sentence of approximately 5 years (Durose & Langan, 2007). Often justified as a deterrent, there is ample evidence that incarceration does not reduce criminal behavior and some evidence that it may actually increase it. This chapter explores the impact of incarceration and the need for effective classification and treatment within our correctional institutions.

The Impact of Incarceration

Theoretically, people are sent to prison in an effort to prevent them from committing future crime. The "get-tough" movement of the 1980s was largely premised on the notion that imprisonment could have a deterrent effect. That is, increasing the cost of crime would prevent people from engaging in future criminal activity. However, there is little evidence that this is the case. In fact, it is clear that those leaving prison often engage in subsequent criminal behavior. In 2002, researchers at the Bureau of Justice Statistics (BJS) released a report detailing the recidivism rates of approximately 300,000 offenders who had been released from prison in 1994 (Langan & Levin, 2002). They found that 68% of prisoners were rearrested for a new crime within 3 years of their release and more than half returned to prison during that same time period for either a new crime or a technical violation. Many of those who reoffend do so quickly upon their release from prison; the same study found that 30% of those released from prison were rearrested within 3 months of their release.

The Pew Center on the States and the Association of State Correctional Administration conducted a survey of states to collect recidivism data for prisoners released in 1999 and in 2004 (Pew Center on the States, 2011). States were asked to report reincarceration rates using a 3-year follow-up period. The results were not much more encouraging than those of the BJS study. As illustrated in Figure 10.1, 45% of prisoners released in 1999 and 43% of those released in 2004 returned to prison within 3 years of their release.

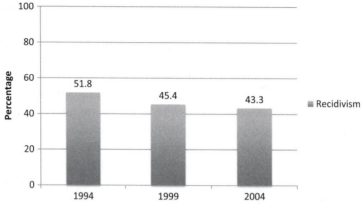

FIGURE 10.1 Recidivism rates of prisoners. *Source: Langan, P. A., & Levin, D. J. (2002). Recidivism of prisoners released in 1994 (NCJ 193427). Washington, DC: Bureau of Justice Statistics; and Pew Center on the States. (2011). State of recidivism: The revolving door of America's prisons. Washington, DC: Pew Charitable Trusts.*

A great deal of research has attempted to explain the high rates of recidivism among those released from prison. Some have suggested that the recidivism rates simply reflect the characteristics of those sent to prison. In other words, people sent to prison may be more prone to criminality. However, others have argued that the prison experience may actually have a criminogenic effect. In contrast to the notion that prisoners are simply more prone to recidivism, a criminogenic effect would indicate that prison itself increases the likelihood of recidivism. To test this idea, Cheryl Jonson (2010) conducted a meta-analysis examining the impact of imprisonment and found that incarceration increased recidivism 14% compared to community-based sanctions. These findings suggest there is something about the prison environment that makes people more likely to be criminal upon their release from prison. To be fair, the research on the criminogenic effect of prison is inconclusive. In a review of studies, Daniel Nagin and colleagues found that some findings point to a null effect (Nagin, Cullen, & Jonson, 2009). A null effect means that prison does not make people better or worse; behavior stays relatively stable despite the prison experience.

Although the true impact of imprisonment is yet to be determined, it does seem safe to conclude that prison, as a general rule, does not improve matters, and it often makes things worse. The question, then, becomes Why? As outlined by Daniel Nagin and colleagues (2009), the negative effect of prison may be the result of several factors, including the environment, the stigma associated with incarceration, and the failure to provide appropriate treatment within prison. Although attempts to manage the stigma of incarceration are being addressed through reentry efforts (see Chapter 11), it is important that we consider the role of the prison environment in understanding the high rates of recidivism.

What is it about the prison environment that might make people worse? To answer this question, some have examined the impact of prison security level on recidivism. Although prison security level does not seem to predict misconduct, it does appear to be related to recidivism (Camp & Gaes, 2004). For example, Gerald Gaes and Scott Camp (2009) tested the impact of placing high-risk inmates in level 1 (less secure) and level 3 (more secure) prisons in California. They found that offenders placed in the more secure institutions were 31% more likely to return to prison compared to those who had been randomly placed in the level 1 prisons. This suggests that the harsh conditions associated with more secure facilities may contribute to a criminogenic effect. This is of concern given that less than one-third of state and federal inmates are held in minimum-security institutions (Stephan, 2008).

Others have hypothesized that the prison experience leads to a number of crime-inducing strains, including a loss of autonomy and privacy, limited access to friends and family, the loss of materials and goods, and the loss of heterosexual relationships. In addition to experiencing these deprivations, inmates often struggle to find satisfying work assignments; are housed in crowded conditions; have a great deal of idle time; and are exposed to intimidation, threats, and victimization by both prison staff and other inmates (Blevins, Listwan, Cullen, & Jonson, 2010). To test this, Shelley Listwan and colleagues interviewed more than 1,600 residents of halfway houses in Ohio. They asked residents about their recent prison experience, with an emphasis on whether they had witnessed or experienced victimization. They found that those who viewed prison as hostile were significantly more likely to be rearrested in the community and more likely to return to prison. In addition, the odds of returning to prison were 32% greater for those who had been victimized while in prison (Listwan, Sullivan, Agnew, Cullen, & Colvin, 2013).

The issue of violence in prison is clearly a concern, especially when we consider its link to recidivism. Although the extent of violence is difficult to assess, it is clear that those in prison live with the threat of violence on a nearly daily basis. The *Census of State and Federal Correctional Facilities* (Stephan & Karberg, 2003) revealed that 34,000 inmate-on-inmate assaults were reported in 2000, representing a 32% increase from 1995. During the same year, 606 major incidents (involving more than five inmates) were reported. A review of prison violence by James Byrne and Don Hummer (2007a) suggests that these numbers likely underestimate the true extent of violence in prisons. Their estimates place the true number of assaults closer to 300,000.

As summarized by Byrne and Hummer (2007a), the source of violence in prison is multifaceted. As expected, prison management, staffing, and design issues are all related to the likelihood of violence. However, it is also important to note that both ineffective classification strategies and a lack of effective programming are also related to prison violence. Although much more research is needed in this area, it appears that drawing on the "what works" principles can theoretically help to manage prison violence and reduce subsequent recidivism (Byrne & Hummer, 2007b).

Clearly, it is not sound public policy to continue placing people into prison without considering strategies for success upon release. Although states such as California are taking steps to reduce their prison population, the simple fact remains that a significant number of people are incarcerated each year and approximately 95% of those return to the community (Hughes & Wilson, 2002). As noted in Chapter 11, reentry programs are designed to assist people to successfully return to the community. However, as you will see, many of these programs have relatively low rates of success. Although a number of resources are available aimed at improving reentry services (Pew Center on the States, 2011), it is likely that success is also tied to what happens in prison. Improving the odds of success for those in prison requires a number of changes. Considered from a "what works" perspective, it is important that we use effective classification systems and provide inmates with effective programs aimed at reducing criminogenic needs.

Classification and Assessment

The classification process is of paramount importance for our prisons. Just as treatment programs should assess offenders for risk and needs (see Chapter 2), so should prisons. Although treatment programs primarily use assessment for case management and placement decisions, prisons must be aware of both security and treatment considerations within the facilities. Classification often occurs at two levels: external and internal. External classification refers to decision making regarding custody level (e.g., maximum security and medium security) and is used to assign inmates to a particular institution within the prison system. Once assigned to an institution, internal classification takes place. Whereas many units within a given institution serve the general population, others are specialized and may address specific treatment needs, medical needs, or other considerations. This information, in concert with security concerns and bed space, is often used to assign inmates to a unit within the institution (Austin, 2003).

The role of risk should play an essential part in both internal and external classification. Risk is generally conceptualized as getting into trouble again. Within institutional settings, risk is often conceptualized as risk of escape or other forms of institutional misconduct. Institutions often rely on factors specific to these behaviors rather than the more general set of risk factors. For example, static predictors of prison misconduct include age, gender, and a history of violence. In general, older inmates and women are less likely to get into trouble, whereas those with a recent history of violence are more likely to continue to engage in violent behavior. Dynamic factors associated with misconduct include gang membership, program participation, and recent disciplinary action. As with a history of violence, those who have recently been in trouble or are members of gangs are more likely to be in trouble. In contrast, those who have participated in programming are less likely to get into trouble (Austin, 2003).

One challenge in classifying inmates along risk level is the use of antiquated risk assessments. Although prisons often define risk rather narrowly, they would be well served to use the types of assessments discussed in Chapter 2. The use of assessments that rely on both static and dynamic factors allows prison officials to identify the risk of getting into trouble while in prison and also allows for the identification of treatment needs. As a reminder, examples of these types of assessments include the Level of Service Inventory–Revised (LSI-R; Andrews & Bonta, 1998), the Psychopathy Checklist–Revised

(PCL-R; Hare 1991), and the Violence Risk Appraisal Guide (VRAG; Harris, Rice, & Quinsey, 1993). In addition to these well-known assessments, others have used the HCR-20 (Webster, Eaves, Douglas, & Wintrup, 1995), which, like the VRAG, is designed to predict violent behavior.

A great deal of research has tested whether risk assessments can predict prison misconduct. The results are largely encouraging. Daryl Kroner and Jeremy Mills (2001) tested the predictive validity of the LSI-R, PCL-R, VRAG, HCR-20, and the Lifestyle Criminality Screening Form (LCSF; Walters, White, & Denney, 1991). They found that the instruments predicted institutional misconduct along with convictions and revocations following release from prison. This is important because proper classification can help to reduce in-prison misconduct and subsequent recidivism.

A second challenge regarding the use of assessments involves the unique nature of the prison setting. Some instruments, such as the LSI-R, are not explicitly designed for a prison setting, and many items are less intuitive with regard to scoring. For example, the LSI-R, like most risk/need assessments, has a number of items relating to community involvement, including employment and accommodations. Scoring these items can be challenging because prisoners often have little control over such factors. However, David Simourd (2004) examined the utility of the LSI-R for long-term prisoners. He defined prisoners as those with sentences greater than 2 years and scored dynamic items (e.g., employment) based on the current circumstances. Although he found the sample to be higher risk than community-based samples, he concluded that the LSI-R was predictive of recidivism using a 15-month follow-up period. He cautions, however, that particular attention needs to be paid to the scoring criteria to ensure completed assessments are valid and reliable.

In response to the challenges associated with the "one size fits all" assessment tools, researchers at the University of Cincinnati created the Ohio Risk Assessment System (ORAS; Latessa, Smith, Lemke, Makarios, & Lowenkamp, 2010). As discussed in Chapter 2, the ORAS is different from other tools because it has a unique risk assessment for each point in the criminal justice system. This means that the assessment upon entry into prison looks different from the assessment upon release from prison. By making the assessment specific to the point in time, some of the difficulties in using tools such as the LSI-R are minimized.

Despite the challenges associated with assessment in a prison setting, it is important that assessment be an integral part of the process. In addition to identifying risk level and appropriate security classification, assessments can also identify the treatment needs of inmates. Rather than waiting until prisoners are released to begin treating them, it is important that treatment is provided while in the prison setting.

The Need for Treatment

As has been discussed throughout this text, with regard to changing behaviors, treatment is more effective than sanctions. The same is true within our prisons. Providing effective treatment programs can help to reduce prison misconducts and to increase the likelihood of success upon reentry (French & Gendreau, 2006).

The characteristics of effective treatment programs are similar to those in other settings. A meta-analysis by Sheila French and Paul Gendreau (2006) examined the impact of prison-based treatment programs on misconduct and also explored the characteristics associated with effective treatment programs. Using 68 studies, they found a mean effect size of 14%, indicating participation in treatment can reduce recidivism. Next, they examined the effects of specific types of treatment. Consistent with the literature on effective interventions, they found that behavioral programs had the greatest effect. As illustrated in Figure 10.2, behavioral programs reduced misconduct 26% compared to nonbehavioral programs, which reduced misconduct 10%. Educational and vocational programs, along with those unspecified types of programs, did not have an impact on misconduct.

In addition to examining type of treatment, French and Gendreau (2006) also looked at the treatment targets. As we recall from previous chapters, the needs principle tells us that programs must target factors that are related to the risk of recidivism to reduce the likelihood of future misconduct. French and Gendreau tested this principle in the prison setting by comparing programs based on the number of needs they target. As shown in Figure 10.3, programs that target three to eight criminogenic needs reduced misconduct by 29%. Those that targeted one or two criminogenic needs reduced misconduct by 16%, and those that failed to target criminogenic needs did not significantly reduce misconduct.

It is not surprising that the research on prison-based programming is consistent with the more general literature on effective interventions. However, although it has been clearly established that treatment can help to reduce misconduct and recidivism, there are relatively few programs available for inmates. The BJS periodically conducts a census of prisons and other secure facilities to learn more about the institutions in the

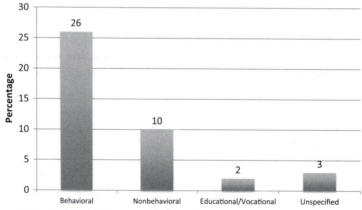

FIGURE 10.2 **Mean effect of treatment type on misconduct.** *Source: French, S., & Gendreau, P. (2006). Reducing prison misconducts: What works! Criminal Justice and Behavior, 33, 185–218.*

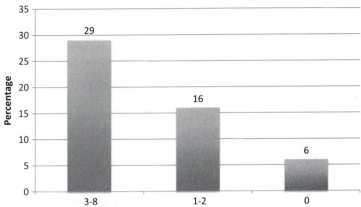

FIGURE 10.3 Effect of number of criminogenic needs on misconduct. *Source: French, S., & Gendreau, P. (2006). Reducing prison misconducts: What works!* Criminal Justice and Behavior, 33, *185–218.*

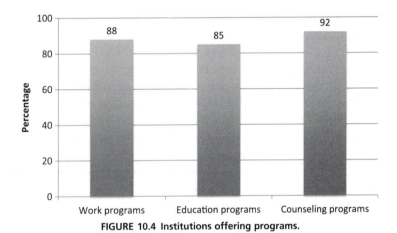

FIGURE 10.4 Institutions offering programs.

United States. The most recent census was conducted in 2005 (Stephan, 2008). Institutions were asked to report on the types of work, educational, and counseling programs provided to inmates. As indicated in Figure 10.4, the majority of institutions provide work, educational, or counseling programs. All but 40 institutions offer some type of counseling program. The most common types of programs are life skills and community adjustment, drug/alcohol dependency, and employment training (Figure 10.5).

Although it is clear that many programs target criminogenic needs, it is important that prisons make a distinction between *programs* and *activities*. For our purposes, programs refer to services aimed at reducing recidivism. In contrast, activities refer to services aimed at helping to manage the pains of imprisonment by keeping people busy (e.g., recreation, yoga, and puppies on patrol). In the following sections, we review the evidence on the effectiveness of treatment programs in prison.

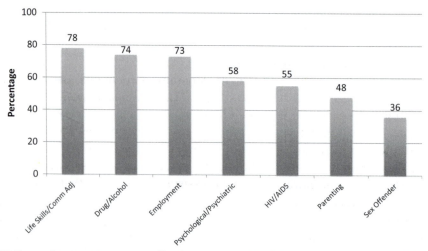

FIGURE 10.5 Types of treatment programs offered in correctional facilities. *Source: Stephan, J. J. (2008).* Census of state and federal correctional facilities, 2005 *(NCJ 222182). Washington, DC: Bureau of Justice Statistics.*

Drug Treatment Programs

As noted previously, nearly 75% of correctional facilities offer some type of substance abuse treatment (Stephan, 2008). The types of programs offered within prisons range from 12-step programming and drug education to group counseling and medical management programs. Although there is limited support for drug education programs and self-help programs (Pearson & Lipton, 1999), a meta-analysis conducted by Mitchell and colleagues (2007) found support for residential substance abuse treatment (RSAT), therapeutic communities (TCs), and group counseling. Specifically, they concluded that participation in drug treatment was associated with a 42% recidivism rate for the treatment group compared to a 50% recidivism rate for the comparison group. Let us examine each of these types of programs in more detail.

Established in 1994, RSAT is administered by the Bureau of Justice Assistance, which provides funding, training, and technical assistance to criminal justice agencies. The RSAT grant program is designed to assist jurisdictions in implementing prison- and jail-based substance abuse programs, along with aftercare and post-release treatment programs. To date, more than $500 million has been spent on RSAT programs throughout all 50 states, along with the District of Columbia and U.S. territories (Bureau of Justice Assistance, 2005).

According to the grant program, RSAT programs should last between 6 and 12 months and are designed to isolate prisoners from the general population. This occurs in two ways. First, program participants are housed with other participants and away from the general population. Second, only those nearing their release date are eligible for participation. Because of this, participants are released to the community upon program completion instead of returning to the general prison population. It is expected that these programs target substance abuse along with other related needs, including cognitive skills, social skills, and vocational skills. Although each program is unique, they are expected to provide individual and group counseling.

As we recall from previous chapters, treatment programs are most effective when they target higher-risk offenders. A review of program participants between April and September 2012 indicates that more than 95% of the participants were identified as high risk and having high substance abuse treatment need (Steyee, 2012). More than half of the program funding was spent on substance abuse treatment and cognitive and behavioral services. In addition to SA and cognitive behavioral therapy (CBT), the programs also provided employment, housing, mental health services, and other services (Steyee, 2012). A report prepared for the Bureau of Justice Assistance indicated that nearly 50,000 individuals entered RSAT services between January 2012 and March 2012. Among these, 71% successfully completed the program and 72% remained arrest-free in their first year of release (CSR Incorporated, 2012). In 2012, the majority of jail participants were released from the program within 6 months, whereas prison-based participants generally took 4–9 months to complete the program.

Although the nature of RSAT programming varies across institution, Mitchell and colleagues (2007) found that the bulk of RSAT programs could be described as TCs. In fact, they found that virtually all of the RSAT programs in their meta-analysis could be described as a TC. A TC is an intensive drug treatment program in which all participants are housed together in a separate treatment unit. This helps to minimize the influence of other inmates who are not participating in treatment, thereby reducing the criminogenic effect of prison. In contrast to a basic counseling group, a core component of a TC is the involvement of the program participants in running the program. TC participants often help to lead treatment groups and hold other members accountable for their behavior. A typical TC lasts between 6 and 12 months (Mitchel et al., 2007).

Harry Wexler, Gregory Falkin, and Douglas Lipton (1990) conducted an evaluation of the Stay'n Out program, a prison-based TC that opened in 1977 in New York. They compared recidivism rates of those who participated in the TC to those who received traditional counseling, participated in milieu therapy, and those who volunteered to participate in the TC but never entered it. Although many point to this study as evidence of the effectiveness of the TC model, the findings are actually mixed. Wexler and colleagues found that both male and female TC participants had lower rates of arrest than members of the other groups. However, the groups did not differ in terms of successful completion of parole or time to arrest, and multivariate analyses, controlling for factors such as age and criminal history, were not significant. Thus, these early findings provided some preliminary support for the model.

As a result of the early findings, a great deal of support was provided to the development and implementation of TCs. The Bureau of Justice Assistance funded Project REFORM and the Office of Treatment Improvement created Project RECOVERY, both of which were aimed at helping states develop programs for prison-based treatment (DeLeon & Wexler, 2009). These initiatives, along with RSAT funding and the early empirical support, led to a number of TCs being implemented throughout the United States. One example of a TC is the Amity TC in California. It was implemented as a demonstration project in 1990 and has been subject to a great deal of research.

Like many TCs, the Amity program was designed for inmates nearing the end of their prison sentence and generally lasted 9–12 months. The program consisted of three phases. The first phase included observation, assessment, and orientation to the TC. Participants were expected to assimilate to the TC through encounter groups and an introduction to the TC process. Encounter groups are often run by more senior participants to discuss the progress, or lack of progress, among other participants and to bring attention to behaviors and attitudes that are in need of adjustment (Gatson-Rowe, 2011). The second phase consisted of education, counseling, and encounter groups. The third phase of the program consisted of preparing for release from prison and reentry into the community, planning and decision-making skills, and discharge planning. Upon release from prison, some graduates volunteered to go to a residential treatment program for 6–12 months. The Vista program provided a continuation of the Amity TC program.

The Amity program has been subject to a number of evaluations. The early evaluations found that program participants had lower reincarceration rates than the control group at both 12 and 24 months post-release and had longer time in the community until reincarceration. However, program participation did not have a significant impact 36 months post-release (Wexler, DeLeon, Thomas, Kressel, & Peters, 1999; Wexler, Melnick, Lowe, & Peters, 1999). Beyond simply comparing the two groups, Wexler et al. (1999) also examined the role of aftercare. The successful completion of aftercare was significantly related to lower rates of recidivism, even 3 years post-release. As illustrated in Figure 10.6, only 27% of participants completing aftercare returned to prison compared to more than 69% of all the other groups. Michael Prendergast and colleagues (2004) followed the same group for an additional 2 years and found that the trend continued. Participants who had

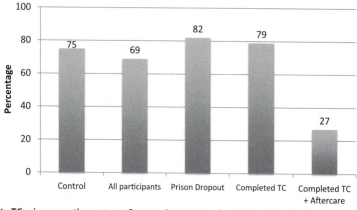

FIGURE 10.6 **Amity TC reincarceration rates at 3 years.** *Source: Wexler, H. K., Melnick, G., Lowe, L., & Peters, J. (1999). Three-year reincarceration outcomes for Amity in-prison therapeutic community and after in California.* Prison Journal, 79, 321–336.

completed aftercare were significantly more likely to have a job and significantly less likely to have returned to prison compared to other members of the treatment group 5 years post-release.

More research is needed on the TC model. To be sure, there are a number of studies in support of the model. For example, Wayne Walsh (2007) conducted an evaluation of five TCs in California and found that participation reduced both rearrest and reincarceration 2 years post-release. A study of a TC in Delaware by James Inciardi and colleagues (2004) found that participation in a TC increased the likelihood of being both drug-free and arrest-free 5 years after release. Similarly, the meta-analysis conducted by Mitchell et al. (2007) found the TC model to be effective overall.

However, other studies have continued to point to deficiencies, particularly those with longer follow-up periods. Like the Prendergast study, Sheldon Zhang and colleagues (2011) evaluated a TC using a 5-year follow-up. As with the Amity findings, they failed to find any evidence of a treatment effect. More than 72% of the treatment group and the comparison group returned to prison within 5 years. Unlike the Amity study, participation in aftercare did not seem to have an effect because 69% of those receiving aftercare also returned to prison within 5 years.

Perhaps one of the challenges for TCs and other drug treatment programs in prison involves the varied nature of participants. Steve Belenko and Jordon Peugh (2005) examined the treatment needs of inmates. They analyzed the data from the 1997 *Survey of Inmates in State Correctional Facilities* conducted by the BJS. Their analyses suggested that 70% of male inmates and 77% of female inmates need drug treatment. However, although prison programs tend to provide identical treatment to all participants, Belenko and Peugh's findings indicate that the type of treatment needed ranges from short-term to residential treatment (Figure 10.7). Just as with community-based treatment programs, it is important that our prisons provide treatment that is matched to the needs of the participants. Doing so will likely increase the effectiveness of these programs.

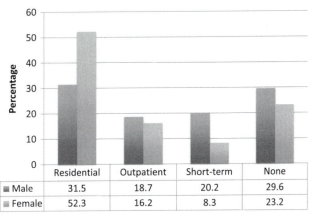

	Residential	Outpatient	Short-term	None
Male	31.5	18.7	20.2	29.6
Female	52.3	16.2	8.3	23.2

FIGURE 10.7 Drug treatment needs by gender. *Source: Belenko, S., & Peugh, J. (2005). Estimating drug treatment needs among state prison inmates. Drug and Alcohol Dependence, 77, 269–281.*

Sex Offender Programs

Whereas a sizable number of inmates are in need of substance abuse treatment, others need sex offender treatment. The number of sex offenders in prison has increased approximately 21% since 2000, and in 2010 there were approximately 160,800 sex offenders in state facilities (Carson & Sabol, 2012). Although the numbers reflect a much smaller population, the need for treatment remains. As indicated in Chapter 8, sex offender treatment can reduce recidivism when done effectively. This is reflected in the growing number of treatment programs available for sex offenders. There were only 90 prison-based sex offender treatment programs in 1994 (Freeman-Longo, Bird, Stevenson, & Fiske, 1994). By 2005, however, 662 programs were in place (Stephen, 2008).

As you may recall from Chapter 8, a meta-analysis by Friedrich Lösel and Martin Schmucker (2005) concluded that sex offenders who participated in treatment had 37% less sexual recidivism than those who did not receive treatment. Their study included prison-based programs (25), hospital programs (14), outpatient programs (29), and mixed setting programs (10). Despite the research indicating that prison-based programs often perform worse, Lösel and Schmucker did not find this to be true. Although the effect size for institutional programs was lower than that of other programs, the difference was not significant. This gives us evidence that prison-based sex offender treatment can be successful.

One example of an effective treatment program for sex offenders is the Transitional Sex Offender Treatment Program (SOTP) in the Minnesota Correctional Facility at Lino Lakes (Duwe & Goldman, 2009). The program is designed for inmates in the last year of their sentence and is intended to help them prepare for release into the community. Because of the emphasis on transition, participants continue to receive treatment services in a halfway house following their release from prison. Originally designed as a 30-bed facility in 1978, the program now has more than 150 beds. In addition to sex offender treatment, the program provides chemical dependency treatment as needed. The program is designed to be a cognitive behavioral program and targets moderate- to high-risk sex offenders. Participants are assessed using the Static-99, the Rapid Risk Assessment for Sex Offense Recidivism, and the Public Risk Monitoring tool.

Similar to the TC model, participants are housed separately from the general population and are expected to hold one another accountable. Participants are expected to receive 10–15 hours of treatment per week and remain in the program for 1–3 years. As summarized by Grant Duwe and Robin Goldman (2009), the main components of the program include the following:

- Assessment
- Group and individual therapy
- Substance abuse treatment as needed
- Family/support person education
- Pscyhoeducational groups

- Support groups
- Community meetings

As can be seen, the program adheres to many of the principles of effective interventions. Participants are required to spend an average of 6 hours per week in group therapy, which focuses on sex offending behavior. The psychoeducation groups meet three or four times a week for 12 weeks and include a number of topics, including emotions management, alcohol and drug education, cognitive restricting and criminal thinking, sexuality education, re-offense prevention, victim empathy, and grief.

In a comparison of program participants and untreated offenders, Duwe and Goldman (2009) found that program participants were less likely to recidivate and remained in the community, arrest-free, for longer periods of time. Figure 10.8 illustrates the differences in recidivism rates. Duwe and Goldman also considered the impact of treatment dropout versus treatment completion. Those who completed treatment were 33% less likely to be rearrested for a sex offense compared to those who did not participate. Dropping out of treatment did not have a significant impact. Consistent with other research, this suggests that treatment completion is an important predictor of success.

Similar to the Minnesota program, the Clearwater Program in Canada utilizes a cognitive behavioral approach and follows much of the "what works" literature. Whereas the Minnesota program lasts for 1–3 years, the Clearwater program is designed to last between 6 and 9 months. Participants are assessed on the Violence Risk Scale–Sexual Offender version and the Static-99 to determine risk of recidivism. During their time in the program, participants receive 20 hours of group and individual counseling per week, along with psychoeducational groups. Through the groups, participants' criminogenic needs are addressed. Additional groups may target education, work and life skills, family dynamics, relationships with others, community support, and attitudes and values

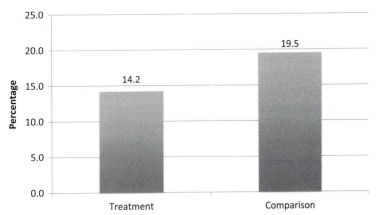

FIGURE 10.8 Average recidivism rates for sex offenders. *Source: Duwe, G., & Goldman, R. A. (2009). The impact of prison-based treatment on sex offender recidivism: Evidence from Minnesota. Sexual Abuse: A Journal of Research and Treatment, 21, 279–307.*

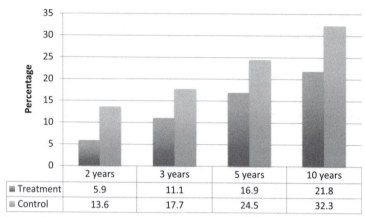

	2 years	3 years	5 years	10 years
■ Treatment	5.9	11.1	16.9	21.8
■ Control	13.6	17.7	24.5	32.3

FIGURE 10.9 Recidivism rates of sex offenders. *Source: Olver, M. E., Wong, S. C. P., & Nicholaichuk, T. P. (2009). Outcome evaluation of a high-intensity inpatient sex offender treatment program. Journal of Interpersonal Violence, 24, 522–536.*

toward women and children as needed. The program also takes responsivity considerations into account when making treatment decisions. As a result of the program's adherence to the "what works" literature, it has been accredited by the Correctional Service of Canada (Olver, Wong, & Nicholaichuk, 2009).

Mark Olver and colleagues (2009) extended an earlier evaluation of the Clearwater program by collecting recidivism data 10 years post-release from the program. The results are illustrated in Figure 10.9. As can be seen, the treatment group performed significantly better than members of the comparison group at all four time periods. Although the treatment effect declined over time, the fact that a significant difference remained at 10 years is noteworthy. This indicates that adhering to the principles of effective interventions can result in a sustained impact on sex-offending behavior, even when the treatment is provided within an institutional setting.

General Counseling Programs

As previously noted, the majority of programs in our prisons tend to emphasize work or education, drug treatment, or general counseling. Although most programs are relatively easy to define, general counseling programs are less so. Indeed, a search of "prison-based treatment" largely reveals a host of research about drug treatment and sex offender treatment programs. Relatively few evaluations exist of other programs, including general CBT, anger management, or life skills.

As discussed in previous chapters, CBT programs generally focus on cognitive skill building (e.g., problem solving, decision making, and understanding the feelings of others) and cognitive restructuring (e.g., reducing thinking errors). As expected, there is evidence that CBT approaches are effective in reducing both prison misconduct and recidivism upon release among prison inmates.

One of the earliest CBT programs in the adult prison system was in Vermont. Kris Henning and Christopher Frueh (1996) evaluated the Cognitive Self-Change (CSC) program to test its impact on recidivism. They found that program participants had 29% less recidivism than nonparticipants 2 years after being released from prison. Although half of the participants recidivated within 2 years, this is significantly lower than the 71% recidivism rate of nonparticipants. A review of the program indicates that it focused on changing thinking errors (e.g., denial of responsibility and victim stance) and developing a relapse prevention plan. A particular emphasis was placed on the identification of high-risk situations and developing strategies for managing those situations. Participants attended group therapy three to five times a week, during which time they completed thinking reports and detailed their thoughts and feelings about a prior antisocial incident. Through this exercise, participants were taught to identify cognitive distortions and practice alternative strategies to managing the situation. On average, participants remained in the program for 9 months and were released to a minimum-security prison upon completion of the program. In contrast to many of the drug treatment programs, participants continued to interact with the general population. Everyone in the group lived in the same unit but mixed with others for recreation, work, and education. This is noteworthy because it suggests that the program was able to have an impact even while participants continued to be exposed to those who were not participating in CSC.

Nancy Hogan and colleagues (2012) evaluated the Cognitive Housing Approach: New Goals Environment (CHANGE), a program based on the CSC program evaluated by Henning and Frueh (1996). The CHANGE program incorporates two curricula promoted by the National Institute of Corrections: (1) Options: A Cognitive Change Program and (2) Thinking for a Change: Integrated Cognitive Behavior Change Program. The first component emphasized intervention, behavior management, communication, and thinking errors, whereas the second component emphasized problem solving, skill building, and cognitive restructuring.

The program was designed to serve high-risk inmates who were younger than 26 years old. The main goal of the program was to reduce prison misconduct. As with many of the other programs we have reviewed, participants were housed separately from the main population.

The CHANGE program consisted of three phases. The first phase was designed to last 6–8 weeks, and participants attended group sessions twice a week. During this phase, participants were taught the basics of cognitive self-change, kept journals, and learned how to do thinking reports. Participants who stayed out of trouble throughout phase 1 could then volunteer to move to phase 2. The second phase was designed to last between 6 and 24 months. During this time, participants attended group sessions four times a week and continue to use thinking reports and journaling to identify their antisocial thinking patterns. Successful completion of phase 2 required the completion of a relapse prevention plan. Upon its completion, participants were eligible to move to phase 3. This phase was designed to last 6–12 months and was focused on community reintegration. Participants met in groups twice a week during this phase.

Although the CHANGE program follows many of the principles of effective interventions, Hogan et al. (2012) found that phase 1 of the program failed to have much of an effect on misconduct. While CHANGE participants were less likely to have violent misconducts 6 months after the program, they did not differ from a comparison group of inmates. The comparison group consisted of individuals who were eligible for participation in the program but were randomly assigned to the control group.

Given the apparent strengths of the CHANGE program, why did it fail? Hogan and colleagues (2012) speculate that part of the reason for the failure was that the first phase was too short (8 weeks) to be effective. As a general rule, we know that treatment should last between 3 and 9 months. Hogan et al. note that 8 weeks may not be enough time for lasting change to occur. Moreover, participants went back to the general population if they decided not to move onto the next phase. There was some anecdotal evidence that correctional officers treated these participants more harshly upon their return.

Despite the failure of the CHANGE program to reduce misconduct, the general consensus is that cognitive behavioral programs are more effective than other approaches. The failure of the CHANGE program is most likely a result of implementation rather than a failing of CBT. Other examples of effective programs include the Strategies for Thinking Productively (STP), which was found to reduce prison misconduct in Michigan (Baro, 1999); a CBT program at the Rideau Correctional and Treatment Center in Ontario (Bourgon & Armstrong, 2005) that was found to reduce recidivism; and Problem Solving developed by Taymans and Pares (1998), which was found to reduce misconduct for women in prison (Spiropoulos, Spruance, Van Voorhis, & Schmitt, 2005).

Education and Vocational Programming

Of all the types of programs we have discussed, participation in educational or vocational programming is probably the most common. However, as previously noted, the meta-analysis by French and Gendreau (2006) revealed that these types of programs do not reduce recidivism. Why not? Both education and employment are considered to be criminogenic needs. Therefore, targeting these needs is appropriate. However, as discussed in previous chapters, education and employment are considered more moderate needs compared to factors such as antisocial attitudes, antisocial associates, and antisocial personality (Andrews & Bonta, 2010).

Despite the failure of education and employment programs to impact recidivism, they still have value when we consider them as a mechanism for helping to manage prison life. As noted previously, participation in programming is associated with reduced levels of violence. Providing these types of programs may both help to minimize the strains associated with prison and help ease the reentry process.

Employment programs can generally be categorized along three dimensions (Bouffard, MacKenzie, & Hickman, 2000). The first consists of vocational education, which includes training and accreditation programs with the goal of providing greater employment opportunities upon release. The second includes correctional industry programs. In these, inmates work in jobs aimed at producing goods and services provided to the state or general public. Finally, some institutions allow work release programs in which inmates go into the community to work but continue living at the institution. Although these programs are more commonly associated with jails or local community corrections centers as opposed to prisons, they provide yet another potential mechanism for inmates to gain work experience.

Examples of educational programs include Adult Basic Education, General Educational Development (GED), and, in some cases, access to college classes. The GED classes often lead to the acquisition of a GED, whereas other prisons work with local school districts allowing inmates to gain a high school diploma. Perhaps one of the most unique education experiences is the Inside Out Prison Exchange program, which brings traditional college students into the prison setting to take courses with inmates. Just as with a traditional college class, these classes meet weekly for a semester and students receive full college credit. Although there is no evidence indicating this type of program reduces recidivism, it has been well received and currently operates in all 50 states.

The role of education and employment should not be discounted. However, at the same time, prison officials must be aware that participation in these types of programs alone is not likely to impact recidivism. Instead, educational and vocational training should be coupled with groups targeting substance abuse and other criminogenic needs to increase the likelihood of success upon release.

Special Considerations

Providing prison- and jail-based treatment is subject to a number of challenges not experienced in the community. Often, there is a tension between the need for security and the need for treatment. In our experience, it is not unusual for treatment groups to be canceled because of custody concerns or for inmates to arrive late for groups because of restricted movement at specific times. Group facilitators may also have to contend with correctional officers who are less supportive of treatment or undermine the positive effects of treatment through shaming and belittling program participants. To counteract this, the state of Pennsylvania provides a session to correctional staff on Reinforcing Positive Behavior as part of the basic training provided to new employees. Participation in the 2-hour session was associated with improved attitudes toward treatment, the need to treat inmates with respect, and a recognition that their own behavior impacts inmate behavior (Antonio, Young, & Wingeard, 2009).

In addition, participants are often exposed to antisocial thinking and behaviors while mixed in with the general population. As previously discussed, the use of separate treatment units or pods can help to minimize the impact of these negative factors. However, the use of specialized housing can lead to additional challenges. For example, let us consider the STP program in Michigan—a two-phase CBT program found to reduce misconduct and assaults. Although the findings are promising, it was revealed that 75% of the program participants quit the program before completing phase 2. Like many of the programs we have reviewed, the STP program moved phase 2 participants into a specialized treatment unit. Although living in a treatment unit has been found to be of benefit to program participants, it served as a deterrent to phase 2 participation for this program. Phase 2 participants were precluded from transferring to minimum-security prisons until they completed the program. Although this is not atypical, the program was designed to last between 6 and 24 months and few participants wanted to wait that long before having the ability to transfer (Baro, 1999). This suggests two points. First, just as with community-based programs, program duration is important. Although high-risk offenders should receive at least 300 hours of treatment, programs should not be so long that they are viewed as punitive. Second, although specialized housing is important for isolating participants from other inmates, prison officials must also be cognizant of the impact that transfers and movement within the prison setting can have on participation.

A Special Note on Juveniles

As noted at the beginning of the chapter, nearly 90,000 juveniles are held in some type of residential facility in the United States (Sickmund, 2010). The types of facilities range from detention centers and diagnostic centers to residential treatment centers and long-term secure facilities, sometimes known as "training schools" and most analogous to adult prisons. In general, secure facilities tend to be much smaller than prisons, with the majority of these institutions holding between 51 and 100 youths. More than 17,000 juveniles are housed in secure facilities.

As with adults, the incarceration of juveniles is often justified as keeping communities safer (DeLisi, Hochstetler, Jones-Johnson, Caudill, & Marquart, 2011). Consistent with this perspective, half of those placed in long-term secure facilities are there for personal crimes. The rest are there for property offenses (26%), public order offenses (11%), technical violations (9%), drug offenses (4%), and status offenses (1%) (Sickmund, Sladky, Kang, & Puzzanchera, 2011).

Although many of the juveniles in long-term institutions are there for serious offenses, the concerns regarding the criminogenic influence of institutions remain. As summarized by Matt DeLisi and colleagues (2011), confinement in juvenile facilities negatively impacts youths' physical and mental health, educational attainments, perceptions of successful reintegration, and family relationships, and it increases subsequent offending. As with adults, juvenile confinement often makes matters worse, not better. In fact, DeLisi et al. found that juvenile confinement was predictive of a future arrest for murder. Although this is not to suggest that confinement causes juveniles to later commit murder, it does suggest that juvenile confinement may have significant negative effects later in life.

The question then becomes how to manage serious juvenile offenders. Many states have taken to waiving these juveniles to adult court and confining them in adult prisons. Although the number of juveniles in adult prisons is declining, the *Prisoners in 2010* bulletin indicates that there were more than 2,000 juveniles in adult prisons that year

(Guerino, Harrison, & Sabol, 2011). The incarceration of juveniles in adult prisons creates additional problems because many prisons end up holding juveniles in isolation for protective reasons. However, long-term solitary confinement can cause both psychological and physical harm.

As with adult offenders, we must do a better job of deciding who to send to prison and ensuring that programs are available for them when sent to prison. The state of Ohio offers hope for reducing the number of juveniles sent to secure facilities. RECLAIM Ohio was established in 1993 as an initiative aimed at incentivizing counties to provide services to juveniles at risk for recidivism. Using a funding formula, counties receive money by keeping youths in the community and diverting them from the Department of Youth Services (DYS). In addition to funding, DYS works collaboratively with counties and provides training to juvenile court staff. By reserving beds for high-risk youths, DYS has been able to close a number of institutions and has dramatically decreased the population from more than 2,600 in 1992 to fewer than 550 in 2012. Other states should consider following the lead of Ohio as a way to reduce the number of incarcerated youths.

Summary

Although it is clear that prison-based treatment can be effective, it is also clear that it is less effective than community-based treatment. Recognizing that some portion of the offender population will continue to be incarcerated, we offer the following suggestions:

- Reserve prison beds for the highest-risk offenders.
- Use effective classification systems and assessment tools to ensure inmates are in the institutions and units best suited to their risk factors.
- Provide programs and activities to help manage the potential criminogenic effect of prison.
- Focus on treatment programs related to criminogenic needs to increase the likelihood of success upon release into the community.
- House treatment participants in separate units to remove them from the peer influence of other inmates.
- Train correctional staff on the importance of respect and the impact of their own behavior on offenders.
- Provide educational and vocational training with an eye toward reentry programming.

References

Andrews, D. A., & Bonta, J. (1998). *The Level of Service Inventory-Revised*. Toronto: Multi-Health Systems.

Andrews, D. A., & Bonta, J. (2010). *The psychology of criminal conduct*. Cincinnati, OH: Anderson.

Antonio, M. E., Young, J. L., & Wingeard, L. M. (2009). When actions and attitude count most: Assessing perceived level of responsibility and support for inmate treatment and rehabilitation programs among correctional employees. *Prison Journal, 89*, 363–382.

Austin, J. (2003). *Findings in prison classification and assessment.* Washington, DC: National Institute of Corrections, U.S. Department of Justice.

Baro, A. L. (1999). Effects of a cognitive restructuring program on inmate institutional behavior. *Criminal Justice and Behavior, 26,* 466–484.

Belenko, S., & Peugh, J. (2005). Estimating drug treatment needs among state prison inmates. *Drug and Alcohol Dependence, 77,* 269–281.

Blevins, K. R., Listwan, S. J., Cullen, F. T., & Jonson, C. L. (2010). A general strain theory of prison violence and misconduct: An integrated model of inmate behavior. *Journal of Contemporary Criminal Justice, 26,* 148–166.

Bouffard, J. A., MacKenzie, D. L., & Hickman, L. J. (2000). Effectiveness of vocational education and employment programs for adult offenders: A methodology-based analysis of the literature. *Journal of Offender Rehabilitation, 31,* 1–41.

Bourgon, G., & Armstrong, B. (2005). Transferring the principles of effective treatment into a "real world" prison setting. *Criminal Justice and Behavior, 32,* 3–25.

Bureau of Justice Assistance. (2005). *Residential substance abuse treatment for state prisoners (RSAT) program* (NCJ 206269). Washington, DC: Bureau of Justice Assistance, Office of Justice Program.

Byrne, J. M., & Hummer, D. (2007a). Myths and realities of prison violence: A review of the evidence. *Victims and Offenders, 2,* 77–90.

Byrne, J. M., & Hummer, D. (2007b). In search of the "tossed salad man" (and others involved in prison violence): New strategies for predicting and controlling violence. *Aggression and Violent Behavior, 5,* 531–541.

Camp, S. D., & Gaes, G. G. (2004). Criminogenic effects of the prison environment on inmate behavior: Some experimental evidence. *Crime and Delinquency, 51,* 377–387.

Carson, E. A., & Sabol, W. J. (2012). *Prisoners in 2011* (NCJ 239808). Washington, DC: Bureau of Justice Statistics.

Incorporated, C. S. R. (2012). *Residential Substance Abuse Treatment Program closeout report, January 2010–March 2012.* Washington, DC: Bureau of Justice Assistance.

DeLeon, G., & Wexler, H. (2009). The therapeutic community for addictions: An evolving knowledge base. *Journal of Drug Issues, 39,* 167–177.

DeLisi, M., Hochstetler, A., Jones-Johnson, G., Caudill, J. W., & Marquart, J. W. (2011). The road to murder: The enduring criminogenic effects of juvenile confinement among a sample of adult career criminals. *Youth Violence and Juvenile Justice, 9,* 207–221.

Durose, M. R., & Langan, P. A. (2007). *Felony sentences in state courts* (NCJ 215646). Washington, DC: Bureau of Justice Statistics.

Duwe, G., & Goldman, R. A. (2009). The impact of prison-based treatment on sex offender recidivism: Evidence from Minnesota. *Sexual Abuse: A Journal of Research and Treatment, 21,* 279–307.

Freeman,-Long, R. E., Bird, S., Stevenson, W. F., & Fiske, J. A. (1994). *Nationwide survey of treatment programs and models.* Brandon, VT: Safer Society.

French, S., & Gendreau, P. (2006). Reducing prison misconducts: What works! *Criminal Justice and Behavior, 33,* 185–218.

Gaes, G. G., & Camp, S. D. (2009). Unintended consequences: Experimental evidence for the criminogenic effect of prison security level placement on post-release recidivism. *Journal of Experimental Criminology, 5,* 139–162.

Gatson-Rowe, L. (2011). Community as change agent: Incorporating peer-to-peer learning in RSAT programs. *Webinar produced by RSAT Training and Technical Assistance National Resource Center.* Retrieved March 2012 from www.rsat-tta.com/Files/Webinars/Peer-to-Peer-Learning.

Guerino, P., Harrison, P. M., & Sabol, W. J. (2011). *Prisoners in 2010* (NCH 236096). Washington, DC: Bureau of Justice Statistics.

Hare, R. D. (1991). *The Hare Psychopathy Checklist–Revised (manual)*. Toronto: Multi-Health Systems.

Harris, G. T., Rice, M. E., & Quinsey, V. L. (1993). Violent recidivism of mentally disordered offenders: The development of a statistical predict instrument. *Criminal Justice and Behavior, 20*, 315–225.

Henning, K. R., & Frueh, B. C. (1996). Cognitive–behavioral treatment of incarcerated offenders: An evaluation of the Vermont Department of Corrections' Cognitive Self-Change program. *Criminal Justice and Behavior, 23*, 523–541.

Hogan, N. L., Lambert, E. G., & Barton-Bellessa, S. M. (2012). Evaluation of CHANGE, an involuntary cognitive program for high-risk inmates. *Journal of Offender Rehabilitation, 51*, 370–388.

Hughes, T., & Wilson, D. J. (2002). *Reentry trends in the United States*. Washington, DC: Bureau of Justice Statistics. Retrieved March 2013 from http://www.bjs.gov/content/reentry/reentry.cfm.

Inciardi, J. A., Martin, S. S., & Butzin, C. A. (2004). Five-year outcomes of therapeutic community treatment of drug-involved offenders after release from prison. *Crime & Delinquency, 50*, 88–107.

Jonson, C. L. (2010). *The impact of imprisonment on reoffending: A meta-analysis*. Unpublished doctoral dissertation. Cincinnati, OH: University of Cincinnati.

Kroner, D. G., & Mills, J. F. (2001). The accuracy of five risk appraisal instruments in predicting institution misconduct and new convictions. *Criminal Justice and Behavior, 28*, 471–489.

Langan, P. A., & Levin, D. J. (2002). *Recidivism of prisoners released in 1994* (NCJ 193427). Washington, DC: Bureau of Justice Statistics.

Latessa, E. J., Smith, P., Lemke, R., Makarios, M., & Lowenkamp, C. T. (2010). The creation of the Ohio Risk Assessment System (ORAS). *Federal Probation, 74*, 16–22.

Listwan, S. J., Sullivan, C. J., Agnew, R., Cullen, F. T., & Colvin, M. (2013). The pains of imprisonment revised: The impact of strain on inmate recidivism. *Justice Quarterly, 30*, 144–168.

Lösel, F., & Schmucker, M. (2005). The effectiveness of treatment for sexual offenders: A comprehensive meta-analysis. *Journal of Experimental Criminology, 1*, 117–146.

Mitchel, O., Wilson, D. B., & MacKenzie, D. L. (2007). Does incarceration-based drug treatment reduce recidivism? A meta-analytic synthesis of the research. *Journal of Experimental Criminology, 3*, 353–375.

Nagin, D. S., Cullen, F. T., & Jonson, C. L. (2009). Imprisonment and reoffending. *Crime and Justice, 38*, 115–200.

Olver, M. E., Wong, S. C. P., & Nicholaichuk, T. P. (2009). Outcome evaluation of a high-intensity inpatient sex offender treatment program. *Journal of Interpersonal Violence, 24*, 522–536.

Pearson, F. S., & Lipton, D. S. (1999). A meta-analytic review of the effectiveness of corrections-based treatments for drug abuse. *Prison Journal, 79*, 384–410.

Pew Center on the States. (2011). *State of recidivism: The revolving door of America's prisons*. Washington, DC: Pew Charitable Trusts.

Prendergast, M. L., Hall, E. A., Wexler, H. K., Melnick, G., & Cao, Y. (2004). Amity prison-based therapeutic community: 5-year outcomes. *Prison Journal, 84*, 36–60.

Sickmund, M. (2010). *Juveniles in residential placement, 1997–2008*. Washington, DC: Office of Juvenile Justice and Delinquency Prevention.

Sickmund, M., Sladky, T. J., Kang, W., & Puzzanchera, C. (2011). Easy access to the census of juveniles in residential placementAvailable at http://www.ojjdp.gov/ojstatbb/ezacjrp.

Simourd, D. J. (2004). Use of dynamic risk/need assessment instruments among long-term incarcerated offenders. *Criminal Justice and Behavior, 31*, 306–323.

Spiropoulos, G. V., Spruance, L., Van Voorhis, P., & Schmitt, M. M. (2005). Pathfinders and problem solving. *Journal of Offender Rehabilitation, 42*, 69–94.

Stephan, J. J. (2008). *Census of state and federal correctional facilities, 2005* (NCJ 222182). Washington, DC: Bureau of Justice Statistics.

Stephan, J. J., & Karberg, J. C. (2003). *Census of state and federal correctional facilities, 2000* (NCJ 198272). Washington, DC: Bureau of Justice Statistics.

Steyee, J. (2012). *Program performance report: Residential Substance Abuse Treatment (RSAT) program, April–September 2012*. Washington, DC: Bureau of Justice Assistance.

Taymans, J., & Parese, S. (1998). *Problem solving skills for offenders: A social cognitive intervention.* Washington, DC: George Washington University.

Walsh, W. (2007). A multi-site evaluation of prison-based therapeutic community drug treatment. *Criminal Justice and Behavior, 34*, 1481–1498.

Walters, G. D., White, T. W., & Denney, D. (1991). The Lifestyle Criminality Screening Form: Preliminary data. *Criminal Justice and Behavior, 18*, 406–418.

Webster, C. D., Eaves, D., Douglas, K. S., & Wintrup, A. (1995). *The HCR-20 scheme: The assessment of dangerousness and risk.* Vancouver. British Columbia, Canada: Simon Fraser University and British Columbia Forensic Psychiatric Services Commission.

Wexler, H. K., DeLeon, G., Thomas, G., Kressel, D., & Peters, J. (1999). The Amity prison TC evaluation: Reincarceration outcomes. *Criminal Justice and Behavior, 26*, 147–167.

Wexler, H. K., Falkin, G. P., & Lipton, D. S. (1990). Outcome evaluation of a prison therapeutic community for substance abuse treatment. *Criminal Justice and Behavior, 17*, 71–92.

Wexler, H. K., Melnick, G., Lowe, L., & Peters, J. (1999). Three-year reincarceration outcomes for Amity in-prison therapeutic community and after in California. *Prison Journal, 79*, 321–336.

Zhang, S. X., Roberts, R. E. L., & McCollister, K. E. (2011). Therapeutic community in a California prison: Treatment outcomes after 5 years. *Crime & Delinquency, 57*, 81–101.

11

What Works in Reentry

Introduction

The term *reentry* is used to describe the transition offenders make when they leave a period of confinement. However, the period of confinement is not limited to prisons. Jails, residential treatment centers, halfway houses, group homes, or any other residential placement should also be considered in this discussion. In other words, reentry is what inmates experience as they transition back into the community from a period of confinement.

The concept of reentry has increased in popularity during the past decade for several reasons. First, studies suggest that those reentering the community are failing at fairly high rates. For example, studies of parolees find that two-thirds of prisoners are arrested within 3 years, and between 40 and 50% are sent back to prison (Hughes, Wilson, & Beck, 2001; Langan & Levin, 2002). These failure rates are particularly compelling if we consider that during 2011, there were an estimated 1.6 million adults serving time in prison (Carson & Sabol, 2012), and it is estimated that more than 700,000 of those inmates are released back to the community each year (Fontaine & Biess, 2012).

As can be seen in Figure 11.1, those who return to prison represent a staggering number of the new admissions to prison each year. Specifically, of the 668,800 admissions to prison in 2011, 205,787 (30.7%) were parole violators (Carson & Sabol, 2012). To put

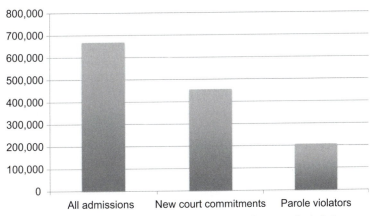

FIGURE 11.1 Prisoners admitted to prison in 2011 by type of admission.

this into further context, an examination of parole trends by Travis and Lawrence (2002) found that

> over the past 20 years, as the number of people sent to prison on new convictions has increased threefold, the number sent to prison for parole violations increased sevenfold. We now send as many people back to prison for parole violations as the total number of prison admissions in 1980. (p. 24)

Second, and related, are the fiscal demands faced by many states. According to the Pew Center on the States (2008), corrections ranks as the second highest expenditure in the United States. In fact, it is estimated that the money spent on corrections by states increased from $12 billion in 1987 to nearly $50 billion in 2007. For some states, this translates into 1 in every 15 state general fund dollars now being spent on corrections. California alone spends an average of $8.8 billion per year on corrections. As a result, many states are facing a financial crisis that means they cannot continue to lock people up at the same rate, even if they want to continue to do so. For example, a news story authored by the Associated Press started with the following line: "When Harry Coates campaigned for the Oklahoma State Senate in 2002, he had one approach to crime: 'Lock 'em up and throw away the key.' Now Coates is looking for that key" (Murphy, 2011). The article discusses how the get-tough movement discussed previously in this book had significant fiscal implications for most states. As a result, in 2010, 18 states planned to close prisons or eliminate prison beds in an effort to save money. Unfortunately, every state also planned to eliminate staff and/or funds for services for prison inmates. See Box 11.1 for an example of how California is struggling.

Third, although much of the previous discussion relies on statistics for adult corrections, the juvenile system is experiencing the same problems. For example, much like the adult system, the use of confinement for juveniles increased more than 40% in the 1990s (Snyder & Sickmund, 2006). The numbers are shifting, however. According the latest statistics, the number of juveniles in custody has declined 12% since 2006 (Sickmund, 2010, p. 1). The decline in the number of juveniles in custody is partly reflective of the reduction in arrests for juvenile delinquency. However, as mentioned at the beginning of the chapter, it is also likely emanating from fiscal issues. A study of community-based programs found that costs were close to $9,000 compared to costs as much as $50,000 to $90,000 per year for incarceration (Lowenkamp & Latessa, 2005).

Finally, the issues facing many of these ex-prisoners can be compelling. Although we have discussed some of these in detail throughout this book, Figure 11.2 highlights some of the needs. It is not surprising that the get-tough movement of the late 1980s and the 1990s did not lead to appreciable reductions in recidivism. Punishment alone fails to change the individual and structural barriers facing many ex-prisoners.

BOX 11.1   SPOTLIGHT: CALIFORNIA'S PRISON CRISIS AND SOLUTION?

California has been under a tremendous amount of pressure to reduce its correctional expenditures. If we look at the numbers, we can see why:

- In 1982, California had 1 in 69 adults under some form of correctional control. In 2009, that number reached 1 in 31.
- In 2008, California spent $9.66 billion on corrections. That figure represents nearly 10% of the state's budget.
- California's prisons are over 200% capacity, with 140,000 inmates in custody.
- California is currently under a mandate from the U.S. Supreme Court to reduce its prison population by 30,000 inmates. The court indicated that the California correctional system was violating inmates' Eighth Amendment right against cruel and unusual punishment.

Under mounting pressure, California passed legislation that effectively barred low-level offenders from being sent to state prisons. Referred to as the Realignment Project, the state gave counties latitude to manage low-level felons, most often in county jails. It is intended that the Realignment Project will give counties greater discretion in how to best manage, treat, and supervise low-level nonviolent offenders. However, some are concerned that the state simply shifted the population to the jail system.

DISCUSSION QUESTIONS

What do you think states should do when faced with these budgetary issues?
Do you think prisons should exist to only serve violent or sex offenders?

Source: California Department of Corrections & Rehabilitation (http://www.cdcr.ca.gov/realignment).

- Housing
  - 10% have a history of homelessness
- Substance Abuse
  - Over half of state prisoners and nearly 70% of jail inmates have substance abuse disorder
  - Only 7% receive treatment in prison

- Mental Health
  - Serious mental illness 4X higher than general population
- Education/employment
  - 40% lack high school diploma
  - Many will remain unemployed in the community

FIGURE 11.2 Reentry at a glance. *Source: Adapted from the National Reentry Resource Center, "Re-entry Facts." Retrieved March 2013 from http://csgjusticecenter.org/nrrc/facts-and-trends.*

Punitiveness Revisited

Why do we continue to incarcerate people if they continue to commit crimes at such a high rate upon release? For some, the costs of confinement can be justified on the grounds of public safety. In other words, if incarcerating criminals leads to a reduction in crime and makes neighborhoods safer, then the costs might be justifiable. However, as we just discussed, the failure rates of those released from the prison are not promising. This brings us to the question of why confinement—or harsh conditions in general—does not deter people from committing crime.

Deterrence studies suggest that it is difficult to have an impact on crime rates by simply increasing the punitiveness of punishment. For example, as discussed in Chapter 1, the U.S. get-tough movement failed to produce the types of reductions in crime we would have expected to see. More interesting, however, are the studies that examine the deterrent effect of prison. For example, a study by Useem and Kimball (1987) examined the factors that led to prison riots. He found that the prison became more violent when the administration eliminated amenities such as programming and television. Other studies have found the same impact. For example, Mark Colvin (1992) examined the factors that led to a particularly violent prison riot in Santa Fe, New Mexico. He found that coercive prison environments increased, not decreased, the chance of inmates rioting. Finally, Shelley Listwan and colleagues found that inmates who reported that prison environments were more coercive and hostile were more likely to have psychological problems and did worse when released back into the community (Listwan, Colvin, Hanley, & Flannery, 2010; Listwan, Sullivan, Agnew, Cullen, & Colvin, 2013).

On the other hand, with regard to rehabilitation, studies suggest that if a prison culture is one that supports treatment services, it can be more effective. Prisons throughout the country offer educational, vocational, or other types of treatment services. However, as discussed in Chapter 10, the reality is that long-term secure institutions often prioritize custody and security over rehabilitation.

Thus, the question becomes, What does work or should work to reduce the failure rates of those reentering the community? Unfortunately, the answer to this question is fairly complex. On the one hand, we know what we should be doing when it comes to treatment. This book has outlined a number of proven strategies. Moreover, as noted by Listwan and colleagues (2006), treatment programs for those reentering the community can provide the following:

- An opportunity to shape behavior through skill-building activities
- An alternative mechanism for dealing with post-release violations than simply returning someone back to prison
- An opportunity to provide services to family members of those reentering the community
- A myriad of services to the ex-inmates that have the potential not only to reduce recidivism but also to increase their overall health and well-being

In order for reentry programs to be successful, however, they must take into consideration all of the treatment issues we have discussed so far in this book. Implementing these principles into practice is not as easy as it might seem. As noted by Christy Visher (2006), a leading expert on the topic, the implementation of these programs is nearly as difficult as changing the offenders' behavior. To get a better understanding of how difficult it can be to implement these programs, let's examine a popular reentry program that produced mixed results.

Serious and Violent Offender Reentry Initiative (SVORI)

In 2003, the **Serious and Violent Offender Reentry Initiative** (SVORI) provided federal grants to states throughout the county in an effort to develop reentry services specifically designed for violent offenders. As noted in a series of publications by Pam Lattimore and colleagues, the SVORI initiative provided more than $110 million to nearly every state with the intent of developing programming and "best-practice"-driven reentry strategies within communities. The funds eventually led to the development of 89 adult and juvenile programs (Lattimore et al., 2012; Lattimore & Visher, 2009).

The initiative, conceived to focus on those who were potentially at the highest need level, was designed to accept only violent and serious offenders. However, as discussed in previous chapters, risk should be defined by a risk assessment tool rather than offense. On the other hand, it is not without merit to focus on serious and violent offenders, particularly given how they are often treated in the community post-release.

The programs were given fairly wide latitude in deciding how and when to deliver services. The model set forth recommended that programs begin offering services 6 months prior to release and then continue those services in a step-down manner, meaning that the participant would continue to receive services at a fairly high dosage post-release and would eventually see those services tapered down as necessary until the participant "graduated" from the program. Sites were also encouraged to use risk and need assessments, utilize graduated sanctions and incentives, and coordinate services with agencies in the community to provide a seamless approach to treatment delivery (Lattimore et al., 2012).

The Research Triangle Institute International (RTI) and the Urban Institute were contracted to provide a nationwide evaluation of state-level reentry programs. As a result, they have provided a "national portrait" of the SVORI programming (Lattimore et al., 2004), which is summarized as follows:

The goals of the initiative are to improve quality of life and self-sufficiency through employment, housing, family and community involvement; improve health by addressing substance use (sobriety and relapse prevention) and physical and mental health; reduce criminality through supervision and by monitoring noncompliance, reoffending, rearrest, reconviction, and reincarceration; achieve system change through multi-agency collaboration and case management strategies. (p. 4)

The national evaluation results of the SVORI programs are mixed. On the one hand, this makes sense if we consider that although similar in some respects, there was considerable variation in how these programs were set up. Moreover, the political will in some states had an impact on service delivery. For example, whereas the national evaluation found that most directors (95%) "reported planning to continue or expand SVORI, and 88% reported that the political climate in their communities was favorable to reentry programming" (Winterfield, Lindquist, & Brumbaugh, 2007, p. 1), other states, such as Nevada, dealt with a number of obstacles when implementing their program. Nevada's program was called Going Home Prepared (GHP).

Although the evaluation in Nevada did not examine recidivism rates, the study did find that more than two-thirds of the GHP program participants failed to successfully graduate. The most common reasons for failure were lack of employment and housing opportunities for clients. Moreover, the program spent considerable funds on crisis management needs such as medical and dental procedures for clients. As illustrated in Figure 11.3, the clients identified a variety of barriers that would exist for them in the community. The money spent on these issues minimized the amount of resources available for direct treatment services. Although program administrators believed they had succeeded in developing a service delivery system that was far better than what had existed before, the resources dedicated to the project were simply insufficient. Once the federal money was expended, the state decided it was not interested in funding the program. As a result, the program was dismantled in 2007.

The national SVORI evaluation developed in a number of stages, with the authors producing a series of process and outcome results. Here are a few highlights of the evaluation:

- SVORI participants were high-need offenders. The vast majority had a lengthy prior record, a lack of vocational skills, high rates of unemployment when in the community, and needed financial assistance upon release.

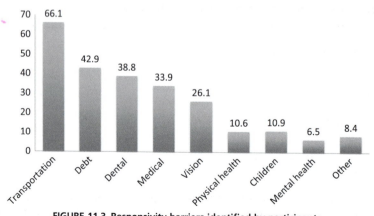

FIGURE 11.3 Responsivity barriers identified by participants.

- Programs nationally struggled with retaining participants in the program post-release from prison.
- SVORI participants were less likely to be arrested and had fewer arrests than comparison group members. However, they were not less likely to be incarcerated.
- Participation in treatment did have a positive impact, but the impact varied. For example, life skills programs and employment services had no impact, but substance abuse treatment, cognitive behavioral interventions, and educational programs had a modest effect.

Although the findings noted here are generally positive, Lattimore and colleagues (2012) argued that some of the programs actually had worse outcomes than their comparison groups. As such, they note "the need for additional research into the sequencing and effects of specific and combinations of reentry services, with an understanding that some programs may be harmful if delivered at the wrong time or in the wrong way" (p. vi).

The question becomes, Why did the programs struggle? There seem to be several issues that impacted these programs. First, many of those enrolled in the program were high-risk and high-need. On the one hand, this is a positive aspect of the program: They should be targeting high-risk clients. However, resources were not necessarily dedicated in a way to respond to the needs of the individuals. Second, the programs did not necessarily rely on effective approaches with their clients. As noted previously, the programs that focused on cognitive behavioral interventions were more effective than those that focused on a more general "life skills" approach.

The risk factors for those who are reentering the community are not unique; rather, they operate differently depending on the inmate's situation. Let's take a moment to examine some of the common and core needs of those reentering the community.

The Core Risk Factors

As discussed throughout this book, research has identified the core risk factors that are known to increase the risk of recidivism (Andrews & Bonta, 2010). As discussed in Chapter 2, there are eight major risk factors or correlates of criminal conduct:

- Antisocial attitudes, values, and beliefs
- Antisocial peers
- Personality/temperament
- Prior criminal record
- Family difficulties
- Vocational/educational difficulties
- A lack of prosocial leisure activities
- Abuse of alcohol or other drugs

We know that those reentering the community are faced with many struggles, most of which were just listed. Although we will not review each of these in detail again, it is

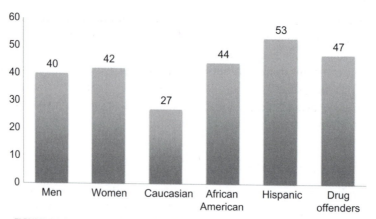

FIGURE 11.4 Demographic profile of inmates without a high school diploma.

important to highlight a few and show how they may be of particular importance to those reentering the community.

First, education and employment are key areas in which inmates struggle. Studies find that more than 40% of state prison inmates do not have a high school education (Harlow, 2003). Figure 11.4 illustrates the demographic profile of inmates without a high school degree or General Educational Development (GED) certificate. Only approximately half of inmates report that they participated in educational courses, with 11% participating in college-level or post-secondary vocational courses. Education and employment are closely linked.

The employment prospects for those reentering the community have only become worse in light of the economic downturn that began in 2008. The Center for Economic and Policy Research released a study in 2008 on the topic of ex-offenders in the labor market (Schmitt & Warner, 2010). It concluded that there are between 5.4 and 6.1 million ex-prisoners in the population. Not surprisingly, the center found that ex-offenders who also did not have a high school diploma were the least employable. The unemployment rate for ex-offenders is estimated to be at least twice that of the general population. Reentry programs often consider employment to be one of their top issues. However, with prior records, incarceration histories, and few skills, it is a struggle to find jobs for ex-inmates.

Another area of particular concern for those reentering the community is family relationships. For those who have been incarcerated, family reunification may be joyous but difficult. Their absence can have a significant effect on the family structure, and their return may be met with ambivalence by those who took over the role of the absent parent. For example, children may feel resentful that they were required to assume an adult role and now the returning parent expects to come back into the family and immediately assert himself or herself as the responsible adult. Youths may feel stigmatized for having an incarcerated parent, or they may have an increased risk of addiction or delinquency themselves.

Even when children are not involved, returning offenders may need to make amends with family members they may have harmed. Returning offenders may also be viewed as a burden to the family if they are unable to support themselves or expect family members to change their lifestyles to accommodate supervision requirements. Marital relationships are often strained and more likely to end in divorce for a variety of reasons, including financial hardship, emotional support, or simply the stress of having an absent spouse (Travis, Chincotta, & Solomon, 2003).

The Model: How Do We Do It?

In an ideal model, reentry programs should include three or more phases designed to transition the inmate into the community (Taxman, Young, & Byrne, 2003). The first phase begins in the institution to prepare the inmate for release. The second phase can assist with transitioning the offender into the community. The third phase focuses on providing services in the community that eventually taper down. As discussed in previous chapters, the assessment results should guide service delivery (type and duration) and include dosage and matching. When the assessment process begins in prison, however, the staff must take into consideration the assessment tool they are using. Let's consider a typical assessment tool such as the **Level of Service Inventory–Revised** (LSI-R) (Andrews & Bonta, 1995). This tool measures 10 areas, including prior record, employment/education, financial status, family relationships, leisure/recreation, accommodations, substance addictions, mental health status, and attitudes. Depending on when this assessment is conducted and depending on the client's situation, it may be that the client's risk level is artificially low. For example, a client may self-report that family will not be a problem for him when he is released. In reality, however, the client may get home and find reunification does not go as planned. It is highly important for the client to be reassessed once he or she returns to the community.

The timing of treatment services is another issue for institutions. For example, some prisons are fond of stating that they begin working toward the client's reentry the first day the client enters the building. For some clients, particularly juveniles or adults who are institutionalized for shorter periods of time, this is absolutely the best approach. Planning for the client's eventual release should be the focus of the program and services.

However, the issue of timing is more problematic when we consider inmates who are incarcerated for long periods of time. For example, for inmates who are serving a 10- or 15-year sentence, when should we time treatment services? The answer lies in the expected outcome. For example, cognitive behavioral treatment in prison can produce more than positive reentry outcomes. Studies have found that those who participated in cognitive behavioral treatment were less likely to have disciplinary infractions in prison (Baro, 1999). However, prison administrators often need to prioritize treatment slots for those who are closer to release.

Clearly, the framework of any reentry process or program should be cognitive behavioral in nature. However, the reality is that reentry is a process that includes more than one type of approach or modality. With that said, there should be a unifying framework that should guide each approach, supervision strategy, and/or court intervention. As noted previously, some of the most significant needs or barriers for those returning home are finding jobs, reuniting with families, and preparing for how to avoid high-risk people, places, and events (a.k.a. relapse prevention).

Finding and sustaining meaningful employment is a significant problem facing many ex-inmates. In a typical jurisdiction, an employment program may consist of providing offenders with resources in the community (e.g., temporary agencies and employment resource centers) or requiring them to engage in certain job-seeking activities (e.g., submit *x* number of job applications per week). Not surprisingly, these approaches are limited and often do not produce leads in sustainable employment opportunities, or they simply lead to no employment at all.

Some employment programs have been found to be more effective. **Transitional jobs programs**, also referred to as transitional work programs, hold some promise in this area. These programs typically provide clients with jobs that are initially subsidized to provide the clients with job skills and training. As noted by Gretchen Kirby and colleagues (2002),

> Like unsubsidized workers, transitional workers earn a wage for actual hours worked and they are eligible for the Earned Income Tax Credit. Most positions are part-time (less than 35 hours per week) with an hourly wage from $5.15 to $8.52. Participants begin earning a wage soon after entering a program; most are paid biweekly or twice monthly. Unlike regular employees, most transitional work participants do not receive employee benefits (for example, employer contributions to health insurance or retirement plans). (p. vi)

The work is temporary and is intended to bridge the client into what is referred to as "unsubsidized" or traditional employment opportunities. An evaluation of the Transitional Jobs Reentry Demonstration found that former prisoners who were placed in a transitional job were more likely to have secured an unsubsidized job upon follow-up (Yahner & Zweig, 2012).

Family reunification is another significant barrier. Although many agencies recognize the importance of bringing family members into the reentry process, the willingness and motivation of the family vary. However, research clearly shows that family-based interventions can strengthen the family support network and provide the appropriate care needed by the offender. Moreover, family-based therapies that rely on behavioral and social learning models have been shown to be highly effective (Gordon, Arbuthnot, Gustafson, & McGreen, 1988; Henggeler & Borduin, 1990; Patterson, Chamberlain, & Reid, 1982).

Engaging families, however, can be extremely difficult. Given the wealth of studies that have found that inmates who have supportive families are far more likely to have positive reentry outcomes (Travis, Solomon, & Waul, 2001), it is crucial to engage and sustain families in the process. The first approach may be to remove the barriers that exist when engaging families while the client is still incarcerated. For example, Naser and Visher (2006) found that issues such as transportation to the facility, cost for collect phone calls from inmates, visitation schedule, and the hostile prison environment were barriers noted by family members for not visiting or engaging with their incarcerated family member. To the extent possible, prison officials should work to remove or alleviate barriers impeding visitation or contact.

Providing individual family-based sessions while the offender is incarcerated allows the family to support the client when he or she is released. The family members should be brought into treatment sessions to not only work on potential issues but also be educated about the client's particular needs and how they can support the family member once he or she returns home. This can be timed to coincide with the family's visitation period. Ideally, the facility may require attendance in treatment as a condition for visitation.

A number of appropriate models are in place, including Family Functional Therapy (FFT) and Multisystemic Therapy. FFT is a family-based intervention that targets youths ages 10–18 years with wide-ranging issues within the family. The intervention is relatively short, lasting on average 3 or 4 months. The program consists of five components:

- Engagement phase: Primarily includes relationship building with the family
- Motivation phase: Development of a positive outlook and begin work on the functioning of the family
- Relational assessment: Primarily focuses on analyzing family dynamics and exploring issues within the family
- Behavioral change phase: A crucial aspect of the therapy and one that focuses on skill-building activities
- Generalization phase: Developing and sustaining existing linkages in the community and assisting families with developing relapse prevention plans

The Multisystemic Therapy program, developed in the 1970s, is an intensive wraparound service-based approach that includes youths and their "system" (e.g., family, school, and their community). The program is designed for youths ages 12–17 years, typically those who have had chronic behavioral problems. The therapist's involvement is very intensive, and meetings occur in the home, schools, and with community agencies to develop a supportive network for youths and their families.

Youths are encouraged to participate in prosocial activities, develop prosocial friendship networks, and improve their academic achievement. Therapists work with parents to increase their problem-solving skills, develop effective communication styles with their sons and daughters, and improve their parenting skills with the use of consistent reinforcement and consequences.

Both of these programs are noted by the Center for the Study and Prevention of Violence at the University of Colorado, Boulder, which developed an information clearinghouse to identify violence and drug prevention programs, policies, and practices in the field. The center's **Blueprints Initiative** is designed to identify effective treatment programs and services that could be replicated in communities throughout the United States.

Readers can learn more about the program at their website (http://www.colorado.edu/cspv/blueprints/index.html).

As discussed throughout the book, the most effective approaches tend to be cognitive behavioral treatments focused specifically on the client's criminogenic needs (e.g., sex offending and substance abuse). Cognitive restructuring therapy attempts to change the antisocial cognitive beliefs or thoughts. Cognitive skills therapy, although similar, is intended to develop a set of skills that individuals can use when confronted with problematic or high-risk situations. The importance of skill building for those reentering the community cannot be understated. As previously discussed, many ex-prisoners are likely to experience many struggles and barriers (some expected and some unexpected). Teaching them how to cope with these issues is imperative. This is where relapse prevention services should come into play with those reentering the community. Relapse prevention strategies are designed to prevent or inhibit the likelihood of criminal behavior in the future. The advantage of working on clients' needs and issues in prison is that clients have a period of time during which they can work on their issues outside of the issues. In other words, they can plan for their release in a supportive environment. The disadvantage of working on release prevention in prison is that prison is an artificial environment. Staff must work to create increasingly challenging situations for inmates to mirror the risky situations they are likely to confront in the community.

Programs that are based on cognitive or social learning strategies view relapse as a temporary setback that can be overcome through learning alternative responses (Dowden, Antonowicz, & Andrews, 2000). Relapse prevention strategies teach clients ways to anticipate and cope with high-risk situations to avoid lapses. Without a comprehensive set of coping and problem-solving skills, it is believed that most offenders are likely to relapse when placed back into the same environment.

In addition, relapse prevention programs attempt to increase the client's sense of self-efficacy. *Self-efficacy* refers to the individual's ability to master a situation and feel confident in his or her ability to handle challenging situations. The client is often taught that the power of change comes from developing skills to handle adversity rather than simply relying on willpower (Parks & Marlatt, 1999). In other words, if the juvenile delinquent is confident that change is possible and can be maintained, then a positive outcome (e.g., abstinence) is more likely.

The complexity of this issue for those reentering the community is managing expectations once released. Let's take a SVORI program example again. In an examination of a reentry program in Maryland, Christy Visher and colleagues (2004) asked participants to report how they felt about their prospects in the community in terms of job availability, pay, family reunification, and housing. The researchers then followed the participants into the community to find out how the adjustment process turned out. They found that

half of the pre-release respondents who thought that finding a job would be easy changed their opinion at the first post-release interview and reported that it actually had been pretty hard or very hard to find a job. Supporting oneself financially and paying off debt (for those who claimed to have debt) were other reentry issues in which more than half of respondents changed their opinion from easy to hard between the pre-release interview and the post-release interview. (p. 159)

Thus, relapse can have a reciprocal effect on self-efficacy. Clients who do not relapse and use their coping skills effectively are likely to increase their sense of self-efficacy or mastery of a particularly problematic situation, whereas those who do not cope well are more likely to feel they are unable to successfully navigate their environment. One strategy taught to clients is that a minor lapse does not need to become a full relapse. In the case of alcohol and other drugs, a minor lapse in drug use can be stopped if clients are taught to accept that failures can happen but that they need to be addressed quickly so that clients can get back into a pattern of sobriety (Marlatt & Gordon, 1985). If a minor lapse is viewed as a failure, the client is more likely to fall into a full-blown relapse that will make it more difficult to recover. Relapse prevention is a common component of substance abuse programs but can also be found in most cognitive behavioral programs and is relevant for all types of problem behaviors.

The issue, however, is attending to all the client's needs once he or she is released back into the community. The core treatment services in the community should be sufficiently intensive and structured around the individual needs of the client. However, many correctional programs are forced to devote resources to crisis management once the client is released. Immediate needs such as housing, medical care, mental health, and transportation supersede more important core treatment needs that are likely to produce long-term change. This is why community collaboration with a number of partners is often one the keys to success for many reentry programs. If these programs are to offer a variety of services at different dosage levels to a variety of clients, they need to have well-constructed collaborations in the field.

A last point in this area is that programs should work to reduce the responsivity barriers that may exist in a client's life. As discussed in Chapter 6, responsivity factors can influence how well a client responds to treatment. Internal factors such as motivation and personality can impact how well clients respond to the counselor or demands of the parole officer. External factors such as child care and transportation can influence their likelihood of attendance. However, other factors, such as serious mental illness and medical problems/medication management, may also need to be part of the treatment plan.

Although in some respects the challenges brought by those reentering the community from prison may seem daunting, the social climate today is far better than it was even a decade ago. The political and social will to change how we deal with ex-inmates exists. The challenge is in the implementation of the principles of effective intervention. Next, we examine some of the policy initiatives that have been developed during the past several years.

Harnessing Support for Reform: Recent Policy Initiatives

The risk in identifying a policy or program as the "solution" to the reentry crisis is that we know that there is no one-size-fits-all approach. It simply does not make sense to expect that all of the people reentering the community (e.g., adults, juveniles, substance abusers, and sex offenders) exhibit the same issues or needs. However, as discussed throughout this book, there are often common risk factors that are important as well as common treatment modalities that give agencies the best chance at reducing recidivism rates and improving the lives of those returning to the community. In that vein, there has been a push by several federal agencies to develop effective reentry models that can be implemented across different types of jurisdictions. Each of these models incorporates many of the strategies we have discussed throughout the book. Let's take a look at a few common models that are using the "what works" framework.

Transition from Prison to the Community and Transition from Jail to the Community Initiatives

As their titles suggest, the **Transition from Prison to the Community** (TPC) and the **Transition from Jail to the Community** (TJC) are initiatives focused specifically on those two populations. The TPC initiative focuses on those returning to the community from prison. Unlike SVORI, the TPC project is not limited to serious and violent offenders. The TPC model was developed in 2001 to be a comprehensive approach to prisoner reentry. This process begins in prison and includes the following:

- Assessment/screening
- Transition planning
- Service delivery

A more interesting version is the TJC initiative, which was developed in 2007 via a partnership between the National Institute of Corrections and the Urban Institute. The need for policies surrounding jail populations reentering the community cannot be overestimated. In 2011, more than 735,000 people were in jails (Minton, 2012). Most of these individuals cycle through the jail very quickly. Although varied, their needs are often similar to those we have already discussed in this chapter.

In general, service delivery in jail is limited at best. This is understandable if we consider that most people in jail are there for only short periods of time. This presents challenges for an initiative such as TJC because, as with the other initiatives discussed so far, the policy calls for services to begin while the individual is still incarcerated in the jail and then continue with the individual once released.

It is still important to target our most intensive interventions to our highest-risk jail population. As such, some jails choose to do a two-pronged approach to assessment that begins by using a risk and need screening tool. If the screening tool indicates that someone is of higher risk or need, this would warrant further assessment with a full risk and need assessment tool. Using this two-pronged approach for this population has several advantages. First, time and money are always a consideration. Screening tools take less time to administer. Weeding out potential clients who may not need a full assessment is a more efficient approach. Second, it assists the agency with intervention dosage plans. For example, it may be that the lower-risk clients can be either screened out for services or offered lower levels of services than those who present with more needs. Reassessment is clearly important to this process as well, given that individuals' risk and needs may change once they are released back into the community.

As mentioned previously, one challenge facing the TJC initiative is the reality that individuals cycle out of the jail fairly quickly. As such, the initiative calls for targeting individuals with a range of services. The components are outlined as follows:

- Pre-release intervention: Brief training programs in key areas (e.g., substance abuse and job training), planning for access to community resources, and case management
- Discharge intervention: Linkages to appropriate community-based services, temporary supplies of medication, and contact information for key resources
- Community-based intervention: Focused service delivery specific to the individual's risk and needs, with reassessment as necessary

The Urban Institute recently released process outcome findings on the TJC initiative and concluded that the program did lead to positive system changes, including an increase in collaboration and knowledge among policymakers and positive changes in policy to sustain the program long term. The evaluators note, however, that one potential problem facing the initiative is how to deliver an appropriate dosage of treatment in a jail environment to those individuals who are high-risk and high-need.

One more note about jails before we move to the next policy initiative: A potential problem that some states are currently facing is the pressure to relieve prison crowding. This may have an unintended consequence of filling jail beds with those who would otherwise go to prison. If this trend continues, reentry programs designed specifically for jails may become as important as those for prison.

Prisoner Reentry Initiative (PRI)

The **Prisoner Reentry Initiative** (PRI) was developed in 2003 to assist nonviolent offenders with their return home. Like the initiative discussed previously, the delivery of services was set to begin in prison and then continue into the community. The key program components include case management, education/employment assistance, and mentoring. According to Douglas Holl and colleagues (2009), the core components are defined as follows:

Counseling and case management usually required the assignment of a "case manager" to guide or counsel the participant throughout participation in the project. Oftentimes, a service plan (called an Individual Development Plan (IDP) or Individual Employment Plan (IEP)) was the adjustable roadmap that would take the participant through the remainder of the reentry process. Projects could use such a plan as a form of behavioral contract.

Job placement assistance was designed to help participants find jobs. This could include the first job after release, a better job after training, or a new job after leaving an old one.

Basic skills and remedial education typically included math and English language classes, GED preparation (for those not already possessing a high school diploma or GED), and workforce readiness classes, such as introductions to the world of work.

Occupational skills training could include on-the-job training, classroom training, and work experience. These range from brief (2- to 3-week) classes on basic computer skills to semester-length (or longer) training at a private or public post-secondary school.

Mentoring was described in the SGA as a key part of the initiative. Mentors were to offer support, guidance, and assistance to help participants deal with their many challenges. Grantees were expected to offer mentors to every released prisoner who desired these services during their first year of enrollment. Participants could be matched with an individual mentor or participate in a group mentoring activity. (p. 9)

Another area to consider in this context is the supervision practices of probation and parole agencies that are responsible for monitoring those reentering the community. In the next section, we examine some newer innovative ideas in this regard.

Effective Community Supervision Practices

Another approach adopted in several states throughout the United States is the **Effective Practices in Community Supervision** (EPICS) model. Paula Smith and colleagues at the University of Cincinnati developed the EPICS approach for both juvenile and adult probation/parole agencies (Smith, Schweitzer, Labrecque, & Latessa, 2012). Their EPICS model is based on the work of James Bonta and colleagues and their Strategic Training Initiative in Community Supervision (STICK) model (Bonta et al., 2010). Officers are trained to provide targeted, short interventions to probationers during the typical face-to-face meeting with clients. In particular, they argue that each face-to-face meeting should include the following:

- Check-in
- Review
- Intervention
- Homework

During the session, the officer focuses on the issues that the client is dealing with that might act as barriers to change. For example, if the client is struggling with finding prosocial peers to spend time with after school and on weekends, the officer can offer suggestions for prosocial activities and work with the youth to develop coping skills to handle high-risk situations. The officer would be able to engage in a short role-play with clients about what to say/how to handle the next time an antisocial peer asks them to attend a party or use drugs. The EPICS approach utilized by probation or parole officers would not be in place of treatment services; rather, it would simply provide a framework for meaningful interactions between the offender and the officer.

Another model, developed by Faye Taxman of Virginia Commonwealth University, is referred to as **Proactive Community Supervision** (PCS). Like the EPICS model discussed previously, the PCS model is based on the "what works" or evidence-based practices for offender change. According to Taxman, Yancey, and Bilanin (2006, p. 1), the PSC model includes five major components:

- Identify criminogenic traits using a valid risk and need tool.
- Develop a supervision plan that addresses criminogenic traits employing effective external controls and treatment interventions.
- Hold the offender accountable for progress on the supervision plan.
- Use a place-based strategy wherein individual probation/parole office environments are engaged in implementing the strategy.
- Develop partnerships with community organizations that will provide ancillary services to supervisees.

Each of these practices and policies attempts to provide avenues for agencies to follow when implementing best practices into their agencies. However, as with the SVORI programs, implementing these programs is not without difficulties. Not only do these programs need multiple levels of support at the state and local levels, but also they must be designed with best practices in mind.

Summary

- The concept of reentry is popular as states rethink the cost of prisons.
- Research supports the use of treatment services for reducing recidivism among ex-prisoners.
- Many barriers exist among those who are reentering the community, including addictions, family dysfunction, education and employment, and mental and physical health issues.
- For reentry programs to be successful, they must take into consideration the barriers that exist for participants and the resources needed to attend to their needs.
- Agencies must plan for how they will assess risk both in the prison and again in the community to assign treatment dosage.
- There are a number of effective strategies, such as transitional jobs programs, that may assist clients as they readjust to the community.

- Relapse prevention strategies are key for assisting with an offender's transition back into the community.
- A number of initiatives exist to guide agencies as they develop reentry services and programs.

References

Andrews, D. A., & Bonta, J. (1995). *LSI-R: The Level of Service Inventory-Revised.* Toronto: Multi-Health Systems.

Andrews, D. A., & Bonta, J. (2010). *The psychology of criminal conduct* (5th ed.). Cincinnati, OH: Anderson.

Baro, A. L. (1999). Effects of a cognitive restructuring program on inmate institutional behavior. *Criminal Justice & Behavior, 26,* 466–484.

Bonta, J., Bourgon, G., Rugge, T., Scott, T. L., Yessine, A. K., Gutierrez, L., & Li, J. (2010). *The strategic training initiative in community supervision: Risk–need–responsivity in the real world.* Ottawa, Ontario, Canada: Public Safety Canada.

Carson, E. A., & Sabol, W. J. (2012). *Prisoners in 2011.* Washington, DC: U.S. Department of Justice, Bureau of Justice Statistics.

Colvin, M. (1992). Penitentiary in crisis. New York: State University of New York Press.

Dowden, C., Antonowicz, D., & Andrews, D. (2000). The effectiveness of relapse prevention with offenders: A meta analysis. *International Journal of Offender Therapy and Comparative Criminology, 47,* 516–528.

Fontaine, J., & Biess, J. (2012). *Housing as a platform for formerly incarcerated persons.* Washington, DC: Urban Institute.

Gordon, D. A., Arbuthnot, J., Gustafson, K., & McGreen, P. (1988). Home-based behavioral-systems family therapy with disadvantaged juvenile delinquents. *American Journal of Family Therapy, 16,* 243–255.

Harlow, C. W. (2003). *Education and correctional populations* (NCJ 195670). Washington, DC: U.S. Department of Justice, Office of Justice Programs, Bureau of Justice Statistics.

Henggeler, S. W., & Borduin, C. M. (1990). *Family therapy and beyond: A multisystemic approach to treating the behavior problems of children and adolescents.* Pacific Grove, CA: Brooks/Cole.

Holl, D. B., Kolovich, L., Bellotti, J., & Paxton, N. (2009). *Evaluation of the prisoner reentry initiative.* Washington DC: Mathematica Policy Research.

Hughes, T., Wilson, D., & Beck, A. (2001). *Trends in state parole, 1990–2000* (NCJ 184735). Washington, DC: U.S. Department of Justice, Bureau of Justice Statistics.

Kirby, G., Hill, H., Pavetti, L., Jacobson, J., Derr, M., & Winston, P. (2002). *Transitional jobs: Stepping stones to unsubsidized employment.* Washington, DC: Mathematica Policy Research.

Langan, P. A., & Levin, D. J. (2002). *Recidivism of prisoners released in 1994* (NCJ 193427). Washington, DC: U.S. Department of Justice, Bureau of Justice Statistics.

Lattimore, P. K., Barrick, K., Cowell, A., Dawes, D., Steffey, D., Tueller, S., & Visher, C. A. (2012). *Prisoner reentry services: What worked for SVORI evaluation participants.* Washington, DC: National Institute of Justice.

Lattimore, P. K., MacDonald, J. M., Piquero, A. R., Linster, R. L., & Visher, C. A. (2004). Studying the characteristics of arrest frequency among paroled youthful offenders. *Journal of Research in Crime and Delinquency, 41,* 37–57.

Lattimore, P. K., & Visher, C. A. (2009). *The multisite evaluation of SVORI: Summary and synthesis.* Research Triangle Park, NC: RTI International.

Listwan, S. J., Colvin, M., Hanley, D., & Flannery, D. (2010). Coercion, social support, and psychological well being among recently released prisoners. *Criminal Justice and Behavior, 37*, 1140–1159.

Listwan, S. J., Cullen, F. T., & Latessa, E. J. (2006, December). How to prevent re-entry programs from failing: Insights from evidence-based corrections. *Federal Probation*, 19–25.

Listwan, S. J., Sullivan, C., Agnew, R., Cullen, F. T., & Colvin, M. (2013). The pains of imprisonment revisited: The impact of strain on inmate recidivism. *Justice Quarterly, 30*, 144–168.

Lowenkamp, C. T., & Latessa, E. J. (2005). Increasing the effectiveness of correctional programming through the risk principle: Identifying offenders for residential placement. *Criminology and Public Policy, 4*(2), 501–528.

Marlatt, G. A., & Gordon, J. R. (Eds.). (1985). *Relapse prevention: Maintenance strategies in the treatment of addictive behaviors.* New York: Guilford.

Minton, T. D. (2012). *Jail inmates at mid-year 2011—Statistical tables.* Washington, DC: U.S. Department of Justice, Bureau of Justice Statistics.

Murphy, S. (2011, January 31). *Republican lawmakers paying for tough crime laws.* Associated Press. Available at http://cnsnews.com/news/article/gop-lawmakers-paying-price-tough-crime-laws.

Naser, R. L., & Visher, C. A. (2006). Family members' experiences with incarceration and reentry. *Western Criminology Review, 7*, 20–31.

Parks, G. A., & Marlatt, G. A. (1999). Relapse prevention therapy for substance-abusing offenders: A cognitive–behavioral approach. In E. Latessa (Ed.), *What works: Strategic solutions: The International Community Corrections Association examines substance abuse* (pp. 161–233). Lanham, MD: American Correctional Association.

Patterson, G. R., Chamberlain, P., & Reid, J. B. (1982). A comparative evaluation of a parent-training program. *Behavior Therapy, 13*, 638–650.

Pew Center on the States. (2008). *One in 100: Behind bars in America 2008.* Washington, DC: Pew Charitable Trusts.

Schmitt, J., & Warner, K. (2010). *Ex-offenders and the labor market.* Washington, DC: Center for Economic and Policy Research.

Sickmund, M. (2010). *Juveniles in residential placement, 1997–2008* (NCJ 229379). Washington, DC: U.S. Department of Justice, Office of Juvenile Justice and Delinquency Prevention.

Smith, P., Schweitzer, M., Labrecque, R. M., & Latessa, E. J. (2012). Improving probation officers' supervision skills: An evaluation of the EPICS model. *Journal of Crime and Justice, 35*, 189–199.

Snyder, H. N., & Sickmund, M. (2006). *Juvenile offenders and victims: 2006 national report.* Washington, DC: U.S. Department of Justice, Office of Justice Programs, Office of Juvenile Justice and Delinquency Prevention.

Taxman, F. S., Yancey, C., & Bilanin, J. (2006). Proactive community supervision in Maryland: Changing offender outcomes *Institute for Governmental Service and Research.* College Park, MD: University of Maryland.

Taxman, F. S., Young, D., & Byrne, J. M. (2003). *From prison safety to public safety: Best practices in offender reentry.* Washington, DC: National Institute of Justice.

Travis, J., Chincotta, E. M., & Solomon, A. (2003). *Families left behind: The hidden costs of incarceration and re-entry.* Washington, DC: Urban Institute.

Travis, J., & Lawrence, S. (2002). *Beyond the prison gates: The state of parole in America.* Washington, DC: Urban Institute.

Travis, J., Solomon, A., & Waul, M. (2001). *From prison to home: The dimensions and consequences of prisoner reentry.* Washington, DC: Urban Institute.

Useem, B., & Kimball, P. (1987). A theory of prison riots. *Theory and Society, 16*, 87–122.

Visher, C. (2006). Effective reentry programs. *Criminology & Public Policy, 5,* 299–302.

Visher, C., La Vigne, N., & Travis, J. (2004). *Returning home: Understanding the challenges of prison reentry.* Washington DC: Urban Institute.

Winterfield, L., Linquist, C., & Brumbaugh, S. (2007). *Sustaining adult re-entry programming after SVORI.* Research Triangle Park, NC: RTI International.

Yahner, J., & Xweig, J. M. (2012). *Which component of transitional job programs work best? Analysis of programs for former prisoners in the transitional jobs reentry demonstration.* Washington, DC: Urban Institute.

12

Making Sure It's Done Right
The Importance of Quality and How to Ensure Program Fidelity

Introduction

Throughout this text, we have provided numerous examples of assessment tools, treatment curricula, and the like. And yet, many well-designed interventions in the criminal justice field have failed, despite being carefully designed and implemented with good intentions (Gendreau, Goggin, & Smith, 1999; Goggin & Gendreau, 2006). On some level, this is not surprising given the number of issues that come into play when designing and implementing correctional treatment programs. However, we know that programs will be more effective if they are well implemented and are able to maintain fidelity to the original model. In fact, in a recent meta-analysis, Mark Lipsey et al. (2010) found that three factors predicted program effectiveness: the type of intervention, the type of offender (high risk), and the quality of the implementation.

Whether due to staff or leadership changes or simply program drift, all programs go through a process of change over time. Implementation should be thought of as an ongoing process rather than something that only occurs at the program's inception. Attending to this change and creating a culture that supports change while maintaining program fidelity is key. In this chapter, we examine the importance of attending to implementation issues, building program fidelity through organizational culture and staff, and outline ways in which programs can develop and use quality assurance processes to improve performance over the long term.

Implementing Evidence-Based Practices

The field of corrections has a long history of what Rothman (1980) describes as conscience versus convenience when implementing various practices. The term *conscience* refers to the fact that agencies strive to do what is best for clients; however, the implementation of evidence-based practices (EBPs) can often suffer from doing what is "convenient" under the circumstances. Budget cuts, high staff turnover, minimal staff training requirements, low morale, and subpar leadership are just a few of the many issues that can influence program development and implementation. Combine these with larger structural issues such as state and local policies, which studies suggest also influence the implementation of EBPs (Henderson, Young, Farrell, & Taxman, 2009), and the whole situation can seem discouraging. At the same time, however, research suggests that there are ways in which agencies can increase their effectiveness by paying close attention to how well they are organized. In that vein, there are two broad categories that can have an impact on implementation: organizational culture and leadership and supervision and training.

Organizational Culture and Leadership

The leadership of the program (e.g., program director) should be involved in the process of translating theory into EBPs for all of the clinical staff members. Having a program director who is not only well versed in the literature in this area but also able to translate that knowledge to staff is key. Agencies can ensure this to some degree by hiring program directors who are educated and experienced in the areas of correctional treatment. However, it should also require that the director read the literature and also be intimately involved in all aspects of the program, which should include direct service delivery (e.g., running groups and conducting assessments).

The program director should be directly involved in hiring and training the staff who are delivering the interventions. This includes developing hiring practices congruent with the interventions employed. For example, staff should have certain therapeutic skills, such as being nonconfrontational and fair but firm, and they should possess certain abilities that will allow them to be effective role models for clients (Dowden & Andrews, 2004). Ideally, directors (and others on an interview panel) would require potential candidates to demonstrate proficiency in certain skills during the interview process (e.g., role-plays and motivational interviewing techniques).

Once hired, the director's involvement with new staff should include translating the organizational climate and practices of the agency. Socializing new staff members on the philosophy of the intended program is important for sustaining the culture. The typical process might be centered on the policies and procedures of the facility, safety issues, first aid/CPR, etc. Training a new staff member on EBPs, however, should augment any necessary training requirements on procedures. We discuss staff training in more detail in the next section.

Research suggests that the leadership within an organization is instrumental in developing the organizational climate. In fact, studies suggest that job satisfaction can be influenced by how well the workplace functions (e.g., clear mission statement, counselor cohesion, and communication) (Joe, Broome, Simpson, & Rowan-Szal, 2007). Although this finding may not be surprising, the same study suggests that this satisfaction may influence the degree to which employees are open to receiving training on EBPs. In particular, George Joe and colleagues (2007) found that "counselors who feel integrated into their jobs and work environments would be more likely to have received, used, and be satisfied with training" (p. 179). This finding has been found in other studies of organization, albeit those serving non-criminal-justice populations (Bradley, Schlesinger, Webster, Baker, & Inouye, 2004).

Staff turnover can derail the implementation of a program because it takes considerable resources to train new staff. Certain factors inherent in correctional environments, such as safety concerns, low pay, and difficult clients, lead to high staff turnover. However, as we should expect, the leadership style and culture of the organization impact staff turnover as well. For example, studies have found that those who reported high levels of job satisfaction, which included high ratings of director leadership, were less likely to leave the organization (Garner, Hunter, Godley, & Godley, 2012). Perhaps more compelling are studies that have found that these organizational climate measure are also correlated with client retention (Broome, Flynn, Knight, & Simpson, 2007). In other words, if the environment is healthy, the clients are also more likely to benefit.

The program director must also be key in the development of a **therapeutic alliance** among staff. The therapeutic alliance is a term often used to describe the relationship between the client and therapists. However, it is also used to describe relationships among multiple staff members and the clients. In an institutional setting, we might describe a therapeutic alliance as the relationship among staff, including counselors and security staff, and the clients. In this context, the therapeutic alliance can be seen as similar to the organizational climate of the organization. Studies suggest that ratings of support among leadership are associated with positive ratings of organizational climate and therapeutic alliances and ultimately positive attitudes toward EBPs (Aarons & Sawitzky, 2006). With that said, organizational climate is still only one facet of the implementation of EBPs. The supervision and training of staff is another key aspect.

Staff Supervision and Training

As noted previously, staff members should be required to undergo a relatively intensive initial training period during which they become familiar with the organization's mission, goals, and interventions. This initial orientation should also include training on assessment tools, curricula, group dynamics, and treatment planning. However, staff members also need to receive ongoing training and supervision. The ongoing training can occur through a number of avenues, such as staff meetings, conferences, workshops, and other content-related trainings.

As noted previously, however, simply exposing staff to training is different than creating an organizational culture supportive of EBPs. How we implement interventions can have an impact on how well staff receive and buy into the mission. According to Simpson (2002), four steps should be considered when implementing interventions. These steps may increase the support or buy-in among staff:

Exposure: Training, an introduction to evidence supporting its use
Adoption: Period of time during which the intervention(s) is discussed and buy-in is created
Implementation: The piloting of the intervention begins, with feedback from staff; resources and staff support critical at this stage
Practice: Continued implementation and modification, with the sustainability of the intervention taking precedence

Regarding the first step, exposure, it is recognized that the "messaging" of the practice is key for buy-in among staff. For example, do the staff members understand why the particular practice (e.g., curriculum, program structure, and behavioral system) is being implemented? Do they have a say in how it will be implemented (while maintaining fidelity to the model)? Are there adequate resources for implementation and opportunities for training and feedback? Motivating staff for change becomes a core facet of the implementation strategy. This may be achieved through building leadership teams that can shoulder initial responsibility for fleshing out ideas and then presenting them to the organization. The leadership team should be as multidisciplinary as necessary to achieve the particular goals in mind. In that vein, the leadership team should include administrators and line staff and, in some circumstances, involve clients to receive their feedback and concerns regarding the implementation.

From there, the leadership teams should build organizational commitment to the model or practice. This may include a top-down approach with regard to understanding why decisions are being made, but it should also include a bottom-up feedback loop where line staff and others feel comfortable sharing their concerns and suggestions during the adoption and implementation stages. Ideally, staff should be rewarded for their participation and support. These rewards may be traditional (recognition and promotions) or less traditional (tokens of appreciation via raffles or other means). Building organizational culture also includes having adequate staff to implement the program as designed. Although the result is perhaps not surprising, Henderson and colleagues (2009) found that adequate staffing levels and resources within substance abuse treatment programs led to an increased chance that the staff would use EBPs.

The training of staff members cannot be overemphasized and should be geared toward providing opportunities for staff to practice skills. Often, employees are handed the keys (or the treatment manual) and told to not let the ship run aground. To implement a highly structured behavioral or cognitive program, however, staff should be trained by teaching them the skills they will need to facilitate group intervention in addition to the knowledge underlying the intervention. In that context, staff should be given the opportunity to practice their skills and receive feedback to increase their proficiency.

Feedback should come via regular clinical supervision. The clinical supervisor should be on hand to provide continual support and feedback to the staff members as they implement the practices. We should not forget that staff members' decisions to buy into training and use what they learn is influenced by their views of the organization (Joe et al., 2007). The clinical supervisor and/or director should be supportive in their feedback and coaching. In an effective model, coaching and continual training are key to making sure that staff members are implementing the program in a way that ensures fidelity to the model (Landenberger & Lipsey, 2005).

As mentioned previously, the process of implementation should include a piloting and monitoring phase. As we discuss in the next section, monitoring the process of implementation can occur through a variety of performance and outcome measures. The monitoring of the process is key for making necessary changes and minimizing design flaws. In the next section, we discuss how programs should monitor themselves to ensure fidelity to the interventions and practices adopted.

Monitoring Program Performance

One of the hallmarks of EBPs is the use of data to monitor and improve program performance. This can occur at different levels. For example, outcome studies are designed to determine if a program or intervention is having the desired effect on recidivism or some other outcome measure. These studies usually require some type of comparison, typically either to a comparison group or to some other standard, such as an ideal or preprogram status. Process evaluations are more concerned with the inputs of a program: Is the program doing what it says and how well is it doing it? The one thing that is clear is that effective programs evaluate what they do, often at different levels.

Before an agency embarks on implementing a system for assessing quality, it should first define what it means by quality. There are a number of definitions of quality, but there are at least two defining characteristics. The first is that the services offered are based on current professional knowledge. In other words, does the organization use evidence-based treatment approaches? The second is that the services produce desirable outcomes. For correctional treatment programs, one such desirable outcome is reduced recidivism. Although not discussed here, it is also common for measures of cost-effectiveness to be included in definitions of quality.[1]

Recidivism as an Outcome Measure

Although most of the research we have examined focused on recidivism (as well it should), it is important to put this measure in perspective. Recidivism is and should be the primary outcome measure by which we assess correctional program effectiveness. However, recidivism is problematic for a number of reasons. First, numerous definitions are applied, such as arrests, incarceration, technical violations, and convictions. How we define recidivism can determine the rate. For example, using a new arrest as the definition will result in higher recidivism rates than using return to prison. Second, the length of follow-up can be critical. For most offender groups, a 3-year follow-up is sufficient; however, for groups such as sex offenders and drunk drivers, we often need a longer follow-up to adequately gauge recidivism (mainly because these crimes are more hidden and the odds of being detected are low). Third, recidivism rates can be influenced by both internal and external factors. For example, probation departments may change policies, such as increasing drug testing, which in turn can result in higher failure rates (internal), or police departments may focus on specific types of crimes such as drug sweeps (external). Finally, recidivism is often treated as a dichotomous

---

[1]For an example of cost–benefit analysis of correctional programs, see Washington State Institute for Public Policy at http://www.wsipp.wa.gov.

variable—an all-or-nothing measure—when in fact we know that variations in this outcome measure exist. For example, someone who is arrested for public intoxication is a much less serious offender than someone arrested for armed robbery, but we often simply count them both as failures when examining program effectiveness. That said, recidivism is what is usually referred to when someone asks, "Does the program work?"

Intermediate/Performance-Based Measures

In addition to long-term outcome measures such as reductions in recidivism, we may also be interested in examining intermediate indicators. Unfortunately, in corrections we often count activities that have little or no relationship to program or offender performance. An example is counting the number of contacts between a probation officer and offenders. Few empirical studies show any relationship between the two factors, but this is a common measuring stick in probation. The difference between counting an activity and a performance measure is as follows:

Activity: Counting the number of job referrals made
Performance: Number of unemployed offenders at the time of arrest and the percentage employed within 6 months after being placed on supervision

Table 12.1 shows an example of the difference between counting activities and counting results for a juvenile court. One counts tasks, whereas the other counts what we want to achieve. Documenting the performance or progress of program participants will help determine treatment effects. Examples include the following:

- Reduction in antisocial attitudes: This indicator involves administering a standardized validated measure of antisocial thinking at intake and then again at a second point in time (typically discharge) to determine if the client's score decreases over time. This type of measure is important for two reasons: (1) Endorsement of antisocial thinking is one of the strongest predictors of recidivism and (2) antisocial thinking is the primary treatment target for cognitive behavioral programming. This means that this type of indicator can indicate whether a program is reducing the risk to reoffend for its clients and if its cognitive behavioral programming is effective.
- Reduction in risk scores: This indicator is measured by administering a validated risk assessment tool at intake (e.g., the Level of Service Inventory [LSI], Ohio Risk

Table 12.1   Communicating What a Juvenile Court Does: Activities Versus Results

Counting activities	Counting results
No. of contacts	Increase in no. of school days attended
No. of drug tests	Percent drug free
No. of youth on electronic monitoring	Reductions in runaways

Assessment System [ORAS], or similar tools) and then again at a second point in time. Again, the goal is to determine how many clients reduce their scores, thereby demonstrating proof that the program is reducing the probability that clients will commit future offenses.

- Increase in treatment readiness: This involves administering a standardized measure of treatment readiness (e.g., the Client Motivation and Readiness Scale or the treatment readiness scales contained in the Texas Christian University Client Evaluation of Self and Treatment).[2] The goal here is to determine whether clients' scores increase, or improve, over time. This might be an important measure for programs that are using motivational interviewing as a strategy for increasing client motivation for treatment.
- Educational improvement such as increase in grade point average or improvement on standardized achievement tests: This is an important intermediate outcome measure for programs that offer education services.
- GED: This is similar to the previous indicator.
- Employment: This is also typically an intermediate outcome measure for programs that stress employment. Indicators can include the employment rate, days employed, and improvement in employment.
- Reduction in mental health symptomology: This is an important intermediate outcome measure for programs that provide their own mental health treatment to clients—for example, days hospitalized (pre/post-treatment).
- Reduction in substance use: This indicator is often used as both an intermediate measure and a long-term measure. In other words, programs want to know whether clients have stopped using drugs while they are in treatment but also want to determine whether they continue with sobriety after they have left the program. The most common method of measurement for this type of indicator is urinalysis or drug tests.
- Improvements in institutional adjustment as measured by incident reports or days in segregation.
- Completion of behavioral objectives (meeting treatment plan).
- Acquisition of new prosocial skills: Program participants can demonstrate new ways to handle risky situations.
- Program completion: This can be an important measure but ideally would include at least four components: attendance, participation, progress, and completion.

By focusing on performance rather than activities, a correctional program can develop intermediate goals that, if achieved, can serve as a prelude to reductions in recidivism. Osborne and Gaebler (1992) identified seven principles for results-oriented management:

1. What gets measured gets done.
2. If you don't measure results, you can't tell success from failure.
3. If you can't see success, you can't reward it.

[2]See the Texas Christian University Institute for Behavioral Research web site at http://www.ibr.tcu.edu.

4. If you can't reward success, you're probably rewarding failure.
5. If you can't see success, you can't learn from it.
6. If you can't recognize failure, you can't correct it.
7. If you can demonstrate results, you can win public support.

Of course, before we begin to discuss performance measures, it is important to make sure the program or intervention is designed around research and the existing evidence to support a positive effect. Throughout this book, we have discussed what works in reducing recidivism. It should be abundantly clear that effective programs do not just happen. They are designed and implemented around some principles. Fortunately, there has been considerable progress in identifying the hallmarks of effective correctional programs (Latessa & Holsinger, 1998). The question now is, "How can we measure whether or not a correctional program is in fact meeting these principles?" Let's now turn our attention to measuring program integrity.

Assessing Quality

Examining the "input" of a program is usually referred to as a process evaluation. A process study helps determine whether the program is operating as designed. The problem, of course, is that a program may in fact be operating efficiently but not effectively. For example, a drug education program may be doing a great job of teaching offenders about the harm that drugs can do to them without being effective in reducing drug usage. Likewise, a boot camp may be very well implemented but will not reduce recidivism for the reasons stated in Chapter 5.

The other problem with traditional process studies is that they often do not provide a "quantitative" measure. One way to think of this is to consider the example from offender assessment. Some assessment processes gather a great deal of information about the offender (e.g., criminal history, employment, drug use, family, and education). The problem is that when they are performed as a "clinical" assessment, they do not really have a good way to pull it all together to quantifiably measure risk. Now compare that to using the ORAS, LSI, or another instrument. The same information is gathered, but when you are finished you produce a score that in turn helps tell you the probability of recidivism, as well as whether or not the offender scores "high," "medium," or "low" in each domain.

So how do we quantifiably measure program integrity, and what factors are examined? One tool that is used was developed by Gendreau and Andrews (1989)—the Correctional Program Assessment Inventory (CPAI). This instrument is based in part on the results from meta-analyses of correctional effectiveness studies. It is a tool for assessing correctional programs based on empirical criteria. However, unlike traditional process evaluations or audits that simply measure if you are doing what you say you are doing, this process examines the degree to which a correctional program is meeting the principles of effective intervention. This tool has been used to evaluate programs throughout the United States and Canada.

A number of studies of the CPAI found strong correlations with measures of individual outcomes for both domain areas and individual items (Holsinger, 1999; Lowenkamp, 2004; Lowenkamp & Latessa, 2003, 2005a, 2005b). Based on these studies, researchers from the University of Cincinnati developed the Evidence-Based Correctional Program Checklist (CPC). Only those indicators that were found to be positively correlated with outcome were retained on the CPC.[3]

The Correctional Program Checklist

The CPC is a tool developed to assess correctional intervention programs and is used to ascertain how closely correctional programs meet known principles of effective intervention. Several studies conducted by the University of Cincinnati on both adult and juvenile programs were used to develop and validate the indicators on the CPC.

The CPC is divided into two basic areas: content and capacity. The capacity area is designed to measure whether a correctional program has the capability to deliver evidence-based interventions and services for offenders. There are three domains in the capacity area: Leadership and Development, Staff, and Quality Assurance. The content area focuses on the substantive domains of Offender Assessment and Treatment and the extent to which the program meets the principles of risk, need, responsivity, and treatment. There are a total of 77 indicators, worth up to 83 total points that are scored during the assessment. Each area and all domains are scored and rated as "highly effective" (65–100%), "effective" (55–64%), "needs improvement" (46–54%), or "ineffective" (45% or less). The scores in all five domains are totaled, and the same scale is used for the overall assessment score.

Data are collected through structured interviews with selected program staff and program participants and through observation of groups and services. In some instances, surveys may also be used to gather additional information. Other sources of information include policy and procedure manuals, schedules, treatment materials, manuals, curriculums, a review of a sample of case files, and other selected program materials. Once the information is gathered and reviewed, the program is scored, and a report is generated that highlights the strengths, areas that need improvement, and recommendations for each of the five areas. Program scores are also compared to the average from across all programs that have been assessed. The following is a brief description of the areas examined and some of the attributes of high-quality correctional programs:

- Program leadership and development: Effective programs are characterized by the strong direct involvement of the program director in designing the programming;

[3]These studies involved more than 40,000 offenders (both adult and juvenile) and more than 400 correctional programs ranging from institutional to community based. Since that time, we have developed several versions, including the CPC–Drug Court, CPC–Group, CPC–Community Supervision, and CPC–Mental Health Court.

selecting, training, and supervising staff; and in the provision of services to residents. Experience and formal education in a helping profession are also important attributes of effective correctional leaders. The development of effective programs has several dimensions: They are designed to be consistent with the treatment literature on effective programs; interventions and program components are piloted before full implementation; the values and goals of the program should be consistent with existing values in the community; and funding is adequate to sustain the program as designed.

- Staff: High-quality programs have qualified, experienced, and well-trained staff selected for their skills and values. They should be regularly assessed on service delivery and receive clinical supervision. Staff should also meet regularly to discuss cases, have input into the program, and follow ethical guidelines.
- Offender assessment: The selection and assessment of program participants is another aspect of high-quality programs. Criteria for inclusion should be developed and followed, and all offenders should be assessed on risk, need, and responsivity factors using valid assessment tools.
- Treatment: It is important that correctional programs target criminogenic behavior and use evidence-based treatment approaches. The types of treatment used to target these behaviors, specific treatment procedures, the use of practice and skill development techniques, positive reinforcement and punishment, and methods

Table 12.2   Types of Programs Assessed with the CPAI and CPC

Boot camps
Community correctional facilities
Correctional education programs
Day reporting centers
Drug courts
Diversion programs
Group homes
Halfway houses
Institutional sex offender programs
Institutional treatment programs
Intensive supervision units
Jail-based substance abuse programs
Mental health courts
Outpatient substance abuse programs
Residential correctional programs for parolees
Residential correctional programs for women
Residential substance abuse programs
Residential substance abuse programs for habitual drunk drivers
School-based programs
Sex offender programs
Therapeutic communities, both institutional and community based
Work release facilities

used to prepare residents for return to the community are all hallmarks of effective programs. Other important elements of effective intervention include the ratio of rewards to punishers; matching the offender's risk, needs, and personal characteristics with the appropriate treatment programs, treatment intensity, and staff; and relapse prevention strategies designed to assist the offender in anticipating and coping with problem situations.

- Quality assurance: Effective programs develop both internal and external quality assurance processes, survey client satisfaction, reassess on target behaviors, track participant outcomes, and examine other indicators of program performance.

Each of these areas has multiple indicators and defined criteria that are used to determine the final scores and ratings described previously. In one large-scale study of the relationship between program integrity and outcome, Lowenkamp (2004) found a strong correlation (.60) with reductions in recidivism. All the areas are important, but assessment, treatment, and program leadership and development are particularly important.

Advantages to the CPC

There are several advantages to the CPC. First, it is applicable to a wide range of programs (adult, juvenile, community, institutional, etc.). Second, all of the indicators included in the CPC have been found to be correlated with reductions in recidivism. Third, the process provides a measure of program integrity and quality; it provides insight into the "black box" of a program, something that an outcome study alone does not provide. Fourth, the results can be obtained relatively quickly; usually the process takes 1 or 2 days, and a report is generated within a few weeks. Fifth, it identifies both the strengths and the weaknesses of a program and provides recommendations designed to improve the integrity of the program and to increase effectiveness. Finally, it allows for benchmarking. Comparisons with other programs that have been assessed using the same criteria are provided, and because program integrity and quality can change over time, it allows a program to reassess its progress. Types of programs that have been assessed with the CPAI and CPC are shown in Table 12.2.

Results from Program Assessments

Researchers at the University of Cincinnati have assessed more than 600 programs nationwide and have developed a large database on correctional intervention programs. Figure 12.1 shows the overall results from these assessments. Approximately 6% of the programs assessed have been classified as "very effective," 17% "effective," 33% "needs improvement," and 43% "not effective." The average scores in each of the areas are shown in Figure 12.2. The areas of leadership and development and staff were the highest rated, followed by assessment. The treatment and quality assurance areas were rated much lower, indicating that there is considerable work to be done to improve the quality of the correctional treatment programs offered to offenders.

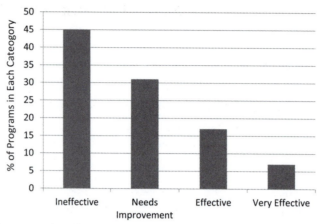

FIGURE 12.1 Results from more than 600 correctional program assessments. This includes a wide range of correctional programs using the CPAI or the CPC.

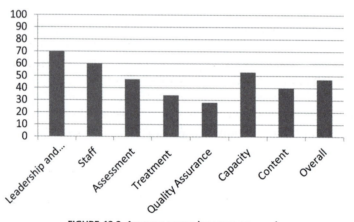

FIGURE 12.2 Average scores by areas assessed.

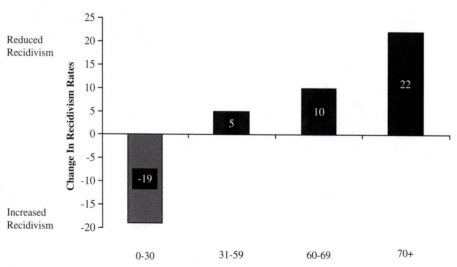

FIGURE 12.3 Program integrity—Relationship between program integrity score and treatment effect for residential programs.

Program Integrity and Recidivism

In three large-scale studies examining a wide range of correctional programs for both adults and juveniles, University of Cincinnati researchers found strong support between overall program quality and recidivism. Figure 12.3 shows the results from residential programs for adult offenders: The poorest quality programs increased recidivism by 19%, whereas the best program reduced recidivism by 22% (Latessa & Lowenkamp, (2006). Figure 12.4 shows a similar pattern for correctional supervision programs[4]; the low-quality programs increased recidivism by an average of 15%, whereas the highest quality programs reduced recidivism by an average of 16%. Finally, Figure 12.5 shows the results for juvenile programs, including institutional, residential, and community. The juvenile offenders in this study were categorized by risk level, and as can be seen in the figure, low-quality programs had higher recidivism rates than high-quality programs regardless of the risk of the youth.

Although we have seen that it is very important to design and implement programs well, we also see similar effects from some well-known evidence-based models for juveniles. Figure 12.6 shows the results from a study conducted by the Washington State Institute for Public Policy (WSIPP, 2004), which examined Functional Family Therapy (FFT) and Aggression Replacement Therapy (ART). When competently delivered, these interventions significantly reduced recidivism; however, when not competently delivered, they actually increased recidivism. Figure 12.7 shows the WSIPP results on the

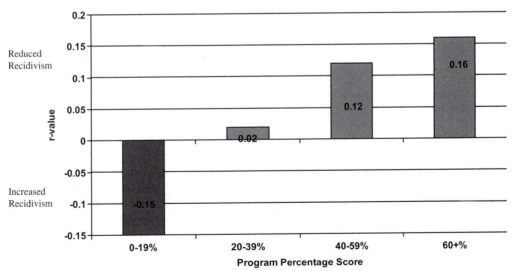

FIGURE 12.4 Program integrity—Relationship between program integrity score and treatment effect for community supervision programs.

[4]Supervision programs included intensive supervision, day reporting, and electronic monitoring.

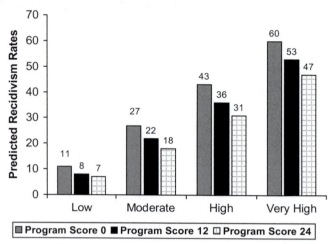

FIGURE 12.5 Program integrity—Relationship between program integrity score and treatment effect for juvenile programs.

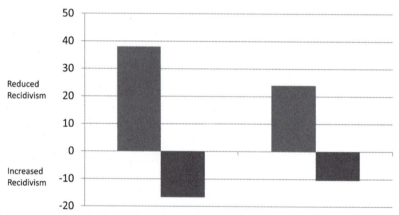

FIGURE 12.6 Effects of quality delivery for evidence-based programs for juvenile offenders. *Source: Washington State Institute for Public Policy. (2004).* Outcome evaluation of Washington State's research based program for juvenile offenders. *Olympia, WA: Author.*

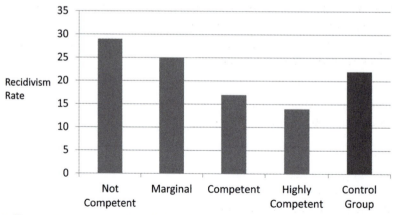

FIGURE 12.7 Staff competency ratings and recidivism. *Source: Washington State Institute for Public Policy. (2004).* Outcome evaluation of Washington State's research based program for juvenile offenders. *Olympia, WA: Author.*

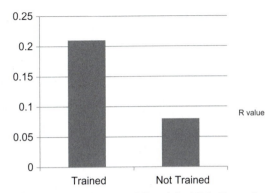

FIGURE 12.8 Importance of training: validity of the LSI-R. *Flores, A., et al. (2006).*

importance of having competent staff deliver the program. When staff were rated as highly competent and competent, they reduced recidivism; however, when rated as not competent or only marginally competent, they increased recidivism. In a study involving adult offenders, Latessa, Brusman, and Smith (2010) found that delivering groups poorly was worse than not having them at all. This was true for cognitive behavioral, domestic violence, and gender responsive groups.

Similar results were found with regard to assessment training—for example, a study by Flores, Lowenkamp, Holsinger, and Latessa (2006) on the importance of training when using an assessment tool such as the LSI-R (discussed in Chapter 2. As seen in Figure 12.8, Lowenkamp reported a larger correlation of LSI-R score and recidivism among agencies whose staff were formally trained in its use.

The Upkeep of Change: Monitoring and Evaluating the Program

It is important that correctional systems monitor and evaluate the programs they offer. This should include developing processes to ensure that the assessments, services, and interventions provided by the program are delivered consistently and as designed, including services delivered by contractors or outside services providers. The following are some of the techniques that can be used:

- Case file audits
- Video- or audiotaping sessions
- Client satisfaction surveys or exit interviews
- Clinical supervision of staff
- Program audits
- Site visits and group observations
- Certification processes
- Evaluation of staff on service delivery

Table 12.3   Checklist for Group Observation

1. Did the group start on time?
2. Did the facilitators settle the group down to start?
3. How did they settle the group down?
4. Did the facilitators review the homework?
5. Was the homework review conducted during the 1st quarter?
6. Did all offenders participate in the homework review?
7. Did the facilitators issue reinforcement for those who completed the homework?
8. Did the facilitators issue consequences for those who did not complete the homework?
9. How long was the homework review?
10. Did the facilitators present the didactic information?
11. Was the didactic information presented during the 2nd quarter?
12. Did the facilitators review each step of the skill during the presentation?
13. Did the facilitators review an action and a thinking step?
14. Was the information presented in an understandable fashion?
15. Did the offenders pay attention during the didactic information?
16. If no, how did the facilitators handle the situation?
17. Was the new skill modeled correctly by the facilitators? (Each step used in an understandable fashion)
18. Did the facilitators ask how the skill could apply to offenders? Or did they personalize the skill?
19. How long was the didactic presentation including the modeling demonstration?
20. Did the offenders practice in the 3rd quarter?
21. Was the new skill role-played by all offenders?
22. Did the facilitators assist the offenders to differentiate between a thinking and an action step if needed?
23. Did the facilitators stop a role-play when it was performed wrong or it got out of hand?
24. Did they require the offender to practice the skill correctly after the redirection?
25. Did the facilitators assign others to watch for the steps? (Must be all role-plays)
26. Was feedback given after each role-play? (Must be all role-plays)
27. Was feedback given in the correct order? (Must be all role-plays)
28. Did the facilitators redirect on the feedback when needed?
29. Was the 4th quarter reserved for graduated rehearsal?
30. Did all offenders practice the graduated rehearsal?
31. Was a script used for the graduated rehearsal?
32. Did the facilitators provide assistance when needed to the actors during the graduated rehearsal?
33. Did the facilitators stop a graduated rehearsal when it was performed wrong or it got out of hand?
34. Did they require the offender to practice the graduated rehearsal correctly after the redirection?
35. Did the co-facilitator assign steps for the graduated rehearsal? (Must be each role-play)
36. Was feedback given after each graduated rehearsal? (Must be all role-plays)
37. Was feedback given in the correct order after each graduated rehearsal? (Must be all role-plays)
38. Was homework given for the offenders to practice the skill outside of group?
39. Did facilitators use positive reinforcement during the group?
40. Were they specific in their reinforcement?
41. Did the facilitators use punishments if needed during the group?

Group observation is an important tool in monitoring program delivery. Table 12.3 is an example of the indicators that should be examined for a cognitive behavioral group. It is recommended that group observation be done at least once during the cycle of the curriculum. Another example comes from the EPICS model discussed in Chapter 4. After

Table 12.4   Areas Rated from Probation Office–Client Interactions from the EPICS Model

Check-In
Relationship with the client
Assessment of crisis/acute needs
Assessed for compliance with conditions
Review
Set or reviewed goals
Discussed community agency referrals
Enhanced learning by reviewing previous interventions
Reviewed previous homework assignment
Intervention
Behavior chain
Cognitive restructuring
Cost–benefit analysis
Social skills
Graduated rehearsal/practice
Homework
Generalized to other situations
Assigned appropriate homework
Behavioral Practices
Effective reinforcement
Effective disapproval
Effective use of authority
General Ratings
PO was anti-criminal model
Use of reflective listening statements
Communication was clear and concise
Engaged the client throughout the session
Length of session
Made outside referrals
Role clarification

probation officers are trained in the model, they are required to audiotape sessions and send them in electronically for review. Each tape is then coded to determine how well the officer is following the model. Coaching sessions are then held through video conferencing, and skills are reviewed and practiced as needed. Table 12.4 shows some of the areas that are reviewed for quality.

Effective programs have several additional characteristics in the area of evaluation:

- They track recidivism.
- They develop and monitor performance measures.
- They have evaluators work with the program.

In 2002, Latessa, Cullen, and Gendreau wrote an article on professional quackery in corrections. They noted four common failures of correctional treatment programs:

1. Failure to use research in designing programs
2. Failure to follow appropriate assessment and classification practices
3. Failure to use effective treatment models
4. Failure to evaluate what we do

It is clear that we can indeed design and implement correctional programs that reduce recidivism. However, it is equally clear that we need to design programs using the research and make sure they are delivered with integrity.

Summary

This book examined a number of principles of effective correctional programs: Who to target (risk), what to target (needs), and how to target (responsivity and treatment) are the keys to reducing recidivism. However, perhaps the greatest challenge facing correctional programs is the constant need to monitor and ensure that the programs are being conducted with fidelity and integrity. This chapter examined the importance of doing it well. The following are the major points of this chapter:

- If a program is not well implemented, it may appear as if the program did not work when in fact the program was never implemented correctly.
- Implementing evidence-based practices requires an organizational climate that is supportive of treatment and leadership that is knowledgeable of evidence-based practices.
- Staff training and supervision are key to implementing evidence-based practices, but so is creating buy-in among staff members.
- Recidivism is the primary measure by which correctional programs are evaluated, but how it is defined and how long we follow offenders are important considerations in gauging rates.
- Performance measures should focus on intermediate objectives that are related to long-term goals. Examples include reductions in risk scores, improvements on pre/post-tests, gains in employment and educational achievement, negative drug tests, and the acquisition of new prosocial skills.
- The CPAI and CPC are designed to assess correctional programs and focus on program integrity. Areas examined include leadership and development, staff, assessment, treatment, and quality assurance.
- The vast majority of correctional programs that have been assessed with the CPAI or CPC have scored poorly, indicating that there is a strong need to infuse research and fidelity into existing correctional programs.

- Studies have found a strong correlation between program integrity and offender outcome.
- Poorly designed and implemented programs, even those considered evidence based, can result in increased recidivism.
- Programs can monitor quality in multiple ways, including file reviews, group observation, audits, and taping sessions.

References

Aarons, G. A., & Sawitzky, A. C. (2006). Organizational culture and climate and mental health provider attitudes toward evidence-based practice. *Psychological Services, 3,* 61–72.

Bradley, E. H., Schlesinger, M., Webster, T. R., Baker, D., & Inouye, S. K. (2004). Translating research into clinical practice: making change happen. *Journal of the American Geriatrics Society, 52,* 1875–1882.

Broome, K. M., Flynn, P. M., Knight, D. K., & Simpson, D. D. (2007). Program structure, staff perceptions, and client engagement in treatment. *Journal of Substance Abuse Treatment, 33,* 149–158.

Dowden, C., & Andrews, D. (2004). The importance of staff practice in delivering effective correctional treatment: A meta analytic review of core correctional practice. *International Journal of Offender Therapy and Comparative Criminology, 48,* 203–214.

Flores, A., Lowenkamp, C. T., Holsinger, A., & Latessa, E. (2006). Predicting Outcome with the Level of Service Inventory-Revised: The Importance of Implementation Integrity. *Journal of Criminal Justice, 34,* 523–529.

Garner, B. R., Hunter, B. D., Godley, S. H., & Godley, M. D. (2012). Training and retaining staff to competently deliver an evidence based practice: The role of staff attributes and perceptions of organizational functioning. *Journal of Substance Abuse Treatment, 42,* 191–200.

Gendrea, P., & Andrews, D. (1989). *The Correctional Program Assessment Inventory.* St. Johns, New Brunswick, Canada: University of New Brunswick.

Gendreau, P., Goggin, C., & Smith, P. (1999). The forgotten issue in effective correctional treatment: Program implementation. *International Journal of Offender Therapy and Comparative Criminology, 43,* 180–187.

Goggin, C., & Gendreau, P. (2006). The implementation of quality services in offender rehabilitation programs. In C. R. Hollin, & E. J. Palmer (Eds.), *Offending behaviour programmes, development, application, & controversies* (pp. 209–246). Chichester, UK: Wiley.

Henderson, C. E., Young, D. W., Farrell, J., & Taxman, F. S. (2009). Associations among state and local organizational contexts: Use of evidence based practices in the criminal justice system. *Drug and Alcohol Dependence, 103,* 23–32.

Holsinger, A. M. (1999). *Opening the "black box": Assessing the relationship between program integrity and recidivism.* Cincinnati, OH: Doctoral dissertation, University of Cincinnati.

Joe, G. W., Broome, K. M., Simpson, D. D., & Rowan-Szal, G. A. (2007). Counselor perceptions of organizational factors and innovations training experiences. *Journal of Substance Abuse Treatment, 33,* 171–182.

Landenberger, N. A., & Lipsey, M. (2005). The positive effects of cognitive–behavioral programs for offenders: A meta-analysis of factors associated with effective treatment. *Journal of Experimental Criminology, 1,* 451–476.

Latessa, E. J., Brusman, L., & Smith, P. (2010). *Follow-up evaluation of Ohio's community based correctional facilities and halfway house programs: Program characteristics supplemental report.*

Available at http://www.uc.edu/content/dam/uc/ccjr/docs/reports/project_reports/Program_Characteristics_Supplementary_Report_FINAL.pdf.

Latessa, E. J., Cullen, F. T., & Gendreau, P. (2002). Correctional quackery: Professional responsibility for evidence-based practice. *Federal Probation, 66*(2), 43–49.

Latessa, E. J., & Holsinger, A. M. (1998). The importance of evaluating correctional programs: Assessing outcome and quality. *Corrections Management Quarterly, 2*(4), 22–29.

Latessa, E. J., & Lowenkamp, C. (2006). What works in reducing recidivism. *St. Thomas Law Journal, 3*(3), 521–535.

Lipsey, M. W., Howell, J. C., Kelly, M. R., Chapman, G., & Carver, D. (2010). *Improving the effectiveness of juvenile justice programs: A new perspective on evidence- based programs.* Washington, DC: Center for Juvenile Justice Reform, Georgetown University.

Lowenkamp, C. T. (2003). *A program level analysis of the relationship between correctional program integrity and treatment effectiveness.* Cincinnati, OH: Doctoral dissertation, University of Cincinnati.

Lowenkamp, C. T. (2004). *Correctional program integrity and treatment effectiveness: A multi-site, program level analysis.* Cincinnati, OH: Unpublished doctoral dissertation, University of Cincinnati.

Lowenkamp, C. T., & Latessa, E. J. (2003). *Evaluation of Ohio's halfway houses and community based correctional facilities.* Cincinnati, OH: Center for Criminal Justice Research, University of Cincinnati.

Lowenkamp, C. T., & Latessa, E. J. (2005a). *Evaluation of Ohio's CCA programs.* Cincinnati, OH: Center for Criminal Justice Research, University of Cincinnati.

Lowenkamp, C. T., & Latessa, E. J. (2005b). *Evaluation of Ohio's RECLAIM funded programs, community correctional facilities, and DYS facilities.* Cincinnati, OH: Center for Criminal Justice Research, University of Cincinnati.

Osborne, D., & Gaebler, T. (1992). *Reinventing government.* Boston: Addison-Wesley.

Rothman, D. J. (1980). *Conscience and convenience: The asylum and its alternatives in progressive America.* Boston: Little Brown.

Simpson, D. D. (2002). A conceptual framework for transferring research to practice. *Journal of Substance Abuse Treatment, 22,* 171–182.

Washington State Institute for Public Policy. (2004). *Outcome evaluation of Washington State's research based program for juvenile offenders.* Olympia, WA: Author.

Index

Note: Page numbers with "f" denote figures; "t" denote tables; "b" denote boxes.